The Sacred Dance

of

Venus and Mars

Michele Finey

The Wessex Astrologer

Published in 2012 by
The Wessex Astrologer Ltd
4A Woodside Road
Bournemouth
BH5 2AZ
England

www.wessexastrologer.com

ISBN 9781902405810

A catalogue record of this book is available at The British Library

Cover design by Tania at Creative Byte, Poole, Dorset

For Neil

Contents

Acknowledgements

I wish to express my deep gratitude to the many people who have assisted me during the process of writing of this book.

Firstly, I want to thank Martin Lewicki who set my course on the day he told me about the 32-year cycle of Venus and Mars. I am grateful to fellow astrologers Roderick Kidston, for urging me to write this book, and Michelle Proctor for her friendship and enthusiastic encouragement during my early stages of research.

I wish to express my appreciation to Bil Tierney for taking the time to read a large section of the manuscript and providing many useful suggestions. Thanks also to John Martineau for granting permission to reproduce his exquisite illustrations and to Astro.com for supplying the data on Venus. Paul Westran and Adam Gainsburg took the time to respond to my emails and I'd like to extend a special thank you to 'Amelia' and 'Tom' for allowing me to use their birth charts.

I'd like to acknowledge a special group of wonderful friends and fellow writers; Mandy Burton, Carol Challis, Kim Challis, Lynne Siejka and Blaise Van Hecke, for their insightful feedback, encouragement and support.

I especially wish to mention the invaluable assistance given to me by my partner Neil Dennis, who created many wonderful diagrams from my pencilled layouts. In addition he provided editing suggestions and feedback. He also explained the copper-iron relationship to me and helped write the material on electro-magnetism in Section Two. Neil has guided me throughout this project with his vast knowledge, practical skills and patient understanding.

I am truly blessed by his support and generosity and the wonderful relationship we share. Nine months after I first began investigating the Sacred Dance of Venus and Mars, he opened my heart to love.

Foreword

My personal journey in writing this book began some years ago when I happened to notice that Venus and Mars were about to make a conjunction. This is not unusual, for the cosmic lovers often unite, on average once a year. But just how regularly do Venus and Mars kiss? It was a question I had never asked myself before.

Planets move in cyclic patterns and align at regular intervals; Neptune and Pluto unite every 492 years, Saturn and Jupiter align every 20 years, the Sun and Moon once a month, but the Venus-Mars cycle seemed to defy explanation. Conjunctions between Venus and Mars can occur several weeks apart, several months apart, up to almost two years apart. Unlike other planets, their periodic conjunctions jump back and forth through the zodiac in a seemingly random way.

As I began researching their orbital cycles and synodic relationship, I quickly became engrossed. I couldn't find a pattern to their motion, and yet there must be one.

After some fruitless enquiries, astronomer Martin Lewicki told me that Venus and Mars have a 32-year cycle. This tweaked my curiosity further, for how could Venus and Mars possibly have a 32-year cycle when neither of their orbits is anywhere near this long? Intrigued by this mystery, I embarked on a quest to investigate the Venus-Mars cosmic dance.

In a way it should come as no surprise that the Venus-Mars synodic cycle is complicated; after all, their celestial dance mirrors the complex nature of our personal relationships: as above; so below.

When I began investigating the Venus-Mars cycle I had been single for more than ten years. For me, relationships had always been hit and miss affairs, mostly miss. In my heart I was secretly hoping that if I could comprehend the Venus-Mars cycle it might also help me find love. Then I noticed that I was having a Venus Return and a Mars Return on the same day! Without a doubt this was a clear signal of encouragement from the cosmos.

In less than a year I found love. Finding the love of my life in the midst of researching the relationship between Venus and Mars has made me realise the importance of getting the cosmic timing right. Yes, synastry is important; as is the condition of our natal Venus and Mars, but comprehending their cyclic motion in the heavens brings a whole new dimension to our understanding of relationships.

The mystery of love is mirrored in the timeless paths these celestial lovers travel in the heavens. Their heavenly relationship, like love itself, is complex and mysterious, but its beauty and power is revealed to us when we take a closer look.

Michele Finey can be contacted via her website
www.celestialinsight.com.au

Introduction

The world has changed and we have evolved. Both women and men have become more conscious. Over recent decades gender roles have drastically altered and relationships have too. Our ancestors could never have imagined the many different types of relationship and family structures that exist today. While much has changed, one thing about relationships remains the same; they are often rather complicated.

Despite the many changes we have seen since the social revolution of the 1960s, women are still the ones who give birth. Men, by virtue of their physiology, are still more remote from parenting than women.

This gives rise to different psychological dynamics in girls and boys as they mature.

Developmental psychologists recognise the importance of two primary factors in childhood; children need to feel secure and loved by having their basic needs met, and at the same time they must be allowed to separate from their parents in order to grow into a healthy, happy adults.

One of the main challenges in terms of this process of development is connected to our relationship with the parent of the same sex. Mother-daughter and father-son relationships are generally more complex than mother-son and father-daughter relationships because children need to identify with, as well as separate from, the parent of the same sex.

Mothers, as primary care-givers, often behave more protectively towards their daughters, because they more closely identify with them than with their sons. Girls get their sense of self from their mothers, which is why it is often difficult for mothers and daughters to separate psychologically from one another.[1]

Consequently, girls have to work harder than boys to establish their independence. In order to do this, and forge their own identity the main task girls face is to separate from their mothers.

Of course boys need to psychologically break free from mother too, but since they are biologically different from her, subconsciously they are already aware of being separate.

Boys need a positive male role model to give them an idea of what it is to be a man, but they often have a hard time *connecting* with their fathers who in one way or another are often absent or more remote from the family. The main challenge for boys is to learn to *connect*.

Girls need a positive father image in order to develop healthy personal relationships with the opposite sex, but a girl's relationship with her father is not tied to her personal identity like it is for boys.

Though gender roles have changed over the years, it is still true that women identify more personally with Venus and men with Mars.

As the first planet inward from Earth, and our closest planetary neighbour (apart from the Moon) Venus is the key feminine archetype. Symbolising beauty and love, self esteem and relationship, Venus represents the law of attraction, our core values and the need for closeness and connection.

Mars is the key symbol of masculine strength. As the next planet orbiting outward from Earth and natural ruler of the Ascendant, Mars represents our sense of individuality, independence, self expression and autonomy.

These critical aspects of life are mirrored in the cyclic journey of Venus and Mars in the heavens, whose glyphs are identical to those we use to distinguish the sexes. Biologically too, every one of us is the product of these cosmic lovers whose intimate union creates new life.

Regardless of our gender, or sexual orientation, Venus and Mars are found in every birth chart and so every one of us needs to experience love while being free to be ourselves and act independently.

Today women are much more independent and in touch with their Mars nature than they once were. Men have also grown in their capacity to express love and connect emotionally. Yet the challenge we all face is to find the right balance between self and others.

This book examines the planetary synodic cycles of Venus and Mars and other facets of their movement in the heavens. These patterns mirror our relationships and can tell us a great deal about ourselves. In the first Part, Rhythm of the Dance, we explore the nature of love and learn the basic dance steps of the planets. In Part two we take a closer look at the Sun-Mars cycle and the Sun-Venus cycle. Mars describes our journey towards becoming a separate individual and is akin to the Hero's Journey. The Mars 'phase' tells us a great deal about how we express ourselves as individuals. The Sun-Venus cycle is associated with our desire for self expression too, but has more to do with values, what and who we are attracted to and how we connect and evaluate. Rather than action-based, like Mars, Venus seeks quality, interaction and cooperation. These cycles with the Sun show how we develop and consciously express our Venus and Mars natures.

In Part three we examine the special relationship between Venus and Mars. We'll look at the way Venus and Mars dance together in the heavens. By exploring their chemistry, their sacred geometry, aspects and synastry we get a clearer picture of how Venus and Mars see one another and interact.

Part four is an in depth exploration of Venus-Mars conjunctions spanning more than 1000 years. This Venus-Mars *Saros* cycle highlights the vast scope of the Venus-Mars Sacred Dance that has mundane implications yet can also tell us the best time to start a new relationship. Part five includes a number of case histories.

Though technically not an eclipse cycle, the Venus-Mars Saros gives us a fuller appreciation for the scope and beauty of planetary motion and has wide-ranging implications. It may hold the key to understanding why people are so passionate about specific things, why relationships start and end, and even why some karmic connections and soul unions transcend time. Beyond the personal level, I believe this cycle has mundane implications. It is clear that together Venus and Mars are incredibly powerful.

Note that throughout this book I have opted to call the Sun 'father', though the Sun might equally be assigned to mother, or to both parents, guardians, care givers, grandparents, foster parents, or other people who helped raise us. The Sun is also a symbol of the more conscious Self we are destined to become. Similarly, Venus is referred to as she and Mars as he, though I should emphasise that they represent yin and yang forces in all of us regardless of our gender.

All charts are calculated using either 0 Aries houses, or Placidus with Mean Node. Data sources include Solar Fire databases, AstroDataBank and Astrotheme.com

Footnotes
1. Nancy Friday, *My Mother My Self*, Fontana/HarperCollins, London, 1979. pp.39-40

Part One
Rhythm of the Dance

The Fairy Tale Romance

In *Beauty and the Beast* a young maiden falls in love with an ugly beast and her love transforms him into a handsome prince. In *Cinderella*, a handsome prince falls in love with an ordinary girl and whisks her away from her life of poverty and hardship. Like the Beast, or Cinderella, the odds might be stacked against us but deep down we know that love will transform us.

Love stories, fairy tales and romance novels transport us to another world where love always triumphs and everyone lives happily ever after. But before love wins the day, there is generally an obstacle to overcome, or an evil spell to break. In real life, we often face the same twists and turns in our journey towards love.

The origins of romantic love date back to the Age of Chivalry, around the 12th century. Fascinatingly, the original meaning of the word 'romance' seems to have more in keeping with Mars, than with Venus, for it simply means 'the story of a hero's adventures.'[1] To find love we need the courage of Mars. The courage to know what we want and go after it. Romantic adventures generally tell how a hero or handsome prince must confront danger before he can rescue his damsel in distress. The prince and the princess must overcome insurmountable challenges before they can be united. She is locked in a tower and he must slay dragons and rescue her. Along the way, our hero proves himself worthy of the hand of his fair maiden.

In real life however, a damsel who is waiting to be rescued is not in touch with her faculty for independent action. She places all her faith in the potential relationship, and the hero who will save her.

Similarly, a hero who is hell-bent on slaying dragons and battling enemies is not capable of entering into a relationship, let alone sustaining one. He is only focused on himself and places no importance on other people.

The interplay between Venus and Mars in the heavens shows us how we can balance these two opposing forces. The Venus-Mars dance is beautiful, creative and incredibly powerful. Their motion reveals just how these opposing magnetic polarities of self and others oscillate and how we can integrate them. When we understand a little bit about their celestial dance, Venus and Mars can teach us about their point of view. It is their role to help us to function independently while at the same time experiencing the joy of a wonderful loving partnership.

Cosmic Choreography

Before we can begin to learn the intricate and complicated manoeuvres Venus and Mars perform, and decipher what this might mean, we first need to learn some of their basic dance steps. We need to understand a little bit about the way the planets move in time with the music of the spheres.

When Galileo turned his telescope to the sky in 1610 he discovered the phases of Venus, thus confirming that the Earth was in orbit around the Sun. This was to be a defining moment leading to the eventual acceptance of the Copernican heliocentric view of the solar system. Yet what concerns astrologers most is the way we see the planets from Earth.

Phases are important because they are related to the position of the planets in relation to the Earth as well as the Sun. Understanding phases also helps us to interpret aspects.

The word 'phase' has two meanings, and they are connected. A 'phase' is a distinct stage in a process of development, and it also describes the aspect 'phase' one planet makes in relation to another planet. In this context planetary aspects are not fixed, but are part of a process of ongoing development.

It is also important to recognise the difference between zodiacal motion which is anti-clockwise as planets through the zodiac, and diurnal motion which is clockwise as planets rise in the east and set in the west.

But it is the third type of planetary motion that has to do with phase. This is the movement we see when we compare one planet's motion to another planet that is moving at a different pace; this is synodic movement. This can be clearly seen when you 'animate' a chart using an astrological software program. You will see the planets dance around one another and from this you can tell what phase a planet is in, relative to another. A planet's synodic cycle with another planet begins with the conjunction, waxes as it approaches opposition, then wanes as the cycle returns to the next conjunction.

When it comes to understanding this planetary motion, and phases, there are three categories of planets. These are the inferior planets which lie inside the Earth's orbit; the superior planets that lie outside Earth's orbit; and the Moon, which is in a category of its own.

As astrologers we tend to model our understanding of phases on the lunation cycle of the Moon, but there is one important difference; *the Moon is the only body which is waxing when in a latter degree of the zodiac than the Sun and waning when in an earlier degree.*

The planets beyond Earth's orbit, the superior planets, move in a *clockwise* direction around the chart wheel relative to the Sun. This is because the Sun is moving faster through the zodiac than these planets. It is only the Moon which moves *anti-clockwise* in her lunation cycle with the Sun.

The inferior planets, Mercury and Venus differ because they are never in opposition to the Sun. Mercury and Venus wax when they are morning stars, between inferior conjunction and superior conjunction, and wane when they are evening stars, after superior conjunction and before inferior conjunction.

So, except for the Moon, all planets, both inferior and superior, are waxing when in an earlier zodiacal degree than the Sun, and waning when in a latter degree.

'The rule is simple: two planets are considered to be in their waxing or lower aspect phase when the faster planet is approaching the opposition point of the slower planet according to the natural sequence of signs.'[2]

In his classic book, *Dynamics of Aspect Analysis*, Bil Tierney explains clearly how waxing aspects differ from waning aspects.

According to the *Oxford English Dictionary*, the term 'wax' means, having a progressively larger part of its visible surface illuminated. To 'wane' means having a progressively smaller part illuminated.

Although the term 'waxing' specifically relates to the progressive illumination of a planet's disc, astrologically planets are also said to 'wax' without any reference to the Sun.

For example, a waxing square between a slower moving planet, let's say Pluto, and a faster moving planet, for example Uranus, occurs when the faster planet is 90 degrees *further along the zodiac* than the slower one; as is the case with Pluto in Capricorn and Uranus in Aries. Uranus is said to be 'waxing' relative to Pluto.

The faster planet is separating from the slower one; hence we say Uranus is waxing. Although technically the Sun is not involved in any way, it is still astrologically correct to call this a waxing square.

Note that we are talking about a planet's speed based on its orbital position, rather than its actual daily motion, for example, Uranus' orbit is faster than Pluto.

Celestial Rhythms from a chart perspective

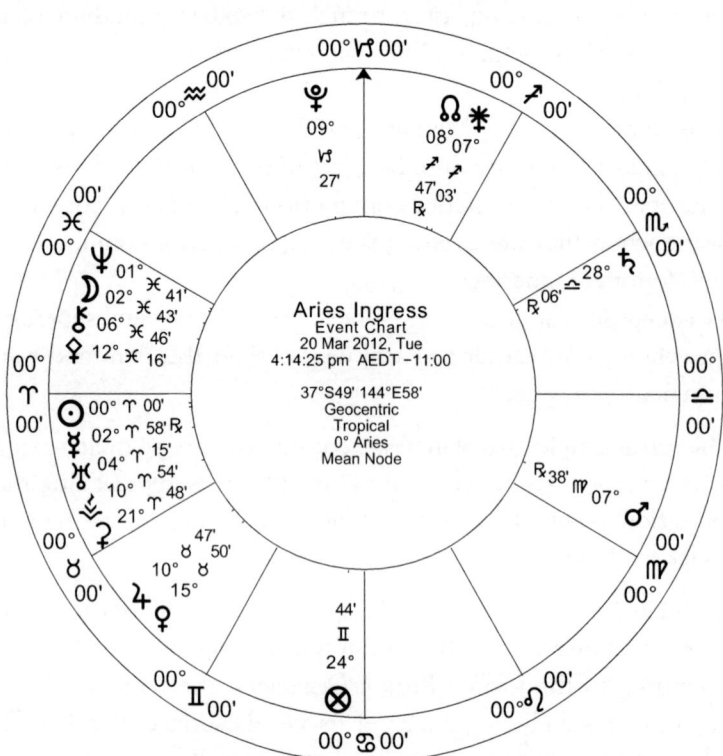

In the previous chart in relation to the Sun…

- Inferior planet Mercury ☿ is occidental (west of the sun), retrograde, waning and about to reach inferior conjunction. Mercury will then begin to wax and become a morning 'star'.
- Inferior planet Venus ♀ is occidental, the evening star, waning and close to greatest (eastern) elongation. Late in her cycle she stations retrograde in May.
- Superior planet Mars ♂ is retrograde, has just passed opposition (full) and has commenced waning. He stations direct in mid April.
- Superior planets Neptune ♆ Pluto ♇ and Saturn ♄ are oriental (east of the sun) and waxing. The Sun is separating from them.
- The Moon ☽ is oriental, but waning and in its balsamic phase, approaching the Sun.

Footnotes
1. http://www.etymonline.com/index.php?search=romance&searchmode=none [May 2011]
2. Bil Tierney, *Dynamics of Aspects Analysis*, CRCS Publications, California, USA, 1983, p.10.

Part Two
Mars and Venus

Mars

Astrologically, like Aries the sign he rules, Mars is impulsive and volatile. Aries has pole position at the beginning of the zodiac and Mars puts himself first too. He is independent and courageous. Psychologically, Mars is the archetypal hero in all of us. He is passionate and forceful and goes after what he wants. He expects to win.

The word 'hero' is from a root word that means 'to protect and to serve'.[1] But young heroes have no real understanding of this. Until life teaches him otherwise, Mars is only focused on himself, not interested in serving others.

In the horoscope it is Mars' role to help us forge our individuality and separate from our parents. Mars is animated, direct and spontaneous. Mars puts himself first, just like the colour red that comes first in the spectrum. The red planet symbolises the active, masculine principle.

> 'Animus, a word used to describe the masculine principle in Jungian terminology, is a Latin word for spirit; it is also a word when used in a particular way, means anger. Animus in its positive, creative form breathes life into situations and objects; it animates them.'[2]

Mars also has a Scorpio side, which makes him deeply emotional, intense and passionate. The eighth sign of the zodiac symbolises the hero's feminine side, his confrontation with death and his ultimate transformation. Mars must pass through dark and challenging times in order to grow in maturity and develop an awareness of others, including the feminine.

Mars' cycle and the aspects he makes to the Sun along the way, describe our journey from infancy, through adolescence, to adulthood, towards maturity and beyond and provides us with the challenges necessary for growth.

The Hero's Journey

In the 19th century anthropologists and psychologists realised that myths from many different civilisations, tribes and cultures were strikingly similar. In terms of their structure, these traditional stories, both oral and written, comprise many of the same elements and archetypal themes.

The hero starts out in an ordinary everyday world. He is called to adventure, where he faces numerous tests and challenges and is transformed by these events, before returning home to claim his reward. In *The Hero with a Thousand Faces*, Joseph Campbell mapped these archetypal patterns for the first time. Campbell's 'monomyth' outlines these various stages in the hero's journey.

This led others to undertake further analysis of mythic structure. In *The Writer's Journey*, Christopher Vogler shows how the many stages in the hero's journey feed the development of character, in storytelling and in our own individual life stories.

Whether by accident or design these maps describing the stages in the hero's journey are virtually identical to the orbit that Mars makes in relation to the Earth and the Sun – and have the same meaning.

As amazing as this might seem, it isn't really that surprising when we realise that this archetypal template is drawn from actual life events handed down through countless generations.

This is just one example of the mysterious links that exist between the macrocosm and microcosm, as above; so below. When we compare the hero's journey to the actual planetary motion of Mars in the sky, the aspects Mars makes to the Sun take on added significance. The hero's journey is our journey.

The Mars phase we were born into correlates with a particular stage in the hero's journey. This enables us to map and interpret aspects, transits and progressions in the context of our life experiences, tests and challenges.

The location of Mars in relation to the Sun – its phase – describes the type of Mars energy we possess and how Mars expresses itself. It tells us how we use our strengths. It helps us recognise there are others who have different ways of expressing their Mars talents, perspectives and points of view.

In numerous myths and stories as the hero sets out on his adventure, he must leave his princess behind. He faces tests of strength to prove

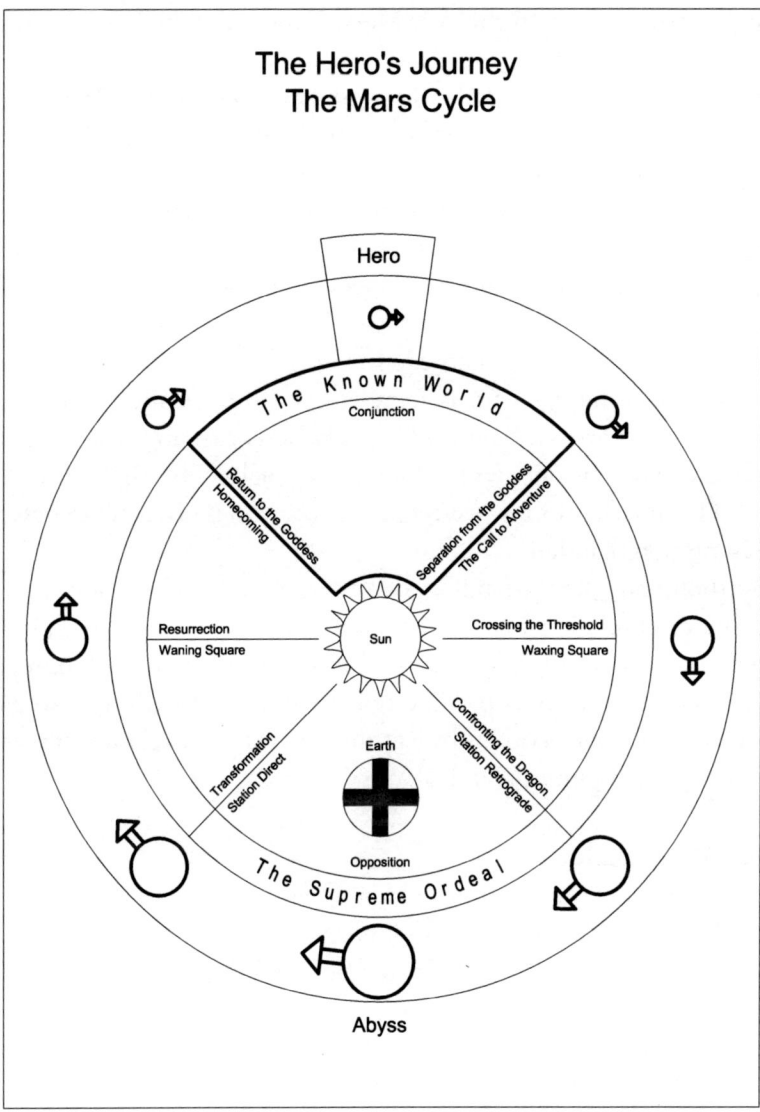

Diagram 1

The Hero's Journey and the Mars cycle. The above diagram shows the Mars-Sun cycle combined with features found in a variety of maps of the hero's journey. I have added two features, which are 'separation from the goddess' and 'return to the goddess', which are key aspects of many stories. These points in the Mars-Sun cycle correlate with the maximum solar orb of Venus; hence the 'known world' is the only region where Venus-Mars conjunctions can take place.

himself worthy of her. In this way Mars matures and the boy becomes a man.

As a rule men easily identify with the hero Mars. Most male archetypal figures generally contain some heroic elements. A woman's journey differs, but it too can contain many of the same features we see in the hero's journey. Women tend to more readily identify with one or more goddesses or heroines. This is reflected in the many differing roles that women undertake at different stages of life, or even throughout the day.[3]

As far as Mars is concerned, his cycle is interwoven with our relationship to 'father' who is represented astrologically by the Sun. Mars' journey starts and concludes when he is conjunct the Sun and culminates when he opposes the Sun at the height of his supreme ordeal which pits him against a powerful opponent, who is often an archetypal representation of father.

Without any understanding of others and no awareness of the importance of relationships, an immature Mars is only interested in his own desires and getting his own way. Ultimately, he becomes lonely and isolated and his victories become hollow. Independent Mars can gain the respect and love of others by learning to relate. His relationship with Venus can teach him a great deal.

The Mars Cycle

Before we explore the meaning of Mars at various stages of his journey, it can help to understand what Mars is actually doing in the sky, especially when he is retrograde. Mars orbits the Sun in 687 days, which is almost two Earth years. Seen from Earth, the journey from one Sun-Mars conjunction to the next is 780 days long. Of these 780 days, Mars spends anywhere between 60 and 82 days retrograde. Retrograde motion is only apparent from Earth. The duration of Mars' retrograde periods vary because Mars has a pronounced elliptical orbit.

The time Mars spends retrograde depends on where Mars is in his orbit. If Mars is retrograde while close to perihelion (making his closest approach to the Sun) this makes for a shorter retrograde period because a planet's speed is faster when closer to the Sun. When further away from the Sun in his orbit, Mars is moving more slowly so his retrograde period is longer.

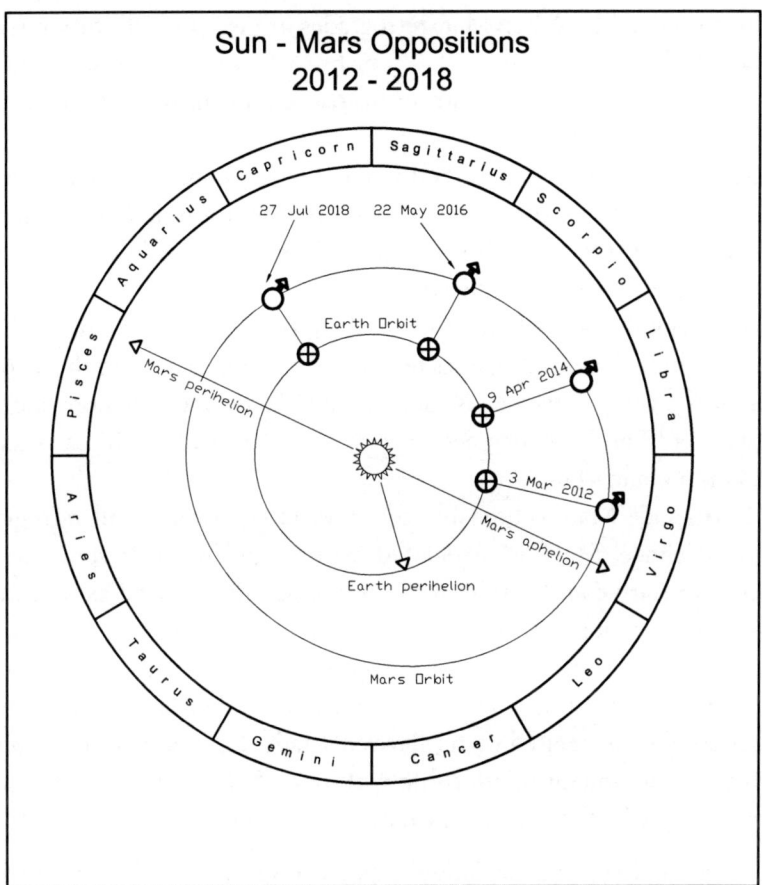

Diagram 2

Some years ago there was a great deal of media attention on Mars because the red planet was making a particularly close approach to the Earth. This took place in August 2003. This retrograde period was short; only 60 days, because Mars was extremely close to his perihelion at the time. Mars reaches perihelion in the early degrees of Pisces.[4]

By contrast the retrograde period of Mars in early 2012 occurred in the opposite sign Virgo. Being close to Mars' aphelion, this retrograde passage was extremely long, spanning 81 days.[5]

Unlike Venus whose orbit is virtually circular, Mars' elliptical orbit means that the point where Mars stations in relation to the Sun can vary quite considerably. When Mars retrogrades in Virgo he will station when only 130 degrees away from the Sun. But when he is in Pisces and his retrograde period is at its shortest, his stations occur when he is around 145 degrees from the Sun.

An extended time spent retrograde, which happens when Mars is retrograde in Virgo, therefore increases the duration and consequently the degree of difficulty of a retrograde Mars, and while in Pisces the duration and severity is reduced.

The region of sky where Mars can be retrograde, relative to the Sun, varies from between 70 degrees to 100 degrees depending on the sign he is in at the time. This means there are two 15 degree segments, located between 130 and 145 degrees away from the Sun where Mars enters a kind of 'no man's land'.

Retrograde Mars is arguably the most challenging of all retrograde planets. Since Mars is associated with impulsiveness, spontaneous energy, initiative and action, when retrograde this natural expression is thwarted. Development of the ego may stall. There can be a tendency to see others as holding all the power and strength. Other people may be seen as competitors with whom Mars must do battle. The seat of this inner conflict associated with Mars retrograde, especially for men, often stems from a difficult relationship with one's father, who is represented astrologically by the Sun. As Erin Sullivan points out...

> 'A natural striving for father's appreciation is quite healthy and usual for all of us in development. However, if our endeavours are not acknowledged we feel that those efforts will not be of any use. If this is the case, or it is felt to be the case, then the inclination is to invert Mars and stop seeking external recognition.'[6]

A retrograde Mars can feel inadequate, or powerless especially early in life. If the young ego is prevented from expressing itself, Mars will either retreat because he knows he cannot win the battle, or he will over-compensate and project his rage onto others, or onto the world.

Over time as the individual matures, natal retrograde Mars can become a great asset, capable of taking on tasks requiring almost super-human strength and endurance leading to lasting achievements. But initially Mars retrograde can hinder natural development and self expression until it finds a way forward.

The relationship, or aspect, between the Sun and Mars determines which 'phase' Mars is in. This tells us a great deal about the condition of the ego and what challenges lie ahead as we express our individuality and grow into adulthood.

Note that planetary positions for the Sun and Mars that enable you to work out your Mars phase can be found in the Appendix.

Phase One: The Action Hero
From Solar conjunction to the waxing semi-square
(Mars 0-45 degrees earlier than the Sun)
Duration: Around five to six months

This is the first stage in the hero's journey. Our young hero is in his 'normal world,' in safe and familiar territory. He is energetic and has an adventurous spirit. He draws on the power of the Sun, (father), but in order to prove himself he must venture out into the world on his own. He wants an adventure. He likes to have his own way and wants to win at all costs. Defeat is not an option.

Mars is moving fastest when conjunct the Sun. It is with a full tank of fuel that he sets off on his journey. While he is ready and eager to test his strength, he has little awareness of the long journey ahead of him.

This Mars is a hero in his own mind, but his scope is limited, at least initially. He tends to overestimate his power and underestimate the challenges that lie ahead. He has no real understanding of what is to come, because he has no practical experience of the world. He is great at taking the initiative, has great zeal and leadership potential, but he does not listen to advice and has great difficulty seeing things from another's point of view.

He may think he is bullet proof and as a result is apt to burn the candle at both ends, especially when young. There's no doubt he is courageous, but he can also be rather foolish and is prone to take unnecessary risks.

Dynamic and impulsive, those with Mars here thrive on action. They are highly creative, but often lack the necessary patience to follow through. It's not surprising that a number of famous thrill-seekers, including Steve Irwin, were born in this Mars phase.

Irwin's last risky adventure, which ended in his death, occurred when Mars was at 27 Virgo.[7] Mars was not retrograde at the time, but it was moving through the 'retrograde Mars area' of Irwin's natal chart, suggesting this was a challenging time.

While staying power is not their strong suit, the individual with Mars in this phase can develop and grow in awareness over time, especially if Mars progresses past the semi-square. Yet many are destined not to grow up and at times can display childish behaviour. In relationships this type can sometimes behave rather selfishly. Their task is to develop more awareness of others.

This Mars has the capacity to maintain their physical fitness well into old age, but can have trouble adjusting to a slower pace in later years.

It is interesting to note that the United States of America was 'born' in this Mars group, which might contribute to its military interventionist policies and ideas about the 'right to bear arms' which are ingrained in its constitution.

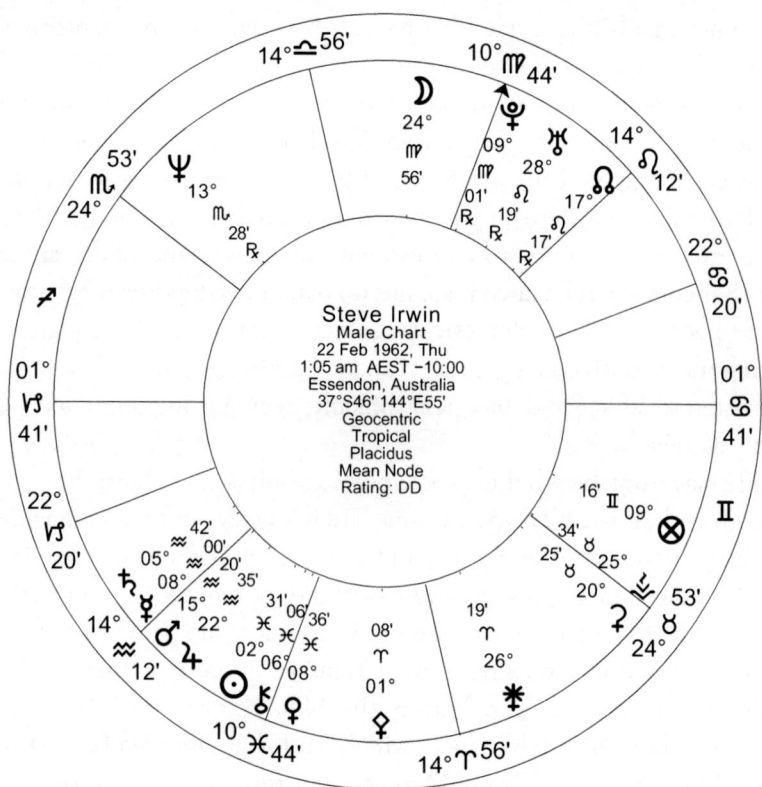

Those born with Mars (waxing) conjunct the Sun include: Liberace, Shirley MacLaine, Johnny Weismuller.

Others born in this group include: Peter Brock, Billy Connelly, Clint Eastwood, Bob Hawke, Jimi Hendrix, Charlton Heston, Sir Edmund Hillary, Jimmy Hoffa, Steve Irwin, Janis Joplin, Evel Knevel, Bruce Lee, Richard Nixon, O.J. Simpson, Margaret Thatcher, Orson Welles, Robin Williams.

Phase Two: Separation from the Goddess
Mars semi-square Sun to the waxing square
(Mars 45-90 degrees earlier than the Sun)
Duration: Approximately four months

Mars travels from the solar semi-square to the square during this phase and all the while he continues to move at about the same pace. This provides him with the means, motivation and staying power to achieve his goals.

This Mars group is more patient and persistent than the first group. Energy is now used in a more practical way. Skills are honed and utilised to achieve a goal.

During this stage of the hero's journey a mentor or teacher often appears. We can associate this with the waxing sextile and quintile.

Those who have these aspects between Mars and the Sun seem to have a fairly healthy relationship with their fathers. Father or another mentor will often guide their development and teach them useful life skills. As a result this Mars type is often gifted in creative, scientific or technical fields where invention, organisation and design are key components. Like the first group they also possess leadership skills but they generally have more awareness. When they are called to adventure they are often guided along by helpers, and they also inspire others to follow.

At the semi-square Mars leaves the 'Venus zone'. He must leave his true love behind, for he is called to adventure. Venus cannot go with him. She is compelled to stay at home and wait for her lover to return.

As they make their way in the world, these Mars types like to know they can depend on the support of family and loved ones. But at some point during the course of life they may experience a degree of disappointment when this support is withdrawn or becomes unavailable.

This has the effect of strengthening their resolve and helping them stand on their own feet. The main test this Mars type will face is finding the courage to journey on alone. Nevertheless, assistance, support and guidance are never far away.

As the waxing square approaches Mars enters a world that is unfamiliar, yet exhilarating. It is a world that he will create and influence. He wants to change it for the better and make his mark upon it.

A number of visionaries, leaders, scientists and inventors were born in this Mars phase. Alexander Fleming's discovery of penicillin revolutionised the treatment of disease. This took place in 1928 when his progressed Mars and progressed Sun were approaching the waxing square, in late Gemini and late Virgo respectively. At the same time, his secondary progressed Mars was making a creative conjunction to his natal Venus in Gemini.

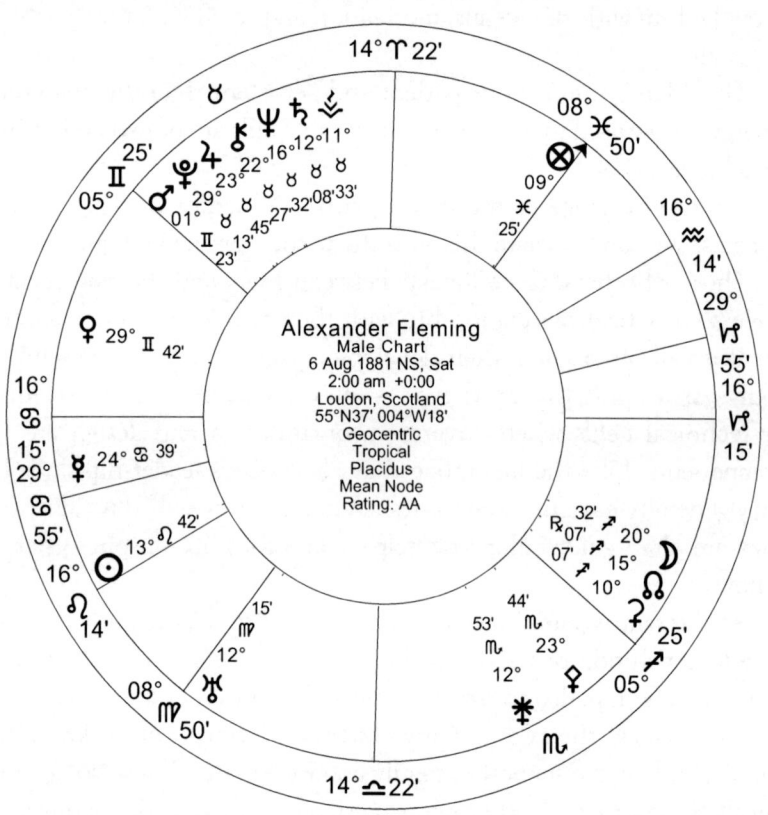

This Mars type often possesses a good mix of determination and adaptability. This persistence coupled with a willingness to experiment, the ability to keep an open mind combined with the right amount of ambition, persistence and good fortune, can lead to great achievements.

Those born in this group include: Maya Angelou, Alexander Graham Bell, Coco Chanel, Winston Churchill, Hillary Clinton, Thomas Edison, Albert Einstein, Alexander Fleming, Indira Gandhi, L. Ron Hubbard, Leonardo Da Vinci, Marilyn Monroe, Jules Verne, H. G. Wells, Oprah Winfrey.

Maria Von Trapp was born just before the waxing square.

Phase Three: Crossing the Adventure Threshold
From the waxing square to station retrograde
(Mars more than 90 degrees earlier than the Sun and direct)
Duration: Between six weeks and twelve weeks

At this point in the hero's journey, Mars faces his first real test. As the red planet heads further away from his energy source, the Sun, he begins to slow down. When Mars squares the Sun, he often stays in the same sign for up to seven months. This provides staying power, but it can equally cause things to stall. Those born in this Mars group can get stuck or bogged down. For while the Sun keeps moving at its regular pace, Mars continues to slow in speed before he stations retrograde in phase four.

The waxing square to the Sun is a crucial turning point for Mars. He can no longer count on the support of family and loved ones, he must travel on alone and find a new source of strength from within.

In the hero's journey, crossing the threshold involves entering a completely new environment and making a commitment to explore it. This is a leap into the unknown and it is risky. As heroes venture out into this new world, they can experience deep seated feelings of insecurity.

The challenge is to somehow overcome these feelings of inadequacy and find the courage to face these fears. This Mars type is capable of reaching great heights, but to get there they must navigate some deep gorges.

When called to adventure, heroes sometimes refuse the call. Christopher Vogler says that this refusal can take the form of making excuses or avoiding life. Fear can paralyse even the bravest hero. On the other hand, this refusal can sometimes be a positive step; allowing time to fully assess the dangers that lie ahead.[8] In this way the hero can make the necessary preparations. Yet in continually avoiding the adventure this Mars can remain trapped in the past.

In some ways Mars' journey is only just beginning, so it is vital for this Mars type to conserve their energy. If they push themselves too far, too quickly, burnouts and crash landings can occur.

Sadly, a number of famous personalities born in this group have died from drug and/or alcohol abuse. The list is a long one: Kurt Cobain, Errol Flynn, Michael Jackson, Elvis Presley, F. Scott Fitzgerald, Jack Kerouac, Johnny O'Keefe, Edith Piaf and Brett Whiteley.

All these talented artists died relatively young after many years of substance abuse.

After the solar square and before station retrograde Mars will trine the Sun. After managing the tension of the square and making a commitment to forge ahead into the unknown, when the trine kicks in our hero may try to take the easy road. His energy or enthusiasm may dissipate. At some point in this phase, Mars needs to rest and recuperate, to build up his energy reserves and confidence, for Mars will continue to slow as he progresses. Summoning the strength needed to keep going can be a real challenge for this Mars type. Those with the trine may find it difficult to harness the motivation and stamina they need to keep the momentum going for long periods.

External pressure to perform and meet others' expectations can bring matters to a head too. This Mars can find it hard to say no; feeling that to do so, is to admit defeat. As a result they can overcommit themselves which further saps energy reserves, that are then unavailable when they are needed most.

Such was the case for Elvis Presley who kept up a relentless tour schedule despite obvious signs of his failing health. Presley died at the age of 42 with progressed Mars at 24 Libra, shortly before it stationed retrograde. By this time Presley's progressed Mars was completing the fourth arm of a cardinal grand cross in his natal chart, squaring Pluto, Mercury and Venus and opposing his 5th house Uranus.

For many people born during this phase Mars will turn retrograde by progression in their lifetime. This generally brings some sort of

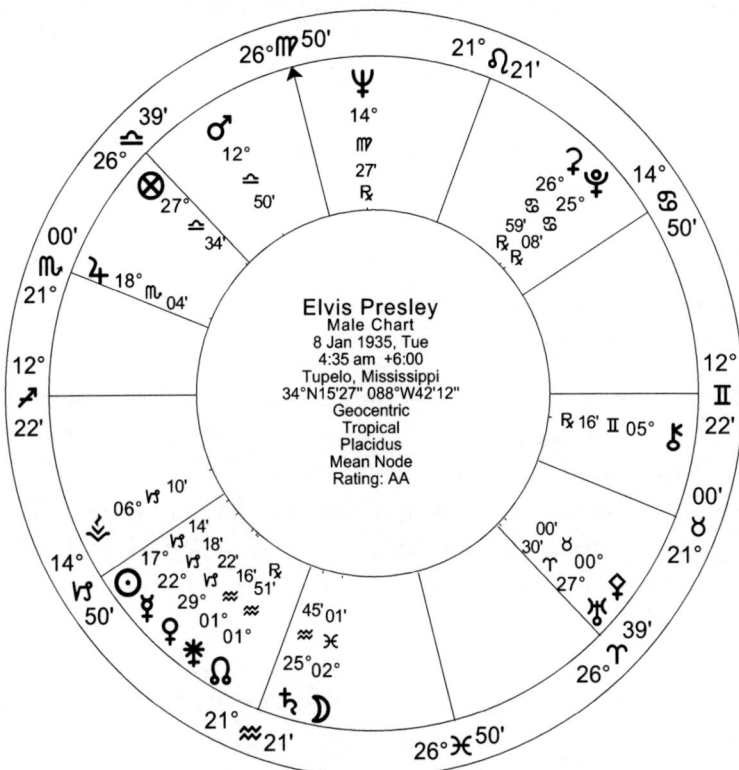

Elvis Presley
Male Chart
8 Jan 1935, Tue
4:35 am +6:00
Tupelo, Mississippi
34°N15'27" 088°W42'12"
Geocentric
Tropical
Placidus
Mean Node
Rating: AA

emotional, material or physical crisis requiring them to alter their course. Yet insecurity or feeling that they must persevere may prevent them from making necessary changes.

These highly creative and talented people will find their struggle easier in the long term if they can find a way to make small adjustments. Instead of embarking on huge projects or tasks they can benefit from breaking them into more manageable segments. The transition from youth to middle age can be a hurdle but learning to be flexible, laugh at life, and eliminating both worry and negative thinking can do wonders.

By conserving their energy and choosing wisely this Mars type can go a long way. They will achieve great feats through persistent application of their creativity and talents and avoid burn out by learning when to say yes, when to say no and when to say maybe.

Those born in this group include: Marie Antoinette, Cheiro, Kurt Cobain, Charles Darwin, Edward VIII, George Eliot, Elizabeth I, F. Scott

Fitzgerald, Errol Flynn, Patty Hearst, Michael Jackson, Jack Kerouac, Abraham Lincoln, Madonna, Kate Middleton, Bette Midler, Michael Moore, Johnny O'Keefe, Edith Piaf, Elvis Presley, Frank Sinatra, Mark Spitz, Brett Whiteley.

Those born just before station retrograde include; Julian Assange, Katharine Hepburn, Vivien Leigh, Rafael Nadal, Laurence Olivier.

Phase Four: Confronting the Dragon
From station retrograde to solar opposition
Duration: 30 to 40 days

As Mars pauses in the sky and begins to backtrack through the zodiac, his challenge is to find a new way to approach his objective; he must find a new path forward. Brute force will not work now.

Mars' very nature is all about action. He does not cope well with frustration, and frustration is exactly what Mars retrograde is about.

Natal Mars retrograde seems to operate in several distinct ways. It can take many years for a retrograde natal Mars to become an asset rather than a liability. By the time Mars retrograde is mastered, the individual is likely to have developed an incredible capacity for endurance and stamina, be it physical or mental, which can lead to mastery of their creative talents and to lasting achievements.

Yet sometimes, particularly early in life, this Mars type can be unsure what he wants from life, let alone know how to go about achieving it. He can feel intensely frustrated because no matter how hard he tries, he never seems able to express himself the way he wants to, nor is he able to meet with success. If at first you don't succeed, try again, the motto says. But try as he might, Mars' expression can be blocked at every turn. How can he possibly concede defeat? Defeat for Mars is simply not an option.

Sometimes there can be a total disassociation from a retrograde Mars and an accompanying tendency to project it onto others. It can foster an inferiority complex for which Mars compensates by overly aggressive behaviour.

Like Mars' two moons, Phobos (fear) and Deimos (terror), retrograde Mars can also manifest as a complete avoidance or negation of anything remotely masculine.

Whatever the case, retrograde Mars is notoriously difficult to master. The fight is often an internal psychological one, but because Mars is naturally inclined to seek out an opponent to battle, or an outer worldly challenge, he seldom looks within for the answers.

Mars is retrograde for up to 82 days – twice as long as Venus – so perhaps Mars retrograde is doubly difficult. It's probably fair to say that Mars retrograde is not as hard to manage for a woman as it is for a man, though women are perhaps more likely to project a retrograde Mars onto men, making their relationships with men extra challenging.

Because retrograde motion is only apparent when viewed from Earth, it suggests that Mars' struggle is somehow related to the reality of matter, but when retrograde his ability to bend matter to his will is tested. Obstacles preventing him from manifesting his desires can cause no end of frustration, but eventually lead him to look within for answers.

The problems associated with Mars retrograde can sometimes be due to medical issues, accidents, or other physical limitations and/or psychological issues associated with the quincunx aspect.

The waxing quincunx is an aspect connected with the earth sign Virgo, the sign of health, suggesting the need for self-analysis, adaptability and healing. Once used positively the intensity with which Mars can focus its energy when retrograde is quite breathtaking. It is interesting that Virgo is the sign in which Mars retrogrades for the longest possible time, again implying the need for healing and self analysis during this period.

An effective method for managing retrograde Mars is seen in the example of Frederick Alexander, who pioneered the *Alexander Technique*. Initially Alexander began his career as a Shakespearean actor but developed chronic laryngitis when performing, though oddly his voice was only affected while on stage.

'For in the mind of man lies the secret of his ability to resist, to conquer and finally to govern the circumstances of his life.'[9]
                    Frederick Matthias Alexander

Determined to fix the problem, he carefully examined his mannerisms in a mirror and noticed he was tensing his neck muscles in a way that was affecting his voice. After painstaking self examination he gradually learned how to alter involuntary muscle movements. Eventually he

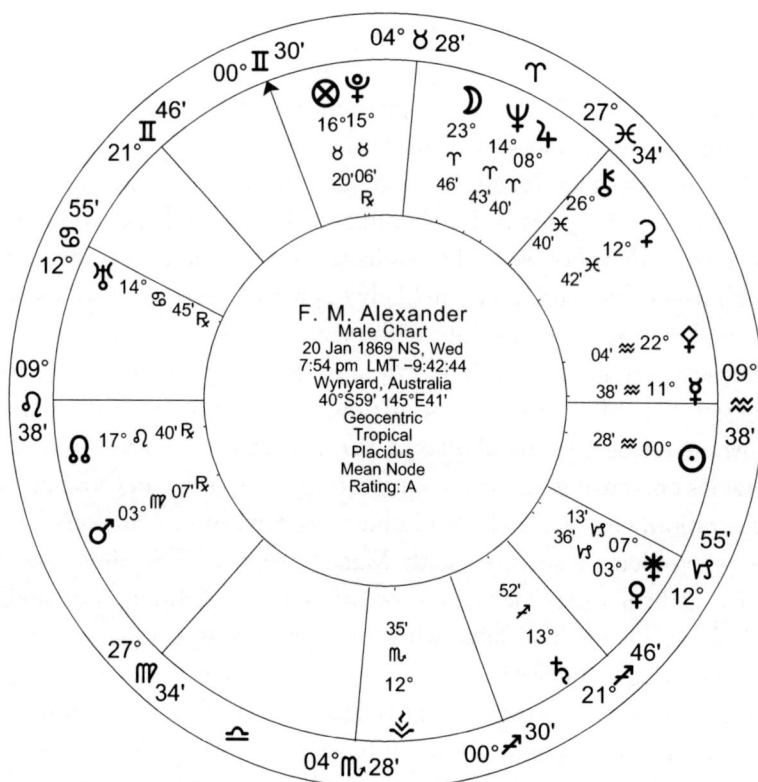

developed a comprehensive system to re-educate the body and the mind, known as the *Alexander Technique*.

His chart shows that his retrograde Mars is in fact in Virgo; the very sign in which Mars retrogrades the longest. Alexander's Mars is very close to its aphelion, which happens in the early degrees of Virgo. His progressed Mars remained retrograde until a few years before his death at the age of 86.

Alexander created a subtle, yet incredibly powerful healing technique which is taught throughout the world.

His willingness to examine and modify his unconscious behaviour facilitated his personal healing.

Those born in this group include: F. M. Alexander, Joan of Arc, Annie Besant, Karen Carpenter, Joan Crawford, Michel Gauquelin, William Hershel, John Howard, Saddam Hussein, John F. Kennedy Jr, Billie Jean King, Lindsay Lohan, Jack Nicholson, Nostradamus, Yoko Ono, Dame Joan Sutherland, Henri Toulouse Lautrec.

Phase Five: The Supreme Ordeal
From Solar Opposition to Station Direct
Duration: 30 to 40 days

This is the Full Moon of the Mars cycle. At opposition Mars is closest to the Earth and in the middle of his retrograde period. This is his ultimate test; the supreme ordeal.

As seen from Earth, Mars is full of light now, like a knight in shining armour, he is brighter than at any other time. His opposition to the Sun pits him in a test of strength with a powerful opponent, symbolised by the Sun.

But as Christopher Vogler explains in *The Writer's Journey*, the hero's greatest opponent is his own Shadow. His real battle is with the forces of the unconscious. These forces seem hell bent on destroying him, yet in hindsight they often turn out to be working in the hero's best interests.[10]

Sometimes Mars must battle with a powerful feminine force, perhaps with the forces of Mother Nature. In other heroic tales the supreme ordeal pits the hero against a father figure, astrologically symbolised by Mars' opposition to the Sun. The position of the Earth between Mars and the Sun symbolises these material, physical and spiritual tests. As seen from Mars, the Earth and Sun are in a conjunction. As far as Mars is concerned Mother Earth and Father Sun are ganging up on him.

With the Earth standing between Mars and the Sun, we see how Mars' ordeal and his retrograde challenge often involves issues relating to physical limitations or other problems managing the material world. Mars begins the waning part of his cycle at this vulnerable time. He is learning humility and learning about relationships too.

In the 1987 movie *Wall Street*, the hero Bud Fox, played by Charlie Sheen, is impatient for success. He sees his hard working father as a failure and instead emulates the greedy and ruthless Gordon Gekko, (Michael Douglas) who becomes his mentor.

Torn between two sets of values personified by his father and Gekko, Bud realises too late that there are no short cuts to success. As his life begins to unravel, Bud receives some words of wisdom from another older and wiser father figure, played by Hal Holbrook. who says to him, 'Just remember something. Man stares in the abyss, there's nothing staring back at him, at that moment man finds his character, and that's what keeps him out of the abyss.'

The 'father' of psychoanalysis, Sigmund Freud, was born in this Mars phase, while Carl Gustav Jung, who followed in Freud's footsteps, and took his pioneering work further, was born at the end of this phase, just after Mars stationed direct. Their legendary falling out over different interpretations of the unconscious was a key aspect of both men's supreme ordeals.

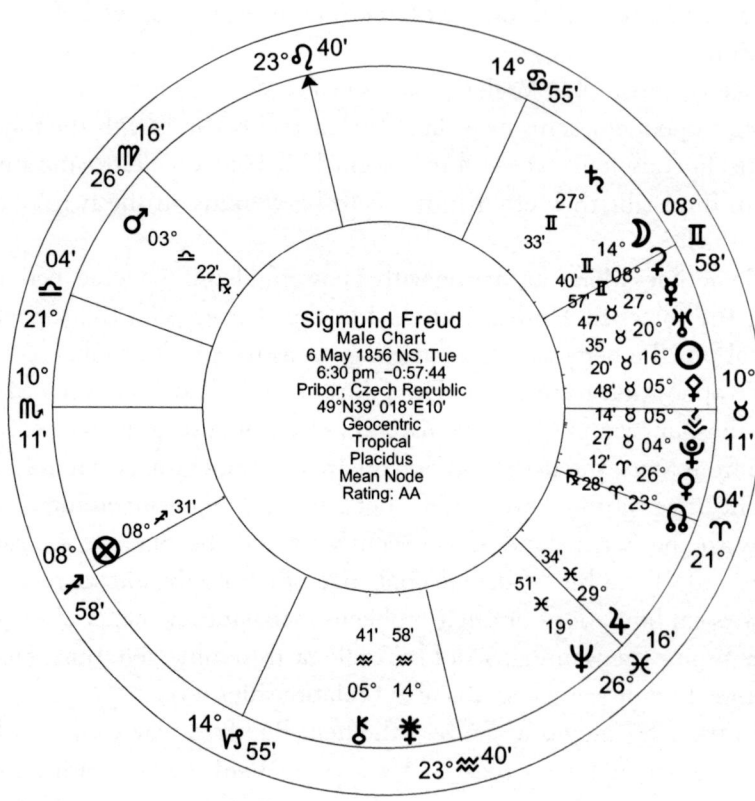

The intrinsic difficulty for Mars retrograde is that he has trouble looking within. Like his glyph ♂ his natural inclination is to focus outward. But what feels right may in fact be completely wrong, just as Frederick Alexander discovered when he looked in his mirror and examined his physical movements.

All opposition aspects including the Sun-Mars opposition facilitate greater awareness of oneself and others, broadening our perspective. But the way that Mars learns about these things is by having the courage to look within. In this way, just as Aries and Libra are opposites, Mars learns about his counterpart, Venus, the unconscious and inner feminine.

Those born close to solar opposition include: Judy Garland, Frida Kahlo, Ludwig van Beethoven.

Others born in this group include: Lord Byron, Lindy Chamberlain, James Dean, Robert Downey Jr, Betty Ford, Sigmund Freud, Steffi Graf, Pope John Paul II, Rodney King, Colleen McCullough, Spike Milligan, Mozart, Jim Morrison, Tiger Woods.

Karen Silkwood was born just before Station Direct.

Phase Six: Transformation
From Station Direct to the Waning Square
(Mars direct and more than 90 degrees later than the Sun)
Duration: Six weeks to twelve weeks

Somewhere between 130 and 145 degrees west of the Sun, Mars pauses to rest. He has travelled a long way and only just survived. He needs to recover his strength and get his bearings before he starts the long journey home. But the story is not over; there are further trials to come.

After he stations direct, Mars slowly starts to gain speed but he is in unfamiliar territory. The strangest part of this landscape is his new reborn Self.

Soon the hero feels a rush of energy and enthusiasm for this new challenge – to find his way home, to find love, and discover where he truly belongs. Yet this Mars can experience reversals of fortune and false starts. The temptation is to revert to old habits, or stay put, when a new approach is called for.

Those born in this Mars phase can seem fragile, shy and awkward especially when young and often appear to be quite content in the background.

There seem to be fewer notable people born in this Mars group than any other. The scorpionic nature of this Mars can lead this type into research or into work behind the scenes in niche areas involving painstaking focus.

This Mars is passionate, and can attain excellence in his chosen field, but at the same time he may never be acknowledged for his hard work and dedication simply because no one knows about it.

This Mars type may become obsessed by their passions as a way to avoid feelings of powerlessness or social awkwardness. Social situations and relationships can be where this Mars feels most vulnerable. He may try to avoid problems by staying isolated so he doesn't have to deal with feelings of inadequacy.

Some heroes born in this phase can encounter deep feelings of foreboding which inhibit the development and application of their talents. They may attempt to hide their true natures, for fear of being hurt or ridiculed. This can lead others to distrust or misunderstand them, complicating matters further.

Storyteller Hans Christian Andersen, author of many children's stories, was born in this Mars group. Andersen suffered several disappointments in love. He never seemed to fit in socially nor get his relationship timing right. His feelings of rejection, frustration and social isolation found an outlet in his stories.[11]

In his tale *The Ugly Duckling*, a young hatchling is taunted and teased so much that he leaves home and wanders the countryside. Wherever he goes he is abused and mistreated. He lives with some wild ducks and geese for a while until hunters slaughter the birds. And when he tries to make a home with an old woman and her cat, he is again abused. After spending a freezing winter out in the cold, miserable and alone, the ugly duckling transforms into a beautiful swan and is finally welcomed into a new flock.

This Mars may feel shy and uncertain but he longs to return to the warmth and safety he once knew. He wants to find love, but fears he will be rejected. Because he expects to be rejected, this can become his self fulfilled destiny. But eventually, as time passes and Mars speeds up he gains confidence. As he learns to share his experiences with others he will come to realise he is not alone. By trusting his instincts and learning to trust others he will be guided along the right path. When conditions are right, he will be transformed into the most beautiful swan and accepted into the flock.

Those born just after station direct include: Truman Capote, Carl Jung, Martina Navratilova.

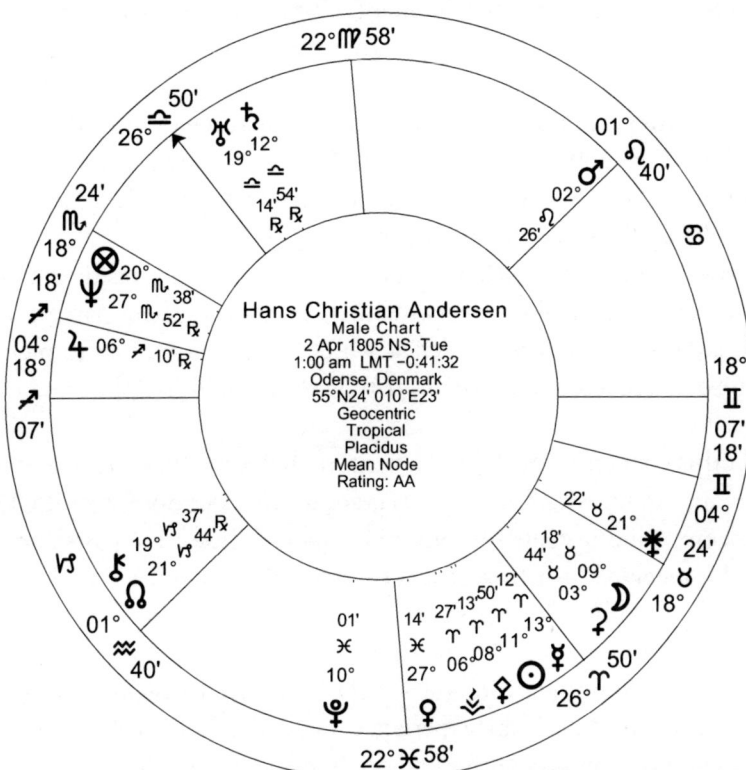

Others born in this group include: Muhammad Ali, Hans Christian Andersen, John Cleese, Brian Eno, John Paul Getty III, J. Edgar Hoover, Sir Charles Kingsford Smith, James Joyce, Julian Lennon, Liza Minnelli, Rupert Murdoch, Sir Isaac Newton, Lee Harvey Oswald.

Those born just before the waning square include; Nikola Tesla, Tina Turner, Shane Warne.

Phase Seven: Resurrection
From The Waning Square to the Waning Semi-Square
(Mars between 90 and 45 degrees later than the Sun)
Duration: Approximately four months

Mars gains speed at the applying square to the Sun. He senses the finishing line ahead, if only he could reach it. His energy is returning, but he must face one last test.

In terms of character development, Christopher Vogler describes the resurrection phase of the hero's journey as being the final attempt at a big change.

Up to this point the hero's transformation may have met with success, but if not, his inability to change will have consequences now. Failure is not an option. Success will bring mastery of the problem, as well as accolades and wisdom. It's all or nothing.

Early in life, those with Mars here may have experienced situations which left them feeling overwhelmed, or indeed their parents may have endured some form of defeat which left them having to pick up the pieces. This fosters a serious attitude to life, self-discipline and early maturity.

In this chapter of the hero's adventure, helpers, allies and guides will often appear, for which the hero is grateful. He does not forget the help he receives and accepts his personal responsibilities. He passes on the help he received, assisting others through difficult times. He does not try to blame others for his shortcomings. He soon learns that worldly achievement is not the only measure of success.

As the waning quintile and sextile bring fresh insights and a new awareness, this Mars can experience rapid psychological growth. As Mars speeds up, an innovative and original approach to life is often seen. In his classic book, *Dynamics of Aspect Analysis*, Bil Tierney describes the waning sextile, or as he calls it the 'upper sextile' as 'indicative of some degree of brilliance or the flashing spark of creative genius.'

This individual may feel as if he is ahead of his time, and so it can be difficult to find a niche into which he fits, especially early in life before he has an opportunity to develop the life skills and knowledge he needs. As he matures he can develop a keen social conscience and passion for humanitarian causes.

The theme of resurrection often plays a key role in the life of these Mars types, who can experience extreme reversals of fortune. However, their journey is not only about their personal resurrection, but in helping facilitate the resurrection of others.

Nelson Mandela was born in this Mars group. Born into a royal dynasty and descended from a tribal king, his struggle against apartheid in South Africa led to his imprisonment in 1962. His personal resurrection came with his release in 1990. He did not hesitate to take the reins of power

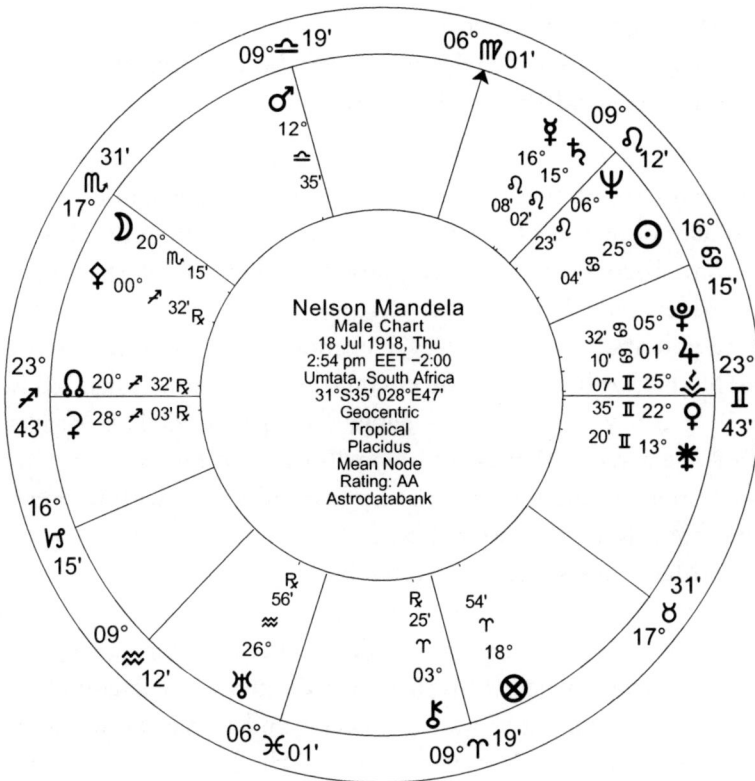

and lead his people towards freedom. He provided the inspiration and means for others to resurrect their lives.

By 1994 when Mandela was elected South African President at the age of 75, his progressed Sun was at 8 Libra, approaching his natal Mars. After five years in power his progressed Sun had reached natal Mars and his journey was complete.

Those born just after the waning square include: Natasha Richardson and Patrick Swayze.

Others born in this group include: Bob Ansett, Richard Branson, George W. Bush, Princess Diana, Charles Dickens, T. S. Eliot, Jane Fonda, Galileo, Ernest Hemingway, Henry VIII, Howard Hughes, Michael J. Fox, Nelson Mandela, Karl Marx, Aristotle Onassis, Christopher Reeve, Dane Rudhyar, Charlie Sheen, Cat Stevens, Pamela Travers.

Phase Eight: Return to the Goddess
From the Waning Semi-square to the conjunction
(Mars between 45 and 0 degrees later than the Sun)
Duration: Around five to six months

When Mars reaches the waning semi-square he re-enters the Venus zone and is reunited with his love goddess. This is his homecoming. Of course Venus may, or may not be waiting for him to return from his quest. She might have become tired of waiting around for her hero and be otherwise occupied, enjoying herself in the morning sky.

The potential reunion however is enough to give Mars a sense of hope. No matter how bleak the circumstances, or how exhausted he is from his journey, he is generally happy and optimistic. This Mars is an idealist. He assumes that everything will turn out for the best. Even if Venus is not waiting for him, and no love interest is within range, he knows that it is only a matter of time.

This Mars is a visionary who often has a sense of mission or 'calling'. Matters of principle are important to him and he is willing to champion causes close to his heart, or on behalf of others. He has staying power and he is often far ahead of his time. Success may come late in life.

This Mars is willing to wait for success and is one the whole more patient than the equivalent waxing aspect. He does not expect rewards to come without putting in the required effort. He is very single minded and can be stubborn. He will persevere despite setbacks. No matter how long it takes, this Mars seeks to master the problems he encounters. Once his mind is made up, he sticks to his guns.

Antarctic explorer Ernest Shackleton is a good example of this Mars type. Shackleton survived three failed expeditions to reach the South Pole. On the third attempt, his ship, aptly named *Endurance*, was crushed in the ice before the Antarctic crossing even got underway.

Shackleton never reached his goal and his self esteem suffered as a result.[12] But his greatest achievement was in the manner of his leadership. Despite incredible hardships and freezing temperatures he managed to lead his party to safety without the loss of a single life.

With this type the progressed Sun will cross natal Mars as the distance between them diminishes. If there is a close applying conjunction in the natal chart between Mars and the Sun, and this conjunction becomes exact by progression before the individual has matured sufficiently, the

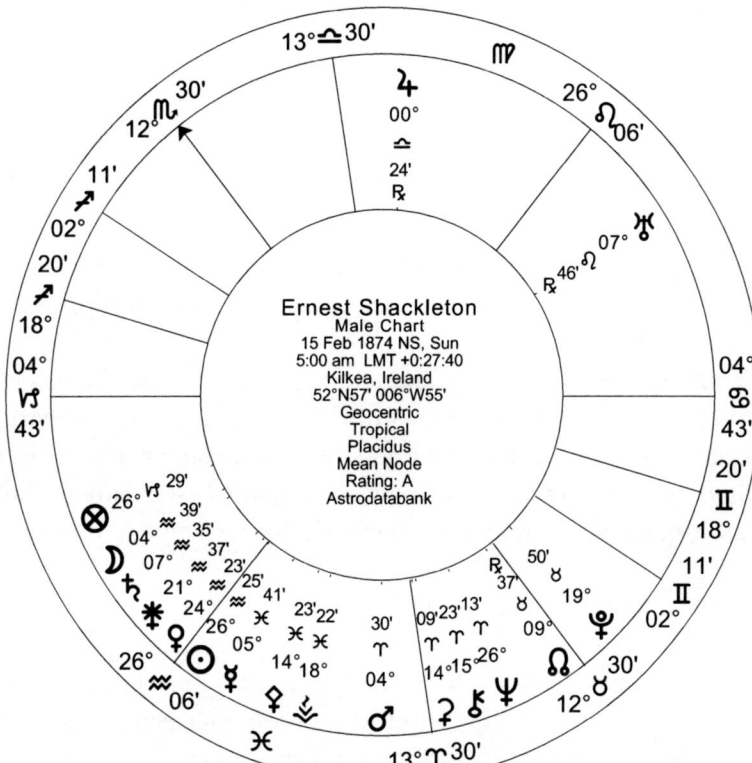

ego can become overblown and further development can be hindered. In some cases it can be difficult to tell the difference between those born in this group and the first Mars group, although this Mars usually has a much broader perspective and benefits from developing a sense of spiritual awareness and understanding.

When he arrives home Mars will tell the story of his heroic adventures and pass on the wisdom he has learned along the way. If he has achieved true hero status, his goddess will embrace him and open his heart to love.

Those born in this group include: Amelia Earhart, Captain William Bligh, Joseph Campbell, Bill Clinton, Walt Disney, Henry Ford, Stephen Fry, Mata Hari, Adolf Hitler, Lleyton Hewitt, Glenda Jackson, Barack Obama, Michelle Obama, Louis Pasteur, Geoffrey Robertson, John D. Rockefeller, Ernest Shackleton, Steven Spielberg.

Those with Mars conjunct the Sun (applying) include: Salvador Dali, Sarah Palin, Dorothy Parker, and Peter Sellers.

VENUS

Venus symbolises love, beauty and fertility. She desires to connect with another because she wants to experience love and relationship, for both pleasure and to procreate.

Venus represents our core values and self esteem, and the qualities we find attractive, valuable and worthwhile. She symbolises everything from personal adornment, to the value we place on our talents and those of others, as well as the deepest and most immutable standards we hold. But most of all Venus wants to experience love; to give it and receive it.

Throughout history Venus has been depicted as having two distinct sides to her nature, as shown by her morning phase and her evening phase. In her morning phase Venus is youthful and innocent and mostly focused on her own values and self expression. Her personal interests and pleasures come first. In this respect Venus as morning star is a bit like Mars. Venus waxes when in the morning sky, hence she is outgoing and takes the initiative. In her evening phase Venus is more sensitive, mature and worldly and has greater awareness of others. Community and spiritual values are a higher priority for evening star types. Venus' dual nature is also shown by her rulership of Taurus and Libra.

The key asteroids Vesta, Athena and Juno and 'dwarf planet' Ceres represent various aspects of the feminine in their own right, but we can also see these archetypes at work in the primary female symbol of Venus.

Jean Shinoda Bolen, in her 1984 book, *Goddesses in Every Woman* describes Venus as an alchemical goddess who embodies all dimensions of the female psyche. Venus incorporates the qualities of all other goddess types including many different virgin goddesses as well as princess, wife, mistress, sister, mother, earth mother and wise woman to name several.

Morning Star

Venus Lucifer (Latin) or Phosphorus (Greek).

The term 'Lucifer' has nothing whatever to do with the devil. Lucifer means 'light bringing'. Venus Lucifer describes the morning star as it rises before the Sun, heralding the light of a new day. Its association with evil is due to an erroneous interpretation of Isaiah 14.12 in the Old Testament.

Evening Star

Venus Vesper (Latin) or Hesperus (Greek).

Vesper is also the name given to the sixth canonical hour of prayer.[13] Hesperus means 'western'. In Greek mythology Eosphorus (Phosphorus) and Hesperus were the gods of Venus. Eosphorus was the god of the morning star, while the Hesperus was the god of the evening star.[14] They were originally depicted as two separate gods, but were later combined.

Venus and the Golden Mean

Venus has a special connection with fertility and the beauty of the natural world. Consistent with the human gestation cycle, the planet Venus spends about nine months as morning star and nine months as evening star.

As seen from Earth, Venus retrogrades five times in eight years, her path drawing a beautiful flower in the heavens.

While Venus symbolises beauty and fertility, the planet itself is hostile to life. Only on planet Earth can we experience the beauty of nature that Venus symbolises.

The intrinsic beauty of Venus is also seen in the near perfection of her circular orbit, as she travels around the Sun in 225 days.

The synodic relationship with Earth is in the ratio of 225:365 or 5:8, and the Earth-Venus' cycle 584 days. 365:584 is in the same ratio, known as the Golden Mean.

The Golden Mean is associated with the Fibonacci series of numbers. Consecutive numbers in this series when added together create the next number; 0,1,1,2,3,5,8,13,21,34,55 and so on. When these numbers are plotted geometrically, a spiral pattern is created. (Diagram 4)

Diagram 3
The beautiful Venus-Earth rosette pattern which is created as Venus
retrogrades. Five Earth years equals eight Venusian years.

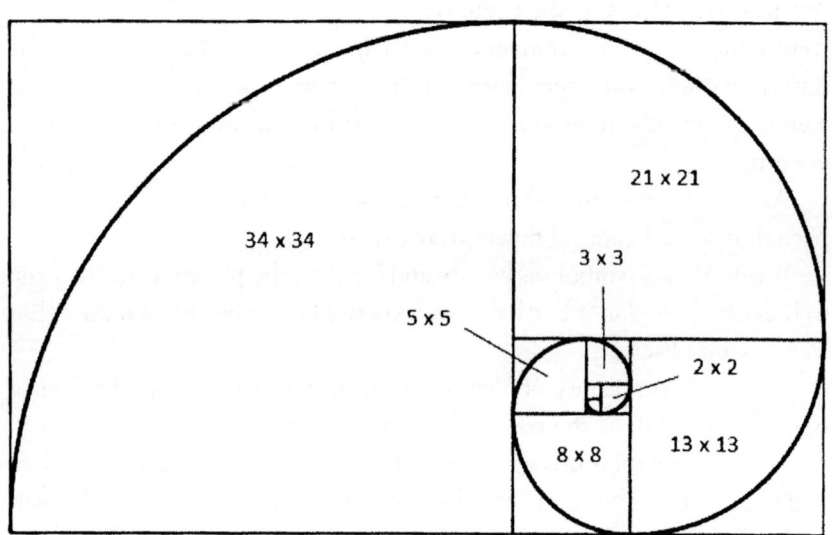

Diagram 4
The Golden Mean Ratio corresponds mathematically to the natural
spiral pattern of growth seen in nature.

The Golden Mean, which is also known as the Golden Ratio or Golden Section, is a naturally occurring pattern of growth which is intrinsic to life itself. Flowers, ferns, plants, shells, and antlers naturally grow and develop in this manner. Indeed all life, from the minute spiralling structure of DNA to the vast reaches of space with its spiral galaxies, is imbued with this beautiful creative pattern.

The Golden Mean was used extensively in classic architecture and art because of the intrinsic beauty of its proportion. It is still seen today in numerous household objects and everyday products and even in the dimensions of the credit cards that we use to purchase them.

Venus has a unique association with the number five. Every fifth conjunction of Venus and the Sun takes place around the same zodiacal position. Venus is connected with the five senses; sight, hearing, taste, smell and touch; for the senses are the methods that we use to evaluate the beauty and merit of all we encounter. This is how we determine our likes, dislikes and personal preferences. What tastes good, what feels nice, who do we find attractive?

In Chinese astrology there are five elements. Venus resonates with the element metal which is said to be the purest of the Chinese elements. It is associated with the colour white, the lungs and the breath of life. The metal element is described as conferring spiritual strength and is also related to our core values and essence. Mars in the Chinese system relates to the fire element, the heart, blood circulation, the muscles and the colour red.

- Venus stations retrograde when she is the evening star.

- Venus stations direct when she is the morning star.

- Venus stations when semi-sextile the Sun (approximate orb 1.5)

- Venus is retrograde 40 days at a time, five times in 8 years.

The Heroine's Journey

There is much more to Venus than just her sign and aspects to other planets. Was Venus the morning star or the evening star on the day you were born? Was she moving towards the Sun, or away from it? How fast was she travelling? What do her phases mean astrologically? What do these things tell us about our personal values and relationship style?

Venus position	Date	Time (GMT)[15]	Degree/Sign	Magnitude/Elongation
inferior conj	2012 Jun 6	01:09	15 GE 44'46"	
transit begin	2012 Jun 5	22:10	15 GE 49'29"	
transit end	2012 Jun 6	04:49	15 GE 38'59"	
morning rise	2012 Jun 12	09:53	11 GE 55' 1"	
direct	2012 Jun 27	15:07	7 GE 29'16"	
greatest brilliancy	2012 Jul 10	20:26	10 GE 32'46"	-4.5m
morning max el	2012 Aug 15	09:07	7 CN 13'45"	45°48'10"
morning set	2013 Feb 16	14:36	18 AQ 8'55"	
superior conj	2013 Mar 28	17:05	8 AR 10'36"	
evening rise	2013 May 6	08:47	25 TA 59'11"	
evening max el	2013 Nov 1	07:59	26 SA 1'29"	47° 4'26"
greatest brilliancy	2013 Dec 10	02:30	26 CP 21'40"	-4.7m
retrograde	2013 Dec 21	21:53	28 CP 58'57"	
evening set	2014 Jan 5	18:51	24 CP 35'44"	

Table A: The cycle of Venus including the 2012 transit.
See Appendix for full list of Venus positions.
Data supplied by Astrodienst www.astro.com

Table A shows key positions of Venus throughout her 19-month cycle. Her cycle commences at inferior conjunction, culminates with her superior conjunction and through to her evening set and next inferior conjunction. To discover exactly where Venus was on your day of birth Appendix A includes all Venus positions for the years between 1921 and 2020.

Venus can never be more than 48 degrees distant from the Sun. Unlike Mars who forms all aspects to the Sun in his heroic journey, Venus moves back and forth relative to the Sun. This arrangement tells us that despite her ability to separate from her 'father' the Sun, Venus maintains relationships. She is able to express herself independently, but also appreciates the value of a special connection.

In her morning phase Venus first separates from the Sun until reaching greatest elongation, then she applies to the Sun until reaching superior conjunction. She separates from the Sun in her evening phase until greatest elongation is reached once more, and then applies to the Sun until reaching inferior conjunction.

Note that when two planets are moving towards one another they are applying, and when moving apart they are separating, but this is not the same thing as an *applying or separating aspect*. An applying aspect is one where the *angle* itself is approaching a zero orb, and a separating aspect is when the aspect has already been exact.

Venus Waxing Phase (Yang)

Morning star – **before** greatest elongation (several weeks duration)
Venus **separates** from the Sun until greatest elongation
- Less than 45 degrees, **applies** to a semi-square
- More than 45 degrees, **separates** from semi-square

Morning star – **after** greatest elongation (several months duration)
Venus **applies** to the Sun until superior conjunction
- More than 45 degrees, **applies** to a semi-square
- Less than 45 degrees, **separates** from semi-square

Venus Waning Phase (Yin)

Evening star – **before** greatest elongation (several months duration)
Venus **separates** from the Sun and if her angle to the Sun is
- Less than 45 degrees, **applies** to a semi-square
- More than 45 degrees, **separates** from a semi-square

Evening star – **after** greatest elongation (several weeks duration)
Venus **applies** to the Sun and if her angle to the Sun is
- More than 45 degrees, **applies** to a semi-square
- Less than 45 degrees, **separates** from a semi-square

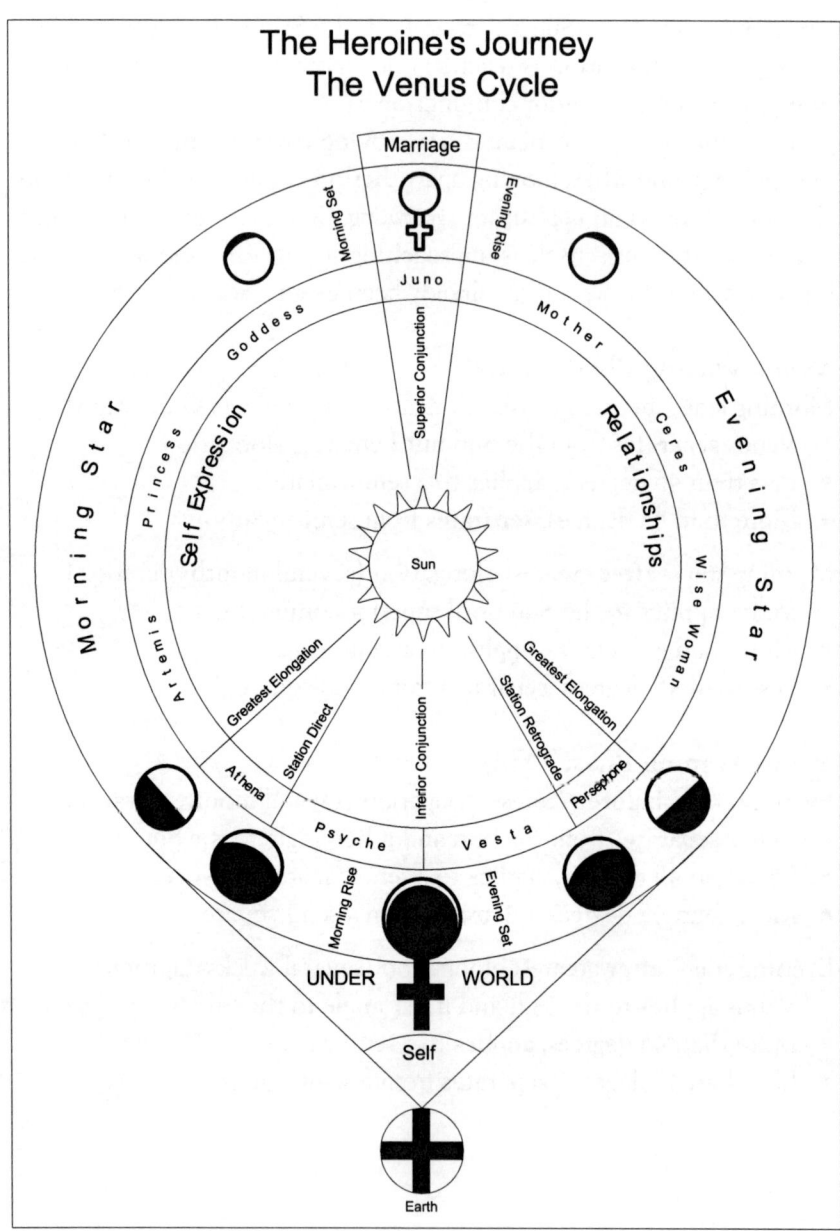

Diagram 5

The Venus Cycle

Phase One: The Birth of Venus
From Inferior conjunction to Station Direct
(0-30 degrees earlier than the Sun)
Morning Star
Oriental Venus Retrograde
Separating from the Sun
Duration: Three weeks

The Venus cycle commences with her inferior conjunction, half-way through her retrograde period. This initial phase takes us through her morning rise, when she first becomes visible before dawn, to her station direct point, when she is semi-sextile the Sun.

These first three weeks of her cycle are akin to Venus' mythic birth in the foaming ocean. Venus emerges youthful, beautiful and fresh, but having only just been born, she must rely to a large extent on her instincts.

Those born in this phase seem to have an air-like quality to their Venus nature. Although lacking experience, this Venus is independent, spontaneous and full of youthful enthusiasm.

Soon after her inferior conjunction Venus and the Sun quickly separate. Venus moves backwards through the zodiac while the Sun travels about a degree each day in direct motion.

This rapid separation from the Sun suggests a withdrawal of parental support, and/or alienation from a father figure, which seems to happen early in life for a significant number of people born in this phase.

Circumstances in early life can indeed be similar to the mythic birth of Venus who was born from the seed of castrated Uranus. Father may have had his power stripped away or he may have died, or departed before a relationship could be established with his offspring. Father may have simply 'deposited his seed'. In one way or another father is often absent, or distant.

Often this Venus has to fend for herself from an early age, or must break free from her parents in order to survive and thrive. There can be impoverished early circumstances, either materially, or in terms of the amount of love and support received. Despite early setbacks or because of them, there is often a powerful need to express creativity and individuality.

To some extent all those born with Venus retrograde are loners because with only seven percent of the population having Venus retrograde they are in a minority group and hence are often misunderstood. Being misunderstood can foster feelings of isolation and introversion. It can be difficult to establish relationships, especially in youth, when peer support is often crucial. But this half of the Venus retrograde group is more likely to take the initiative in relationships than the evening star type.

Despite outward appearances to the contrary, those born in the early part of the Venus cycle are often emotionally fragile, but tend to hide this fragility underneath a vibrant, bubbly exterior. In relationships this Venus can experience a great deal of uncertainty about how much they should compromise for the sake of a relationship.

There seems to be an affinity between those born with Venus conjunct the Sun and those born around greatest elongation. It seems fairly common in couples that one person has Venus conjunct the Sun and the other has Venus-Sun in semi-square; the common denominator being Venus and the Sun in aspect. It appears that those who have Venus and Sun in aspect are apt to enter into relationships with one another.

When Venus transits through this phase it is a good time to perform rituals and visualise the relationship one wants. Since this is the beginning of the cycle, in a way this Venus phase sets in motion the natural pattern of spiral growth and fertility she is known to possess. It is therefore the perfect time to call on the creative power of the unconscious to weave its magic.

About five days after inferior conjunction when Venus is about eight or ten degrees earlier in the zodiac than the Sun, she becomes visible as the morning star. Sleeping Beauty awakens.

Venus's visibility makes her more conspicuous. Despite the fact that she is still in retrograde motion, she is more animated. Young Venus is learning to stand on her own two feet, and fast.

Those with Venus here often become leaders or icons of style. They tend to develop strong opinions and values. Their personal standards are very important especially those formed early in life.

Despite their insecurities, which are generally related to their inexperience and/or lack of support received in childhood, these people often gravitate to positions of leadership. This is especially true for those born after morning rise; just like Venus they are more conspicuous and visible.

Station direct is a significant turning point in the Venus cycle. The station of Venus by transit to one's chart can also herald the start of a new relationship, in particular if this station hits a personal planet, especially Venus or Mars.

The later that one is born in this three week period, the earlier in life Venus stations direct by progression. These first impressionable years can bring a significant event often involving one's parents, which results in a completely different path in life.

Such was the case for Audrey Hepburn whose father abandoned the family when she was six years old, just as her progressed Venus was about to station direct. Audrey later described this as the most traumatic event of her life.

Audrey's father was a brilliant man, a pilot; he spoke thirteen languages and had a passion for humanitarian causes and originality. A virtual cardboard cut out of the Uranus/Promethean archetype, he was a highly restless man and had difficulty remaining in stable employment.

In 1939, when Audrey was ten, her mother moved the family from Belgium to the Netherlands, thinking they would be safe from the advancing German army. Here Audrey studied ballet, with ambitions to make it her career. After the Allied invasion in 1944 freed the Netherlands from German occupation, Audrey almost starved to death in the Dutch famine.

Aid eventually came. Audrey never forgot the help she received. From the 1950s she involved herself in humanitarian work for UNICEF, later becoming a goodwill ambassador.

These early experiences shaped her values to a great extent. After the war she was too malnourished to become a ballerina. Nevertheless, her 'star' just like Venus, rose quickly with a career as a model and actress.

Strongly principled with a caring heart, Audrey Hepburn epitomised the strength, sensitivity and fragility that often go hand-in-hand with natal retrograde Venus.

Audrey's father, just like Uranus, was emotionally and physically absent from her life. Even when Audrey managed to track him down he was not able to express the love, admiration and pride he felt. It was a pattern Audrey repeated in her personal relationships. She was drawn to men who were unable to express their feelings.

Audrey's son Sean writes in his insightful biography of his mother, that her two marriages were in many ways "a continuation of the same dynamic",[16] a repeat of the initial lack of connection she had with her father. He also writes that "the 'emotional hunger' that 'food cannot alleviate'" was how his mother described the children she met in her tours on behalf of UNICEF. He continues, "it was something she knew how to recognise".[17]

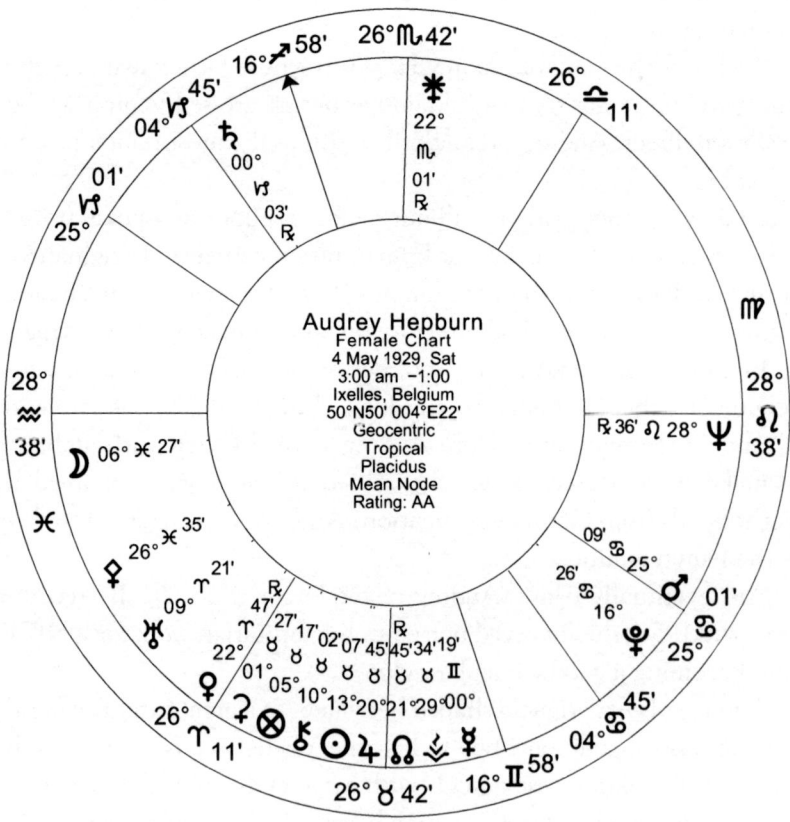

Venus retrograde may be in for a rude shock when she discovers that her standards differ from those which are considered to be social norms, and that cruelty, loneliness and poverty are facts of life. This can foster a passionate response and efforts to redress the situation.

Those born during this Venus retrograde phase want very much to find someone to give their love to, more so perhaps than to receive it.

Others may view this person as a leader, a trendsetter, or role model. They are often greatly admired, although inwardly they may not feel so loved. For better or worse this Venus is destined to stand out from the crowd.

Those born during the invisible morning star retrograde phase include: Kathy Bates, Chrissie Hynde, Chris Isaak, Jack Nicholson, Magda Szubanski, Venus Williams.

Those born in the visible morning star retrograde phase include: Jose Carerras, Jodie Foster, Tom Hanks, Peter Garrett, Audrey Hepburn, Barry Humphries, Saddam Hussein, Julio Iglesias, Carole King, Alan Leo, Courtney Love, Cybil Shepherd, Richard Simmons, Ringo Starr, Gough Whitlam.

Associated Goddess Archetype: Psyche

Phase Two: I am woman
Venus Direct Phase
From Station Direct to Greatest Western Elongation
(30-48 degrees earlier than the Sun)
Oriental Venus
Morning Star
Venus direct separating from the Sun
Duration: About seven weeks

As Venus turns direct she starts to become more animated and conscious. She is more aware of her beauty and desirability and this starts her on a journey towards womanhood and relationship.

This Venus is free and independent and full of youthful enthusiasm. She knows her own heart and mind and actively goes after her desires.

Venus is waxing in her morning phase and now that she is moving direct, she is also more direct in her actions and behaviour. She takes the initiative. She chooses who she will relate to and outlines her terms and conditions. She calls the shots.

Although still young, Venus is more empowered and willingly and eagerly enters into relationships. Her main concern now is having her personal needs and desires met.

There is a carefree quality to Venus expression in this direct separating phase. Eager to experience love, but equally keen to express herself as an individual, she is open and honest about what she wants. What you see, is exactly what you get. She might flirt, but you know she is flirting. If she seems interested in you, she is interested in you. She is keen to see where life will take her and where relationships might go. Equally, those born during this period can sometimes rush into relationships prematurely in their eagerness to experience life and love.

As Venus reaches greatest western elongation she becomes very outgoing and highly animated. Those born with Venus beyond 45 degrees from the Sun and still separating can be quite strident in expressing their views. The Athena archetype can take over.

Germaine Greer was born one day before Venus reached greatest elongation. A leader of the feminist movement, Greer epitomises the lengths to which a waxing Venus will go when separating from the Sun. Highly independent with powerfully expressed opinions, and uncompromising in her values and standards.

Upon publication of her controversial 1971 book, *The Female Eunuch*, Greer was quoted as saying, "women have been cut off from their capacity for action. It's a process that sacrifices vigour for delicacy and succulence, and one that's got to be changed".[18]

This Venus finds expression in breaking down outmoded concepts and standards which need challenging. This is a fiery and Mars-like warrior Venus.

At this point, with Venus so distant from the Sun, independence can be a blessing and a curse. A deep feeling of aloneness can pervade the psyche. It can be difficult to establish connections with others. Venus is unwilling to compromise until after reaching greatest elongation.

About two weeks into this phase, after Venus stations direct she reaches her greatest brilliancy, (this also happens in the equivalent evening star position, about two weeks before she stations retrograde). At these times Venus shines at her brightest. She dazzles. It is worth noting these dates. Significant encounters, opportunities, promotions and recognition can occur if Venus happens to be transiting over a natal planet, or angle when brightest.

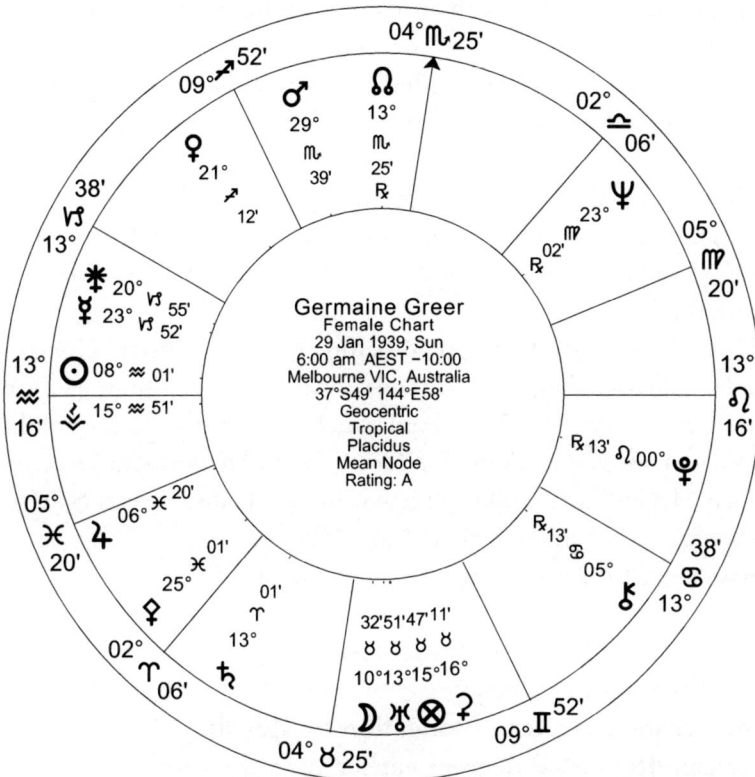

Germaine Greer
Female Chart
29 Jan 1939, Sun
6:00 am AEST −10:00
Melbourne VIC, Australia
37°S49' 144°E58'
Geocentric
Tropical
Placidus
Mean Node
Rating: A

Regardless of whether one has natal Venus in this phase or not, this part of her cycle is a good time to commence a new relationship for Venus has a great deal of forward momentum.

The goddess will bestow her gifts of love, beauty, creativity, fertility and good fortune when she is in a good position herself. This is a creative, expressive and fertile time, similar to a waxing Moon, and seems to be equally good for planting crops, commencing a relationship or starting a creative project.

If a new love relationship begins during these few weeks it does so because both parties are conscious and clear about what they want. Singles are more likely to establish new connections now because a waxing and separating Venus enhances self confidence.

Ideally, two people should use this period to get to know one another and allow love to grow naturally. Assuming both parties are happy with the fast pace, chances are that a connection will develop fairly quickly.

My partner and I had been acquaintances for about five years before our relationship began. Around the time that Venus stationed direct we started spending more time together. Three weeks later, in the middle of this phase we fell in love. Instantly, we both knew without a doubt it was right.

Those born with Venus at the beginning of the visible direct morning star phase include: Julie Andrews (SD), Tony Blair (SD), George Clooney, Mata Hari, Christine Keeler (SD), Julie Walters (SD), Amy Winehouse (SD).

Those born with Venus **just before** greatest western elongation include: Chrissie Amphlett, David Bowie, Melissa Etheridge, Chris Evert, Sarah Ferguson, Betty Ford, Michael J. Fox, Aretha Franklin, Bob Geldof, Al Gore, Germaine Greer, Hugh Hefner, Annie Lennox, Colleen McCullough, Spike Milligan, Robert Plant, Steven Spielberg, Cat Stevens, Margaret Whitlam, Kate Winslet.

Associated Goddess Archetypes: Artemis and Athena.

Phase Three: The Long Engagement
Long Morning Star Phase
From Greatest Western Elongation to Morning Set
(Between 48 and 10 degrees earlier than the Sun)
Morning Star
Oriental Venus and applying to the Sun
Duration: 26 weeks

This phase commences at greatest western elongation when Venus starts applying to the Sun and ends at her morning set when she disappears in the glare of the Sun. This is a six month journey.

A distinct change comes over Venus when she reaches greatest elongation. Her pace quickens but instead of moving further away from the Sun zodiacally, she begins to move back towards it, until they unite at superior conjunction.

Venus at greatest elongation is in some ways a like an opposition aspect, in that Venus and the Sun reach their furthest angular distance from one another. Upon reaching her widest possible aspect to the Sun, Venus has reached a point of culmination, but also limitation. She has no alternative now but to move in a new direction. It is at this point that her lover Mars leaves her and is called to adventure. She cannot go with him. Instead she seeks the security, warmth and safety of the Sun.

Venus is ready to make a commitment at greatest elongation. Though there is no guarantee that a new relationship will endure past its initial phase, transit-wise, this period is a good time for a couple to plan a future together.

Venus is still focused on her personal development and self expression, but not exclusively so. Perspective, priorities and objectives change. Although still in the first half of her cycle, she develops and matures now. She becomes more aware of others and tolerant of different values. Venus is learning that others may have different standards and alternative points of view which are perhaps as equally valid as hers. She is learning the art of compromise and is more willing to meet others half way than she was in the preceding Venus phase. Her goal now is a long term relationship, and she applies herself to finding the right partner, but not just anyone.

One could say that this long journey towards the Sun represents her longing for a union with Sol, a father figure who can provide security. This Venus wants her creative independence, but does not want to journey through life alone.

This Venus has a sense of hopefulness and optimism. This is the natural confidence of youth, which is generally warm and outgoing. When a relationship fails, many of those born in this phase seem to have the natural ability and the confidence to find another partner without too much difficulty.

Jacqueline Kennedy Onassis witnessed the assassination of her husband John F. Kennedy in November 1963. At the time of the assassination, transiting Venus and Mars were together in the sky and both opposed her natal 8th house Venus in Gemini, while also moving over her natal Saturn.

In the years that followed JFK's death she had a number of relationships. Five years later in 1968 her ex-brother-in-law Robert Kennedy was gunned down. Fearing for her life, she fled the US and later that year married Greek shipping tycoon Aristotle Onassis, who was able to provide the security she was seeking.

Her progressed Venus was then at 6 Leo, having just made a conjunction to her natal Sun. Transiting Saturn was moving over her

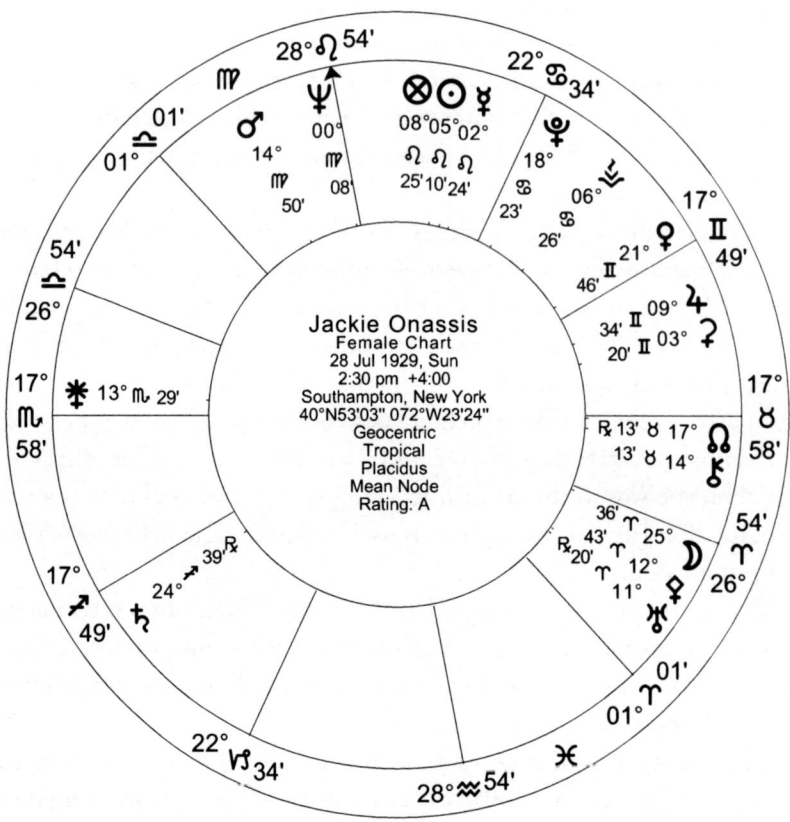

Moon that year too, and in fact stationed retrograde within .03 minutes of her Moon in August 1968, an indication of her fearful state of mind which prompted her to secure her own safety and that of her children.

Those born with Venus just after greatest western elongation include: Woody Allen, Lauren Bacall, Truman Capote, Lewis Carroll, James Dean, Amelia Earhart, Farrah Fawcett, Peter Finch, Queen Elizabeth II, Henry VIII, Billie Jean King, John Lennon, Shirley MacLaine, Helen Mirren, Rupert Murdoch, Greg Norman, Jacqueline Kennedy Onassis, Princess Diana, Keanu Reeves, Eleanor Roosevelt, Barbra Streisand.

Associated Goddess Archetypes: Artemis, Princess, Goddess.

Phase Four: Marriage

Superior Conjunction
From Morning Set to Evening Rise
(Within about 10 degrees before or after the Sun)
Venus invisible
Duration: Approximately 12 weeks

During this time Venus cannot be seen as she is hidden in the glare of the Sun's rays. After morning set Venus approaches her greatest distance from the Earth which happens at superior conjunction about six weeks after she vanishes. Another six weeks or so will elapse before she emerges as the evening star and commences her journey back towards the Earth.

Venus undergoes a process of transformation as she transitions from morning star to evening star. She matures into womanhood, symbolised by the marriage of Venus and the Sun at superior conjunction.

As Venus reaches full maturity and marries the Sun, she is empowered by this commitment, but sacrifices her independence. The virgin goddess ceases to exist. She loses her freedom and autonomy. With marriage to a powerful god like the Sun, there is no choice but to take a back seat and adopt a supporting role.

When a woman marries she joins her partner's family. His genetic line has precedence in the sense that she is the one who changes her name. Of course these days a woman may opt to keep her own name, but even so, marriage for a woman entails a degree of personal sacrifice.

On the one hand Venus is empowered by marriage, but marriage may bring an unwelcome feeling of dependency. As she matures, Venus abandons her youth. In the normal course of events, motherhood means making enormous sacrifices too – huge demands are made on a woman's physical body. Mothers sacrifice their freedom as their children's needs become the number one priority. Venus stops shining. She does become invisible. Yet as Venus reaches fullness, and the most fertile time of her cycle, it is important that she finds a way to shine in her own right.

A significant number of people born in this Venus phase have a powerful desire to be noticed. Equally, they have a strong need to be with people and to be in a relationship, sometimes to the point where they find it emotionally painful to be alone.

This dislike for spending time on their own means that this Venus type will tolerate a great deal of angst because they want to preserve existing relationships. When a partnership looks like it is failing, this Venus type is likely to seek out a new partner before the old relationship comes to an end.

There can be a powerful desire for attention or admiration which can lead these talented people to careers in the entertainment industry where this need can find gratification. These are often highly social people who feel comfortable in the limelight. When operating negatively, it can however develop into a narcissistic streak if they feel they are being ignored or overlooked.

From time to time these people may experience feelings of jealousy, envy or resentment, perhaps stemming from a feeling they must compete with the Sun for attention. Deep down no matter how much they try to shine, these Venus types may never feel they measure up or may feel they are permanently in another's shadow. Perhaps this stems from a dominant parent with whom they cannot possibly compete.

To get what she wants, this Venus is capable of deception and manipulation. Her invisibility suggests she can hide her true motives. But on the whole this is a generous and highly creative Venus.

After superior conjunction Venus starts to wane. Her youth, vigour and autonomy wither in the Sun but then Venus is reborn as the evening star, and a new phase commences. She develops empathy and makes preparations for parenting and taking care of others which are key features of the next cycle.

For growth to occur now Venus must move beyond personal interests and give something to others. If the individual is incapable of this, this person can become overly self involved, and/or increasingly needy and dependent.

Oprah Winfrey was born with Venus one minute of arc past superior conjunction. Her career choice did not surprise her grandmother, who is quoted as saying that ever since Winfrey could talk, she was on stage.

Oprah overcame an impoverished childhood and has risen to become arguably the most successful woman in the world. She chose not to have children of her own, but has empowered and nurtured many thousands.

Those born just before superior conjunction include: Joan of Arc, Jim Carrey, Robert Downey Jr, Billy Graham, Sir Robert Helpman,

Emperor Hirohito, Victor Hugo, James Joyce, Jayne Mansfield,* Charles Manson,* Kylie Minogue, Dolly Parton, Rene Rivkin, Tim Robbins, Percy Bysshe Shelley,* Wallis Simpson, Dame Joan Sutherland, Ian Thorpe, Lily Tomlin.

Those born just after superior conjunction include: Marie Antoinette,* Lucrezia Borgia, Leonardo Di Caprio,* Billy Connolly, Aleister Crowley,

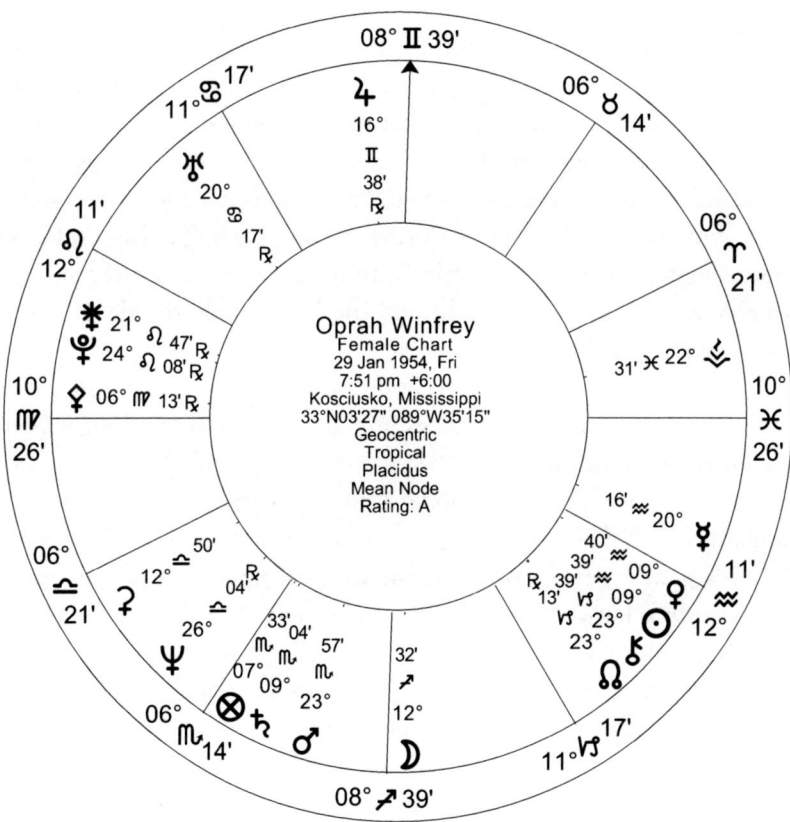

Nicholas Culpeper, Patty Hearst, Jimi Hendrix, Charlton Heston, Paul Hogan, Steve Irwin, Terri Irwin, Johannes Kepler, Jack Kerouac, Stephen King, Glenn McGrath, Dame Nellie Melba, Willie Nelson, Ryan O'Neal,* Louis Pasteur,* Charlotte Rampling,* Diego Rivera, George Bernard Shaw,* Karen Silkwood, John Travolta, Oprah Winfrey.*

Associated Goddess Archetype: Juno

*Venus very close to superior conjunction

Phase Five: Fertility Goddess
The Long Evening Star Phase
From Evening Rise to Greatest Eastern Elongation
(Between 10 and 48 degrees after the Sun)
Evening Star
Occidental Venus separating from the Sun
Duration: Approximately 26 weeks

Venus makes her appearance as the evening star and enters a more mature phase. Each night over the next six months Venus will increase the amount of time she spends in the night sky. Meanwhile her crescent will continue to diminish, though her overall size increases. This suggests an intensification of her energy as she develops a keener focus on a smaller range of interests and activities during the waning half of her cycle. She is more maternal now and settles into a new routine. Other youthful nymphs are taking the limelight and she helps guide the development of a new generation.

This Venus has a more subtle approach to life and love. She is now willing to make personal sacrifices and is adjusting to no longer being the centre of attention.

As Venus develops more understanding of the different values and standards which must somehow co-exist, her role is to establish harmony. She uses gentle persuasion to influence outcomes. She wants greater understanding between people and her style is to subtly guide others, including children.

This Venus type has a strong practical streak. There is an earthy feel to this Venus that fosters a more pragmatic approach to relationships. Patience and staying power are enhanced which help build and sustain relationships even when they are far from perfect.

This Venus type is inclined to wait for her knight in shining armour rather than chase after him. Venus is waning. She is passive rather than active; much quieter and more sensitive than youthful morning star types.

Venus can be overly maternal when she is the evening star. She may give too much of herself without seeming to need love returned. She may undervalue herself and place too much importance on the opinions of others. She tends to put her family responsibilities ahead of her own needs. When taken to extremes this Venus can mother or smother potential partners.

Though they are more sensual, evening star types do not seem to have as much resilience as morning star types. Emotional wounds generally take longer to heal. Yet in a crisis she has the capacity to manage. She is much stronger than she knows.

The late Princess Margaret was born with Venus in Libra in the 7th house, shortly before greatest elongation.

Stunningly beautiful in her youth, the Queen's sister was not known for her ability to sustain long term relationships, rather the contrary. In her youth however Margaret fell in love with Peter Townsend, Equerry to Margaret's father, King George VI. Townsend was divorced with two children and he was much older than the princess. They wanted to marry, but according to British law, Margaret was not permitted to

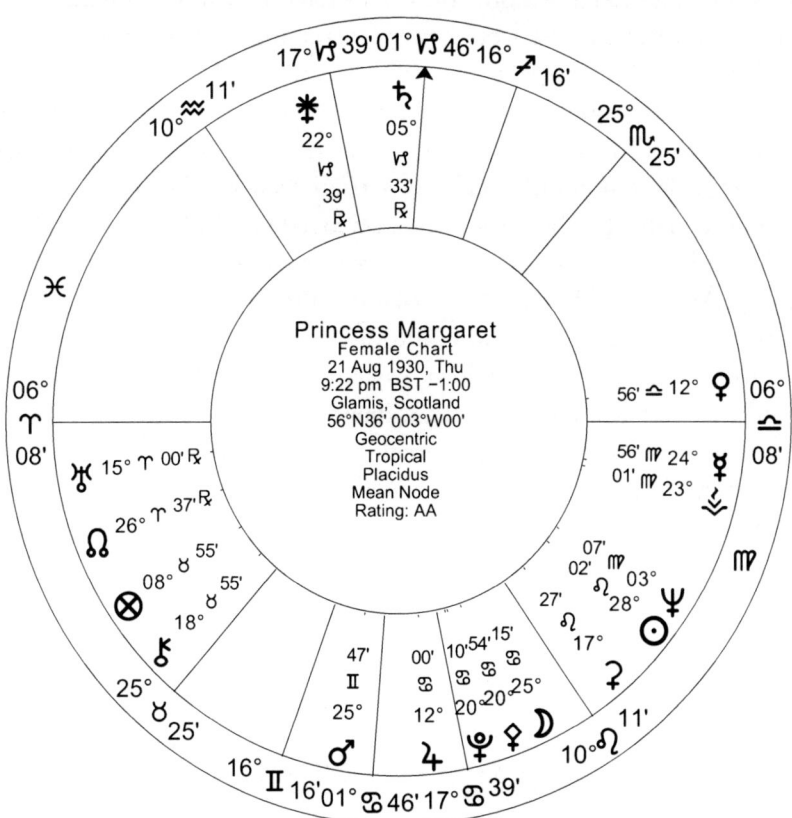

marry a divorcee. After much soul searching in October 1955 Princess Margaret made public her decision not to marry Townsend. Images of her at the time clearly show that she was emotionally devastated.

Margaret's Venus in Libra in the 7th house suggests a personality highly susceptible to outside influence. Venus in its own sign and house of rulership would normally be interpreted as being a positive influence on relationships. But Venus as an evening star accentuated her tendency towards compliance in order to keep the peace and do what was expected of her.

Her chart also shows Venus opposing a headstrong Uranus and squaring Jupiter, aspects which are often associated with a free spiritedness leading to relationship instability.

If Venus had been a morning star perhaps Margaret would have rebelled against the establishment when she wanted to marry. Despite her youth and her position, she would have had more confidence to stand up for herself. She would have given a higher priority to her own needs and personal happiness. Her Sun conjunct Neptune along with her Cancerian Moon and Pluto, show her to be a sensitive woman who would have been impacted deeply by these early events. One wonders how very different her life might have been if she had been permitted to marry the man who she loved, who also loved her deeply.

Those born with Venus just before greatest eastern elongation include: Jeffrey Archer, William Blake, Marlon Brando, Bob Brown, Anita Bryant, Agatha Christie, Bill Clinton, Charles Darwin, Jacqueline Du Pre, Indira Gandhi, Rock Hudson, Angelina Jolie, Sir Charles Kingsford-Smith, Robert Kennedy, Nicole Kidman, Abraham Lincoln, Princess Margaret, Freddie Mercury, Marcel Proust, Helen Reddy, Margaret Thatcher, Maria Von Trapp, H. G. Wells.

Associated Goddess Archetypes: Ceres, Mother, Earth Mother, Wise Woman.

Phase Six: Earth Goddess
From Greatest Eastern Elongation to Station Retrograde
(Venus 48-30 degrees after the Sun)
Evening Star
Occidental Venus applying to the Sun
Duration: Approximately seven weeks

After about six months as evening star, Venus once again reaches her maximum distance from the Sun. At this point she starts to slow in pace and begins to apply to the Sun once more.

During this period Venus is moving closer to the Earth and grows much bigger in overall size, but her crescent shape continues to wane.

We can think of this Venus phase and the next, as being associated with the water element, for Venus is now becoming deeper and wiser.

By this time, late in her cycle, Venus has developed many talents and skills. Her relationship experiences have taught her a great deal.

This period is akin to the time in life when we retire. We may opt to spend more time in the garden or help look after grandchildren. Venus has more time on her hands to pursue her own interests, but less time overall in which to accomplish the tasks she feels passionate about, and this is a deeply passionate and sensual Venus.

Just as Venus' motion is slowing, the pace of life during this phase is also more leisurely. Venus may retreat from interaction with people to some degree for she needs more solitude for contemplation, yet at the same time she seeks an intense, meaningful and intimate union.

Those born during this phase often have very high standards. Principles are important. They set high benchmarks for themselves, their partners, society and the wider world as well. This Venus often has a deep love of nature, children, animals, and the environment and they tend to gravitate instinctively towards causes.

Disillusionment and disappointment are felt deeply, but this Venus is also philosophical. This type may develop strong religious or spiritual views, but there is also a rich sensuality. This potential contradiction can cause inner conflict. The result can be long periods of celibacy punctuated by intervals of deeply passionate intimacy. In relationship and in life, this type is prepared to give everything for love, but expects no less in return. These people expect a lot from themselves, but they are human.

They tend to see others through rose coloured glasses. Evening star types as a whole are apt to be more pliable and give others the benefit of the doubt.

With a big picture mindset they tend to put social, global, philosophical, or spiritual values ahead of their personal needs. Some kind of personal sacrifice, or an extended period of aloneness is sometimes experienced by this Venus type, but so too are relationships which are deeply transcendent, and healing.

Singer Judith Durham is a committed vegetarian and passionate about spiritual development. After leaving the singing group the Seekers in her mid twenties, she married the talented pianist Ron Edgeworth in 1969. She pursued a solo career and worked on musical projects with her husband.

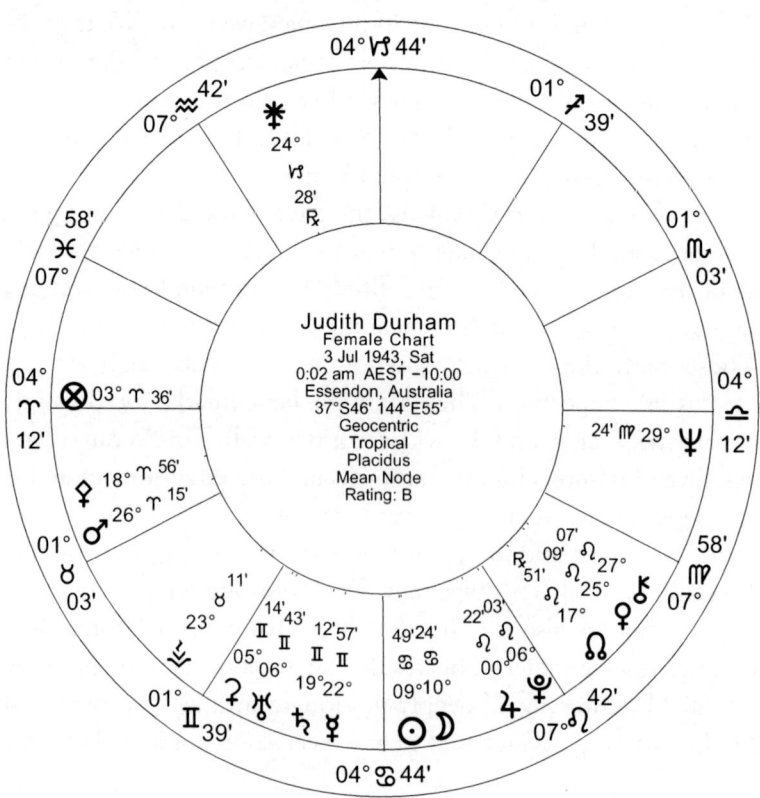

Judith's 5th house evening star Venus in Leo expresses itself musically through her deeply resonant voice. Her Venus also describes the deep love she shared with her husband for over 25 years. In her chart Venus sits close to the North Node between Chiron and Hygeia (not shown), archetypes of wounding and healing. In 1993, with a Seekers' reunion planned close to her Chiron return, and with Chiron transiting over Venus, her husband was tragically diagnosed with motor neuron disease. He died in December 1994. Today Judith uses her talents as a singer and songwriter to heal others through her music.[19]

Transit-wise, a couple of weeks before she stations retrograde Venus is once again at her most brilliant. Major life events and important decision affecting relationships often take place at this time, especially if transiting Venus is in aspect to a natal planet.

When Venus was at its most brilliant in its evening star phase, a client of mine finally decided to end a very unhappy relationship after putting up with years of abuse. At the time she was having a Venus return.

Those born with Venus just **after** greatest eastern elongation include: Frank Abagnale, (*Catch Me if You Can*), Peter Brock, Ludwig van Beethoven, Dr Jim Cairns, Marlene Dietrich, Walt Disney,* Judith Durham, Mia Farrow, Robert Graves, William Herschel, Angelica Huston, Dalai Lama (14th), Sir Isaac Newton, Al Pacino, Oliver Stone, Stuart Wilde.

Those born just **before** station retrograde include: Heidi Fleiss, Michelangelo, Nostradamus.

Associated Goddess Archetype: Persephone Queen of the Underworld.

*Venus very close to superior conjunction

Phase Seven: Sleeping Beauty
From Station Retrograde to Inferior Conjunction
(Between 30-0 degrees later than the Sun)
Evening Star
Occidental Venus Retrograde
Venus applying to the Sun
Duration: Three weeks

As Venus stations retrograde she enters the last phase of her relationship journey. She turns away from the outside world and relationships, but at the same time her desire for a union intensifies as she draws closer to the Sun and Earth.

Venus stations retrograde when about 30 degrees occidental to the Sun. Though she is still visible in the evening sky at this point, she pauses and reflects on the purpose of her life. In this regard this Venus phase is like the Balsamic Moon, having a deep need for a sense of purpose and meaning which can often lead towards an interest in philosophy, spirituality or metaphysics.

As with Venus in the equivalent morning star retrograde position, this Venus may discover that her standards differ from the views held by the majority. When she realises that hardship, poverty, disease, pollution and cruelty are sad facts of life it can elicit a passionate response, spurring efforts to change the world.

The Sun's rapid encroachment towards Venus at this stage of her cycle suggests this person may have a controlling parent who tried to mould their offspring according to their own values, rather than giving their child a balanced measure of freedom and support. In some cases this can skew the personality, as it did in the case of Adolf Hitler, who had a brutal father and an over-protective mother.

In relationships this Venus type is inclined to be very choosey. There can be an all or nothing flavour to relationships. Similarly once love is found, and a relationship embarked upon, these passionate people generally honour their commitments. They have staying power.

Though imbued with empathy towards others, this Venus type is not likely to suffer fools. This Venus will go her own way and even live a hermit-like existence if no relationship is seen to measure up.

This Venus is not only looking for a spiritual union, but she wants a real flesh and blood lover too. She wants someone she can relate to on every level, physical, emotional, intellectual as well as spiritual. If this ideal love is not available she prefers to keep her own company rather than compromise her high standards. She could be waiting a long time.

This Venus is like *Sleeping Beauty* who may be unconscious of what is going on around her. But eventually the prince came along and kissed Sleeping Beauty when it was time for her to awaken to love.

> 'When Venus is retrograde natally, the ability to relate to people on a superficial level is almost non-existent and the world of relationships and values is viewed through either an exalted lens or a jaded glass – the body and its physical, visceral needs is highly responsive and primitive, while the philosophy is often in conflict.'[20]

Vesta seems like an appropriate goddess to represent this last Venus group. Goddess of the Hearth, Vesta's eternal flame provided warmth, safety and sanctuary. The Vestal Virgins of Rome were the human embodiment of the sacred goddess. They tended the eternal flame which the Roman people could access as a source of fire for heating and cooking. The Vestal Virgins were entrusted as keepers of important documents and were highly respected members of Roman society. After thirty years, they were free to marry, though many chose to remain in service. Similarly, this Venus type is very self sufficient and often finds love and personal happiness later in life.

Poet Elizabeth Barrett Browning was born in this Venus phase. Passionate about social justice, with a deep interest in philosophy, religion and theology, she was the eldest of twelve children. Suffering ill health along with grief and guilt over the drowning death of a beloved younger brother, she remained a virtual recluse for many years.

In 1844 a collection of her poems received critical acclaim. This established her as one of the greatest poets of her day. This collection of verse came to the attention of writer Robert Browning, who at that time was not very well known, being six years younger than Elizabeth.

They began corresponding. Five months later they met and immediately fell in love. They exchanged 574 love letters in just 20 months – note the similarity to the Venus cycle, which is 584 days or 19 months long. Elizabeth was almost 40 years old, yet their romance was conducted largely in secret. Elizabeth's father was a religious zealot

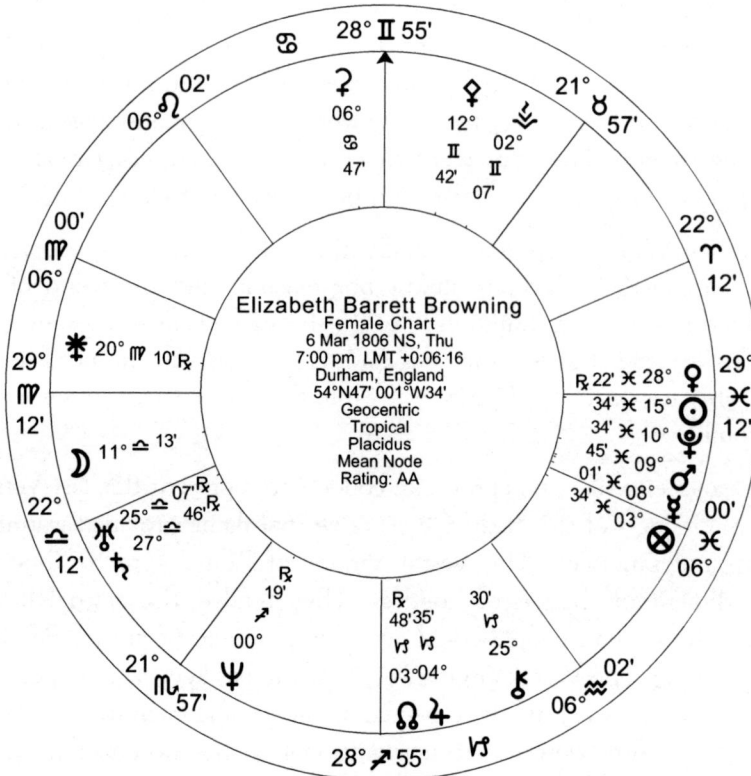

Elizabeth Barrett Browning
Female Chart
6 Mar 1806 NS, Thu
7:00 pm LMT +0:06:16
Durham, England
54°N47' 001°W34'
Geocentric
Tropical
Placidus
Mean Node
Rating: AA

who opposed the marriage; in fact he tried to prevent all his children from marrying. Robert and Elizabeth eloped and moved to Italy in 1846. Her father disinherited her and never spoke to her again. Though she was never physically strong, Elizabeth's health improved in Italy, and incredibly she bore a healthy son at the age of 43.[21] She died in Robert's arms in 1861, aged 55. The last word she ever spoke was 'beautiful'.[22]

Those born during the visible evening star retrograde phase include: Muhammad Ali, Warren Beatty, Elizabeth Barrett Browning, Bjorn Borg, Johannes Brahms, Charlie Chaplin, Sir Winston Churchill, Sally Field, David Hicks (Sr), Adolf Hitler, Tom Jones, David Koresh, Kate Middleton, Lord Mountbatten, Patricia Neal, Sir Peter Ustinov.

Those born during the invisible evening star retrograde phase include: Annie Besant, Olivia De Havilland, Sir John Gorton, Demi Moore, Ted Turner.

Associated Goddess Archetype: Vesta.

Footnotes

1. Christopher Vogler, *The Writer's Journey* (Third Edition), Michael Wiese Productions, California, 2007. p.29.
2. Erin Sullivan, *Retrograde Planets*, Samuel Weiser Inc., York Beach, Maine, USA, 2000. p.166
3. Jean Shinoda Bolen, *Goddesses in Everywoman*, HarperPerennial, New York, 1984
4. The point of perihelion of a planet moves very slowly. As measured along the zodiac it only moves by minutes of arc per orbit.
5. http://cseligman.com/text/planets/marsoppositions.htm [January 2011]. Courtney Seligman's site has some useful and easy to understand diagrams and text on planetary motion and a range of other astronomical data.
6. Erin Sullivan, *Retrograde Planets*, Samuel Weiser Inc., York Beach, Maine, USA, 2000, p.168.
7. Steve Irwin died on September 4, 2006 after being struck through the chest by the tail of a stingray while filming an underwater documentary.
8. Christopher Vogler, *The Writer's Journey* (Third Edition), Michael Wiese Productions, California, 2007 p.108
9. http://www.alexandertechnique.com/fma.htm [February 2011]
10. Christopher Vogler, *The Writer's Journey* (Third Edition), Michael Wiese Productions, California, 2007. p.163
11. http://scandinavian.wisc.edu/mellor/hca_summer/glossary/bachelor.html [February 2011]
12. Christopher Ralling, *Shackleton*, BBC, London, 1983, inside cover.
13. Editors: July Pearsall and Bill Trumble, *Oxford English Reference Dictionary* (Second Edition), revised 2002.
14. http://www.theoi.com/Titan/AsterEosphoros.html [November 2010]
15. GMT. No allowance for daylight saving.
16. Sean Hepburn Ferrer, *Audrey Hepburn; An Elegant Spirit*, Pan Books, 2005, London, p.11.
17. Ibid
18. *New York Times*, 22 March 1971 (From Wikipedia) [December 2010]
19. http://www.judithdurham.com/biography/index.html [January 2011]
20. Erin Sullivan, *Retrograde Planets*, Samuel Weiser Inc., York Beach, Maine, USA, 2000, p.113.
21. www.poets.org/poet.php/prmPID/152 [January 2011]
22. Elizabeth Barrett Browning, *Selected Poems*, Gramercy Books, New York, 1995, p.11.

Part Three
The Venus-Mars Relationship

The Dance of Love

Astrological meaning is derived from symbols, myth, planetary motion and other celestial phenomenon. On these topics Venus and Mars have a lot to contribute.

In this section we'll examine the various ways that Venus and Mars interact and see how their fundamental oppositeness illuminates many aspects of life including our standards, actions and relationship choices.

The pair has a powerful alchemical connection along with a special mathematical and geometric relationship. We'll look at their aspects in detail and follow the route the cosmic lovers take from their opposition to conjunction, and see how this journey can guide us towards love. We'll also consider the role that Venus and Mars Returns play in relationship timing.

Though in every respect Venus and Mars are opposites, ultimately they work together as a team. It is said that love is the most powerful force in the universe. The dynamic relationship between Venus and Mars plays a pivotal role in virtually every aspect of life. Mathematically, alchemically, astrologically, as archetypes, in mythology as well as in biology and physics, this is the law of attraction in action. We are made from their stardust.

The Electromagnetic Dynamics of Venus and Mars

'The meeting of two personalities is like the contact of two chemical substances: if there is any reaction, both are transformed.'

Carl Jung

From the earliest times astrologers and alchemists understood the mysterious connections that exist between the planets and specific metals. These traditional links between metals and planets state that the Sun is associated with gold and the Moon with silver. The planet Mercury is known to represent the fluid metal of the same name, also known as quicksilver. Jupiter has always been associated with tin and the heavy Saturn with lead. More recently, the outer planets have come to represent the radio-active elements uranium, neptunium, and plutonium.

As far as Mars and Venus are concerned, Mars is known for its affinity with iron and Venus with copper. Iron is more heavy and dense than copper, and as befits the archetypal warrior who seeks to conquer the world, iron and steel are used extensively in machines of war, industry and construction. The planet Mars itself has a high iron content which gives Mars its rusty red colour. Copper is more malleable and lighter than iron and also more beautiful. It has many uses, both practical and decorative.

Beyond these functions, iron and copper share a unique relationship. The nature of just how they interact provides us with tangible scientific evidence that confirms their symbolic connection and the traditional astrological meaning of Venus and Mars as handed down through the ages.[1]

Just as Venus and Mars are known to generate sexual energy and magnetism, copper and iron are used to generate electricity and drive our motors and machines.

Put simply, in electromagnetic theory, electricity and magnetism are bound together. They coexist and have a dynamic relationship. Electromagnetic interactions are present wherever electricity is found, including many aspects of the natural world, and in light.

Copper is the most commonly used conductor of electricity. When copper wires are formed into a coil and energised with electricity, a magnetic field is created. If iron is introduced into this magnetic field, it will strengthen, focus and carry this magnetic field. Together, copper and iron then intensify their electromagnetic relationship, far beyond the capacity of either metal on its own.

This strong electromagnetic partnership is the force behind every motor we use in the home and industry, no matter the size. It is also the relationship that binds every transformer that changes electricity from one voltage to another.

The electromagnetic copper-iron relationship is behind most methods of generating electricity too, including generation by nuclear, coal, gas, hydroelectric, geothermal and wind power. The turbines in our power stations operate by spinning magnetised iron inside a frame of copper coils to create electricity. This is simply the reverse of a motor.

Michael Faraday, pioneer in the field of electromagnetism, actually discovered the dynamo principle on 17 October 1831, within days of a Venus-Mars conjunction.[2] This was a crucial discovery which meant that for the first time electricity could be harnessed for practical use.

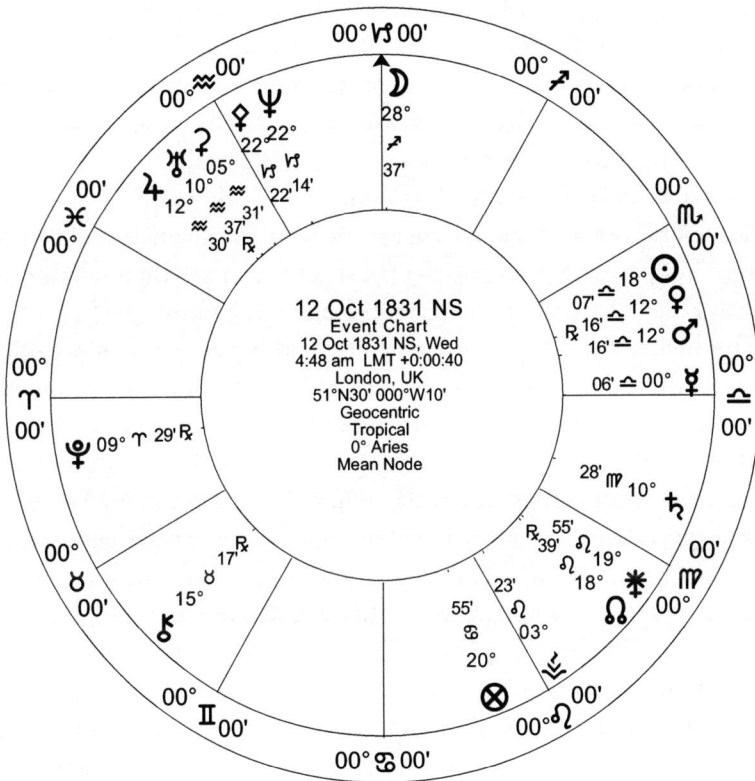

Venus-Mars conjunction 12 October 1831. A few days later Michael Faraday discovered the dynamo principle.

When a circuit is first 'turned on' copper stimulates iron through an inrush of energy that creates the initial magnetism. In electromagnetic theory this is known as the 'in-rush current and initial excitation'. How perfect that Venus turns Mars on and gets him excited! Thereafter the copper-iron relationship settles into a cyclic exchange where energy is transferred back and forth between them, in exactly the same way as in our personal relationships.

The dynamic arrangement between iron and copper is essential in both using and creating electricity, when neither metal on its own is effective. They work better in partnership than independently. The copper conducts the electricity while the iron conducts the magnetism and they are bound together in the physics of their relationship.

The copper-iron relationship works best when both metals are in the right amount for a specific machine. For a machine to function at its best, the amount and arrangement of the copper and iron must be just right. The correct amount of copper and iron generally favours much more iron than copper. In other words, you only need a small amount of copper (Venus) to get the best out of the iron (Mars).

Electrical and magnetic fields also interact in other ways. For example, as the electricity tries to create a magnetic field, the magnetic field creates a force to oppose the changing electrical current. Thus their relationship is always oscillating, as are our earthly human relationships.

The higher the quality of the copper and the iron, the more power can be achieved in terms of the output of our machine. Logically, this reinforces the notion that if our natal Venus and Mars are in good condition, then we will be more adept at relating, be more productive and have a higher output creatively, than if they are debilitated or under-performing. There are many parallels that can be drawn between the iron-copper relationship in electricity and magnetism, and our personal relationships. For example, poor quality iron (Mars) will not produce as strong a magnetic field as good quality iron, and it is also more resistant to the influence of copper (Venus).

However, both copper and iron have their limitations. If copper tries to create too strong a magnetic field, the iron becomes saturated and can take no more. If Venus tries to overpower Mars, Mars will stonewall. As in life, when Venus/copper attempts to establish a closer partnership arrangement with Mars than he wants, she will find that she can no longer influence Mars/iron and he will go his own way. When this happens with metals, copper overheats. Equally, any attempt to get too much power from a machine can cause both the iron and copper to overheat. Ultimately, too much pressure, or demand on the machine will either cause a circuit breaker to trip, or the whole machine will be irreversibly damaged. When the relationship breaks down, more often than not it is Venus/copper that suffers the most. We might be able to repair our 'machine', but it will require a new set of copper wires.

Likewise, when a machine is asked to work harder, or carry a heavier load than it was designed to do, imperfections in the copper and iron become evident. Given enough stress, this will eventually lead to a total breakdown of their relationship, just as external problems can place pressure on human relationships. Stress of one kind or another tends to expose our imperfections. Cumulative stress can eventually lead to a relationship breakdown.

The powerful electromagnetic relationship that exists between copper and iron confirms that Venus and Mars really do generate electricity and magnetism. The energy of love we feel when Venus and Mars connect is identical to the way these metals interact. The physics of their relationship as metals provides us with compelling evidence confirming the ancient metaphysical teachings that were known eons before we ever dreamed of harnessing electricity. The oscillating relationship of copper and iron that makes our machines function and generates power is the identical force of nature that draws two people together. It is the same magnetic energy that courses through us when we fall in love.

Sexuality and Reproduction

In nature, the male of the species must often compete in a test of strength against other males before he can mate with the female. He must impress her, for she is selective. She will choose the best possible mate and together they will create the next generation.

So it is with the hero who in numerous romantic tales must test his strength and prove himself worthy of the love of his fair maiden. Competition is fierce and there can only be one winner.

Just as the Mars glyph denotes the male of the species and the Venus glyph the female, the interplay of Venus and Mars is seen in the process of reproduction and the way that an egg and sperm interact. The egg is larger than the sperm and does not travel very far from her source. She waits for the sperm to arrive. Like the planet Mars, male sperm travel much further and face many challenges before potentially uniting with a female egg. Along the way there are many casualties.

Copper and iron play a role in sexuality and reproduction too. Appropriately, men have naturally higher iron levels than women and women have higher copper levels than men. Interestingly, one of the side effects of the contraceptive pill is to raise copper levels, in fact high copper levels help to prevent pregnancy. Copper IUDs have proven to be highly successful because copper impedes the mobility of sperm.[3]

The mineral copper is found in every living organism and is bound to iron in the way it functions. Iron is one of the most important minerals in the body, but it is not easy to absorb. Only about ten percent of the total intake of iron is actually utilised. In order to work at all, iron (Mars) must form a relationship with copper (Venus).[4]

Venus and Mars are literally in our blood. Copper helps facilitate the body's absorption of iron and production of red blood cells. A deficiency of either copper or iron will eventually result in anaemia.[5] Deficiencies of iron are more common in women than men, due to the loss of blood each month during menstruation.

Regardless of our gender or sexual orientation, Venus and Mars represent fundamental drives that we all possess. They fuel our feelings and passions. When electric Venus and magnetic Mars are aroused, Mars often has sexual conquest on his mind, while Venus prefers a quality relationship where intimacy can develop. It has been said that Mars is the planet most associated with the sexual act; however the goddess of love is just as sexual, and certainly far more sensual. As the saying goes, it takes two to tango. Just as both planets govern one yang and one yin sign, Mars is not the only active principle, nor is Venus just passive. They act upon each other and react to one another. Venus is considered 'fertile' but she cannot create new life on her own. Mars acts on Venus; Venus acts on Mars. Mars responds to Venus; Venus responds to Mars.

Researchers studying the sex life of rats have discovered that female rats will run across an electrified grid in order to copulate with a male, but she'll only mate when the time is right. Female rats require longer mating sessions than males. Male rats prefer a faster pace and many ejaculations, but it is the female that decides when. She needs more drawn out mating sessions in order for fertilisation to take place. After a while, a male rat can become exhausted by all the demands made on his energy, yet if a new female enters the scene, his enthusiasm and sexual response will quickly return.[6]

Venus sexuality differs from Mars sexuality in that Mars is quickly aroused, and since he is impatient and impulsive, it's all over pretty quickly. Venus prefers a tactile and sensual approach.

Astrologically, Venus's sexuality is suggested by her mythic birth when she was spawned in the foaming ocean where the severed genitals of the sky god Uranus had been cast aside. The Greek goddess of love 'Aphrodite' is the origin of the word 'aphrodisiac' meaning 'that which arouses sexual desire'. But the goddess of love didn't just arouse desire in others; she took numerous lovers for her own pleasure.

Greek myth tells us that the lovers Aphrodite (Venus) and Ares (Mars) never married, but they did have five children together, four sons and one daughter. The significance of the number five in connection with Venus must surely have been known when these myths were first described. The most well known of their offspring was Eros, the god of erotic love, who shot his love arrows at mortals and gods alike, making them fall in love. Another of their sons was Anteros, counterpart of Eros, known as the god of reciprocal love.[7] Two more sons were the twins Phobos (Fear) and Deimos (Terror) who represent these powerful emotions. The lovers' only daughter was the goddess of marital and domestic harmony, Harmonia.[8]

The names of these mythic children tell us that when Venus and Mars get together they are capable of creating a wide range of emotional states and feelings including passion, reciprocal love, and harmony, but also fear and terror. Clearly Venus and Mars can bring out the best, or the worst in one another. Indeed recent studies into the nature of hatred have confirmed that this explosive emotion uses the same electrical circuits in the brain as those that are activated when we fall in love.[9] It seems there really is a fine line between love and hate.

Sacred Geometry

The courtship ritual between Venus and Mars takes the form of a beautiful celestial dance. Four Venus-Earth cycles (4x584=2336 days) is almost exactly the same as three Mars-Earth cycles, (3x780=2340 days) so it is that Venus and Mars literally dance around the Earth in 3:4 time; performing a beautiful heavenly waltz. Planet Earth is the dance floor, centre stage, where Venus and Mars embrace.

The ancient symbol for Mars is a cross above a circle, the exact mirror image of Venus, a cross below a circle. These glyphs also describe the position of the planets in their orbits either side of the Earth; Venus on one side of the Earth, Mars on the other, with the cross of matter (Earth) in between. See Diagram 6.

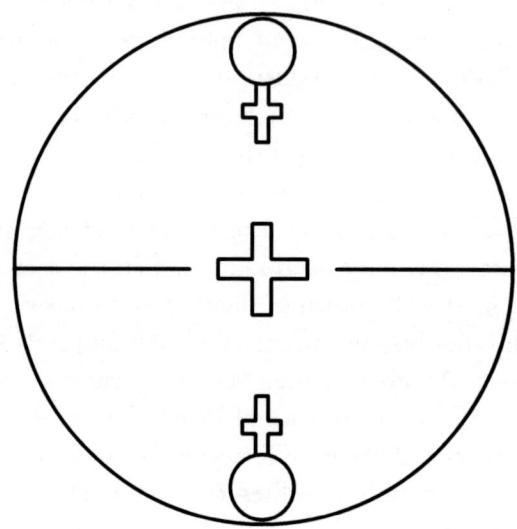

The Venus - Mars Mirror

Diagram 6

The Platonic Solids

Another way that Venus and Mars interface with one another and with the Earth can be seen in their association with the Platonic solids. Platonic solids are characterised by the fact that each has edges of equal length, all angles are equal, every face is identical, and no faces intersect except at their edges. There are only five shapes that fulfil these criteria, and these are the Platonic solids named after the philosopher Plato, Pythagoras was probably the first person to identify these five special shapes. The Greeks believed that each Platonic solid corresponded with a particular element; the tetrahedron was linked to fire, the cube with earth, the octahedron with air, the icosahedron with water and the dodecahedron with ether, or the universe itself.[10]

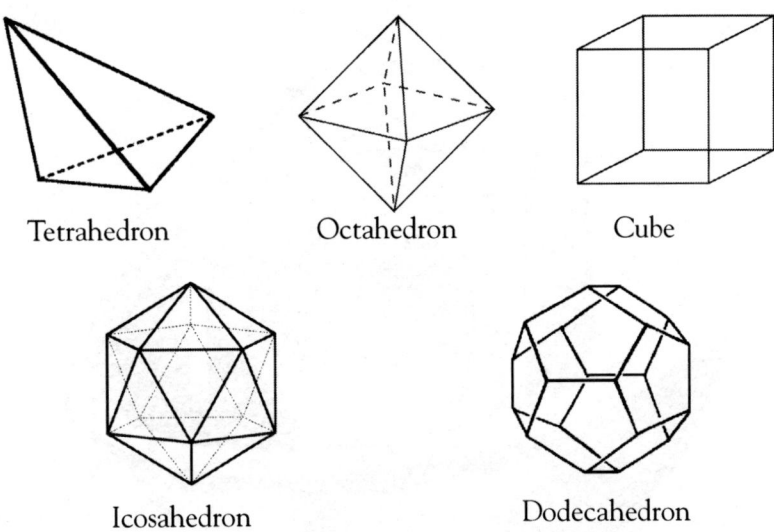

| Tetrahedron | Octahedron | Cube |

| Icosahedron | Dodecahedron |

Diagram 7
The Five Platonic Solids

In the late 16th and early 17th century when Johannes Kepler was working out his theory of planetary motion, he used the Platonic solids to construct a model of the solar system. Kepler discovered that the five Platonic solids closely fit with the orbital ratios between the six known planets. In his model he nested them inside one another to define these planetary intervals.[11]

Though Kepler's scheme was not perfect, he later recalled that this was the sudden flash of insight that helped him work out his theory of planetary motion.

'The earth's orbit is a measure of all things; circumscribe around it a dodecahedron and the circle containing this will be Mars... Now inscribe within the Earth (earth's orbit) an icosahedron, and the circle within it will be Venus...'[12]

The icosahedron, which is associated with Venus, and the dodecahedron, connected to Mars, are the most complex of the five Platonic solids and, as with the metals copper and iron, mathematically these shapes share a special bond.

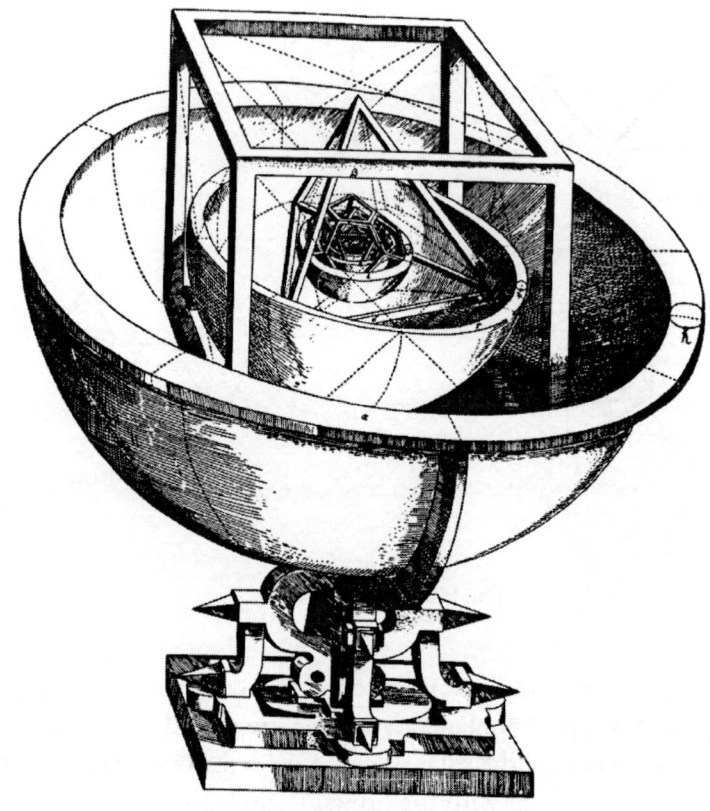

Diagram 8
Kepler's model of the Solar System from
Mysterium Cosmographicum (1600)

If you place a dot at the centre of each face of the icosahedron, and join these dots together, you will construct a dodecahedron. Likewise, by placing a dot in the centre of each face of a dodecahedron, you will build an icosahedron. Just as Venus and Mars create life on Earth, they also create one another. See Diagram 9.

Diagram 9
Cosmic 'Football'. Showing the relationship between Venus, Earth and
Mars and their geometric links to the Platonic solids, the icosahedron
and dodecahedron. Original diagram by John Martineau from *A Little
Book of Coincidence in the Solar System*. Reproduced with permission.

Synastry

One way astrologers examine compatibility is by looking at the synastry between two charts, especially the angles between the planets. In synastry, it helps if one's personal planets, like the Sun, Moon and Mercury have harmonious aspects to the other chart. These aspects enhance all relationships. Difficult aspects, however, such as squares and oppositions, tend to make relationships harder going and can bring about conflict.

When assessing personal relationships that include sexuality and intimacy, Venus and Mars are our primary consideration. All aspects between Venus and Mars heighten desire and passion, some more so than others. Hard angles tend to be more intense than the soft aspects like trines and sextiles. Conjunctions, squares and oppositions between Venus and Mars indicate high levels of sexual chemistry. The semi-squares and sesquiquadrates are also potent and passionate.

Unlike the Sun, Moon and Mercury, where it is helpful to have harmonious synastry aspects, Venus and Mars do not necessarily have to be in a comfortable aspect for the relationship to work. Challenging angles between Venus and Mars can even enhance compatibility. As we shall see, hard synastry angles between Venus and Mars are more commonly seen in intimate relationships than softer aspects. (See Table B)

This apparent liking for hard angles is tied to their intrinsic polarity and the way that Venus and Mars interface with one another in their solar journeys.

Opposites Attract

'Beauty is in the eye of the beholder.'
English Proverb

The polarity of Mars and Venus is seen in virtually every aspect of their astrological symbolism. Mars rules Aries while Venus rules the opposite sign Libra. Venus rules Taurus while Mars governs opposite sign Scorpio. Venus wants peace. Mars wants war. Venus fosters and creates beauty. Mars competes, conquers and destroys. Venus wants to form relationships, Mars wants his independence. Mars revs hard, goes fast and aims to win. He wants to get to his destination as quickly as possible, for he is impulsive and impatient. Venus takes her time and prefers the scenic route.

Mars measures his outward success in terms of *quantity*; the highest, the biggest, and the fastest and so on. Venus on the other hand prefers to evaluate her experiences in terms of *quality*. She appreciates quality in all things and upholds her personal standards. As seen from Earth, Venus moves back and forth in relation to the Sun. She measures the merits and value of her experiences accordingly, more or less against a fixed reference point. Once established this tends not to alter a great deal, though her experiences are evaluated and reviewed during periods when Venus is retrograde. Venus has a more horizontal frame of reference than Mars whose approach is, naturally enough, more vertical.

The motion of Venus and Mars in the sky in relation to the Sun sheds further light on these opposing perspectives and the nature of their relationship. If you overlay the positions of Venus and Mars relative to the Sun as a fixed point in space, you will see that Mars is retrograde in an area of sky which is virtually opposite Venus's complete range of movement, an area that we might call 'the Venus zone'. See Diagram 10.

Mars stations occur when he is between 130 and 145 degrees from the Sun, this varies according to his actual distance from the Sun when retrograde.[13] This averages to about 138 degrees. Since Venus is never more than 48 degrees away from the Sun, this means that Mars stations and Venus elongations are exactly 90 degrees apart. Consequently, when Venus and Mars are in opposition, Mars is always retrograde, or if not, he will be virtually stationary.

- When Venus and Mars oppose and Venus is at her greatest western elongation as the *morning star*, then Mars will be close to his *stationary direct* point.
- When Venus and Mars oppose and Venus is at her greatest eastern elongation as the *evening star*, then Mars will be close to *station retrograde* point.

Mars energy is intense and concentrated when stationary and much more inwardly focused than when direct. Venus meanwhile tends to be freer and more highly animated when she is at greatest elongation than

The Venus-Mars Relationship

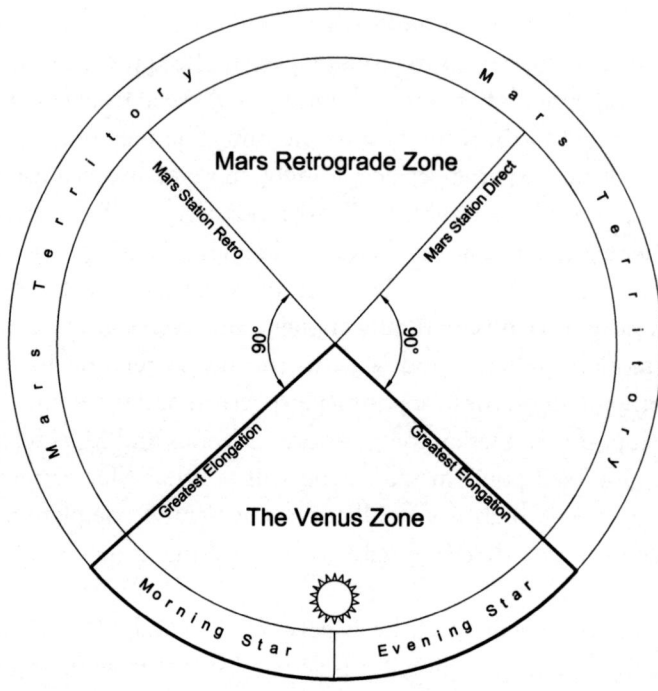

Diagram 10
When Venus and Mars oppose one another, Mars is almost always
retrograde; if not then he is virtually stationary.

at other times. This means that when they are in opposition Venus is
operating in a Mars-like manner, and Mars is more introverted and in
touch with his feminine side. The opposition aspect amplifies their natural
polarity, but at the same time they also have more natural awareness
of one another's perspective. They are capable of understanding one
another, for they are walking in one another's shoes. At the same time the
opposition fosters objectivity and conscious awareness. The opposition
is the aspect we associate with relationship, because it is linked to the
Ascendant-Descendant axis; the axis of self and others. This makes the
Venus-Mars opposition arguably the most dynamic of all their aspects.

At opposition, with the Earth between them, Venus and Mars are
a long way away from one another. They see one another face-on and

begin moving towards one another, reaching out to one another across the lonely empty reaches of space for they know they are destined to be together.

Journey to Love

From the moment they set eyes on one another, it's love at first sight. The opposition is a signature aspect of relationship, but the conjunction of Venus and Mars symbolises the beginning of a new relationship. What has to happen before Venus and Mars unite in a conjunction? How do they cross the vast reaches of space in order to be together? Mars has travelled out into the world and made his mark upon it. But he is lonely. He longs to return to his love. How does he get there from here? What about Venus? Does she encourage him or is she disinterested? The journey Venus and Mars take from their opposition to their conjunction tells us a great deal about what has to happen before Venus and Mars embrace.

Let's follow the journey the cosmic lovers take towards their union at conjunction.

The three scenarios that follow describe how Venus and Mars move in the sky as they travel from opposition to conjunction. When it comes to relationships, timing can be critical.

1. Venus Morning star opposite Mars Stationary Direct

In the chart set for 11 May 2014, Venus and Mars oppose one another. Venus is in the morning sky and has recently begun applying to the Sun. Mars is about to station direct and begin his journey back home towards the Sun and the Venus zone.

At this opposition Venus and Mars immediately start to *move towards one another* and they will keep moving towards one another until they meet in a conjunction. That meeting will take place nine months after this opposition.

In this scenario, it's love at first sight and the lovers seek union. There is no hesitation. They both know what they want and they go for it.

About one month after this opposition, they will be in quincunx aspect. Mars will still be very slow, while Venus is moving fast. She is ready to embrace Mars, but Mars is still in recovery mode after his

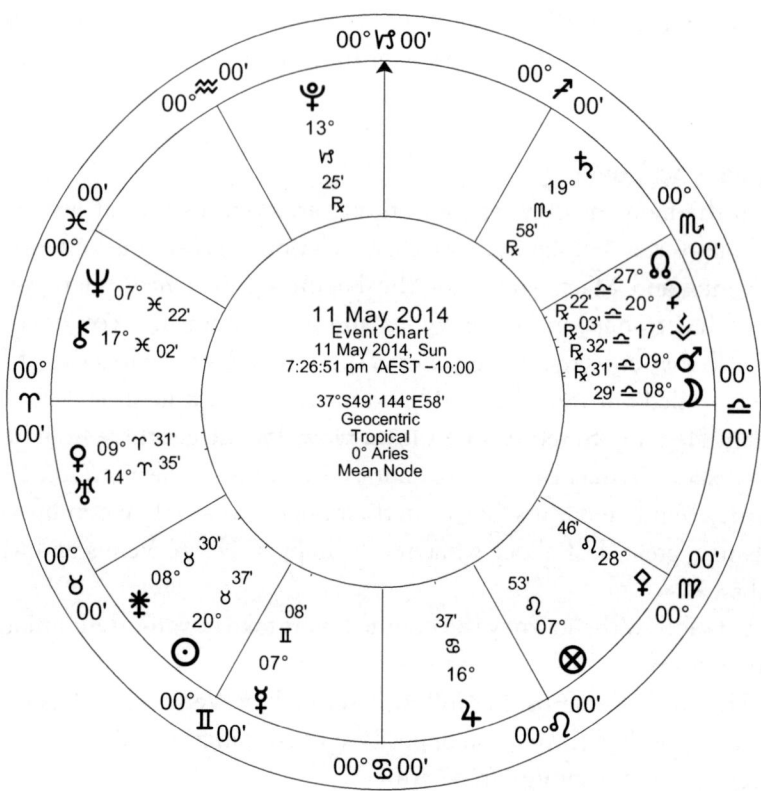

11 May 2014.

Venus reaches Greatest Elongation on 22 March 2014. In this chart she
is still wide of the Sun (morning star) and opposes Mars which stations
direct on May 20.

retrograde phase. He will start to gain speed around July by which time
he will trine Venus. By late August 2014 Venus in Leo and Mars in
Scorpio will square one another. In late October they are in sextile
aspect.

Around that time Mars re-enters the Venus zone, just as Venus is
reaching superior conjunction. She is actually about to marry the Sun.
All the while Mars thought she was interested in him, when in fact she
was only interested in improving her status, or maybe she was always in
love with the Sun, Mars' chief rival for her affections.

But in marrying the Sun, Venus is transformed from morning star to
evening star. Despite her marriage to the Sun, Venus and Mars are still

powerfully attracted to one another and getting closer all the time. In February 2015 around nine months after they first set eyes on each other, they will embrace in the evening sky.

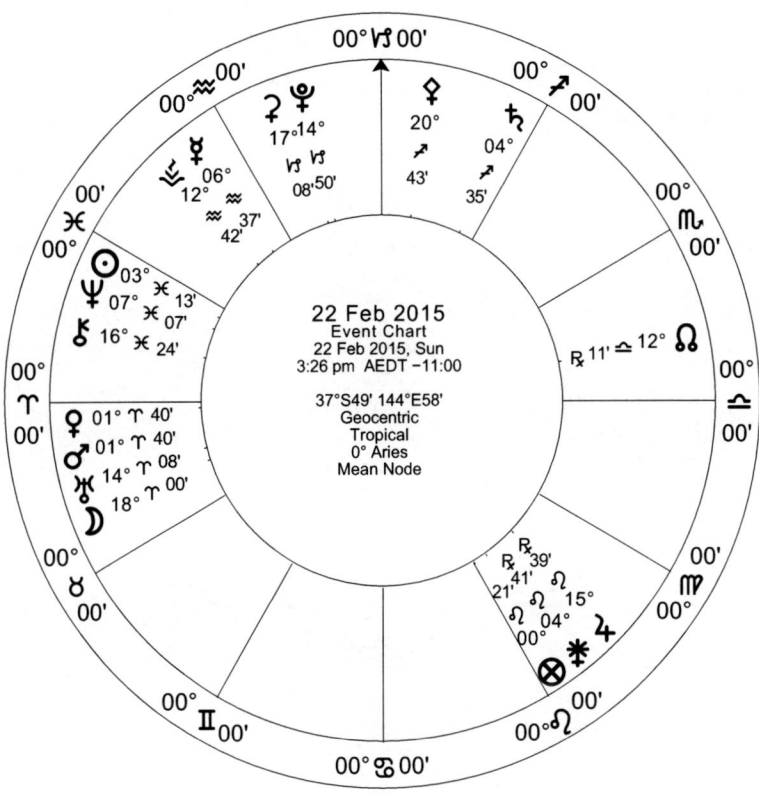

22 February 2015.
Venus and Mars unite after a nine-month courtship, during which time they have been moving towards one another.

2. Venus Evening star opposite Mars Stationary Retrograde
Quite a different love story unfolds if Venus and Mars oppose one another when Venus is in the *evening sky* and Mars is near his *station retrograde* point. Before they can be together, he has a much long journey ahead of him, and so does Venus.

Venus will change direction several times before they rendezvous. First, she will station retrograde, then reach inferior conjunction and transition into the morning sky, then she will station direct. After that

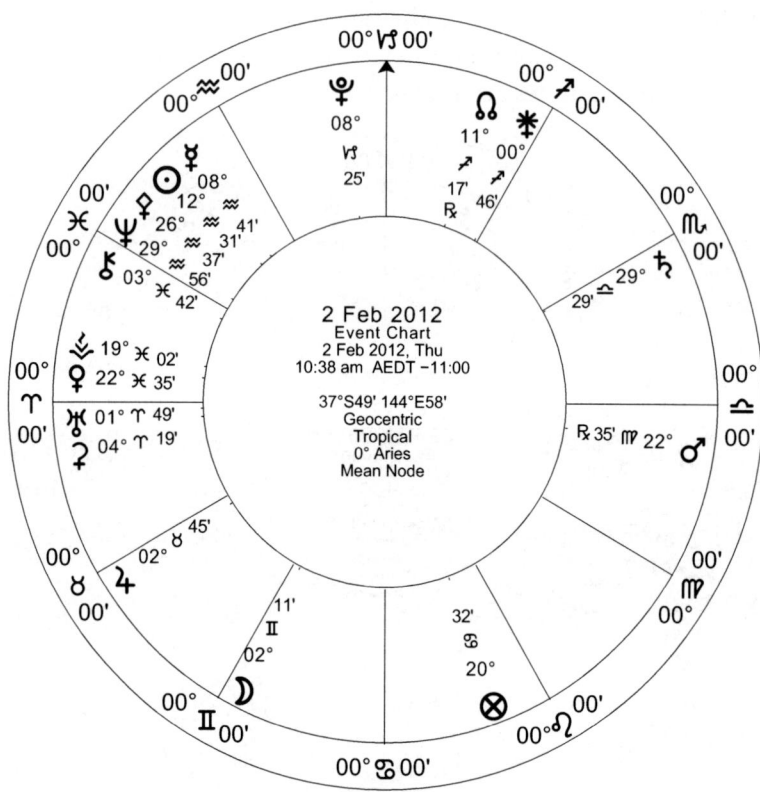

2 February 2012.
Venus-Mars opposition.

she separates rapidly from the Sun, reaches her greatest elongation as morning star. All the while she is moving away from Mars. It is only once she reaches her greatest distance from the Sun that she starts moving towards Mars.

Is she playing hard to get? Is she unsure about what she wants? Is she assessing Mars' intentions? This suggests that Venus as an evening star is more selective in her partnership choices. An evening star Venus does not enter into a relationship with Mars until she has first found her sense of self at her inferior conjunction with the Sun and also had an opportunity to express herself independently in the morning sky. In this way she gets to know herself and what she wants.

What about Mars? He faces many tests before he can be united with his love goddess.

In the chart set for 2 February 2012 Mars is about to face his supreme ordeal. He has yet to prove himself worthy of her love. Her seeming lack of interest may reinforce his feelings of self-doubt.

Like numerous tales of romantic love this story has many twists and turns as the star-crossed lovers attempt to establish a relationship. Not long after this opposition Venus and Mars form a trine, so far so good, except that Mars is still retrograde. Things go from bad to worse in April. Just as he summons up the courage to make an advance towards her they are in square aspect when he stations direct, then Venus retreats from all contact upon turning retrograde in May.

Undaunted, Mars, who is now moving direct, starts chasing Venus, but there is very little progress. Both Venus and Mars are moving slowly, and she is still in retrograde motion. He takes one step forward, she takes two steps back.

Venus reaches inferior conjunction in June, but Mars and Venus are once again in square aspect, on top of which Mars is enduring his challenging resurrection phase.

Shortly afterward Venus transitions to the morning sky and stations direct, but from Mars' point of view no progress has been made at all. Like a recurring dream, the harder he tries to get close to her, the more distance there is between them. It isn't until August when Venus reaches her greatest elongation that she changes her mind about a possible relationship with Mars. At least now things are moving in the right direction! Even so, in September Venus and Mars will form their third square in six months and it will be another six months before they reach a conjunction.

Despite all these obstacles, this story has a happy ending. More than a year after they first set eyes on one another, they finally unite. When they do, they are neither evening, nor morning stars, but both are making a conjunction to the Sun! They are fully conscious of what they are doing. This is a special type of conjunction and we will explore it more fully in Part Four.

While Venus and Mars face many more challenges in establishing a relationship in this longer more convoluted scenario, Mars gets to witness the many different faces of Venus. Over time, he gets to know her many moods. At the same time, Venus sees Mars when he is at his lowest ebb and most vulnerable, and realises that despite his difficulties, somehow he manages to overcome these problems in order to be with her. He never gives up trying, which shows her that he really does love her. They are now ready to make a life-long commitment.

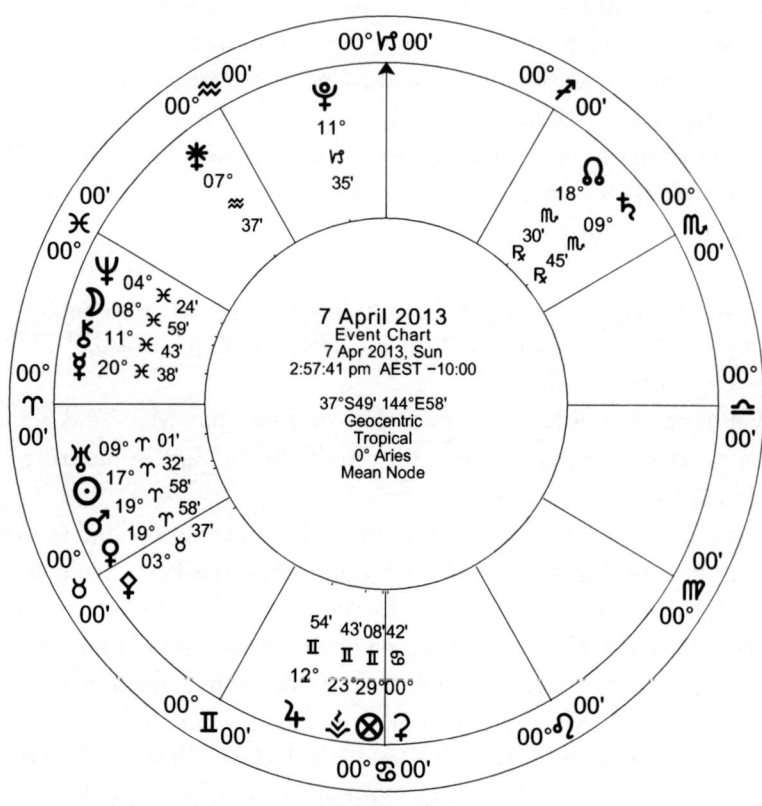

7 April 2013.
Venus-Mars conjunction.

3. Venus conjunct Sun (superior conjunction) opposite Mars Retrograde

This third example shows what happens if a Venus-Mars opposition happens when Venus is close to her superior conjunction and Mars is in the middle of his retrograde cycle, making his closest approach to Earth. In this chart set for 27 January 2010, Venus and Mars are a long way away from one another with Sun and the Earth between them.

Despite the vast distance between them it only takes them seven months to unite. Like long lost lovers they rush towards one another.

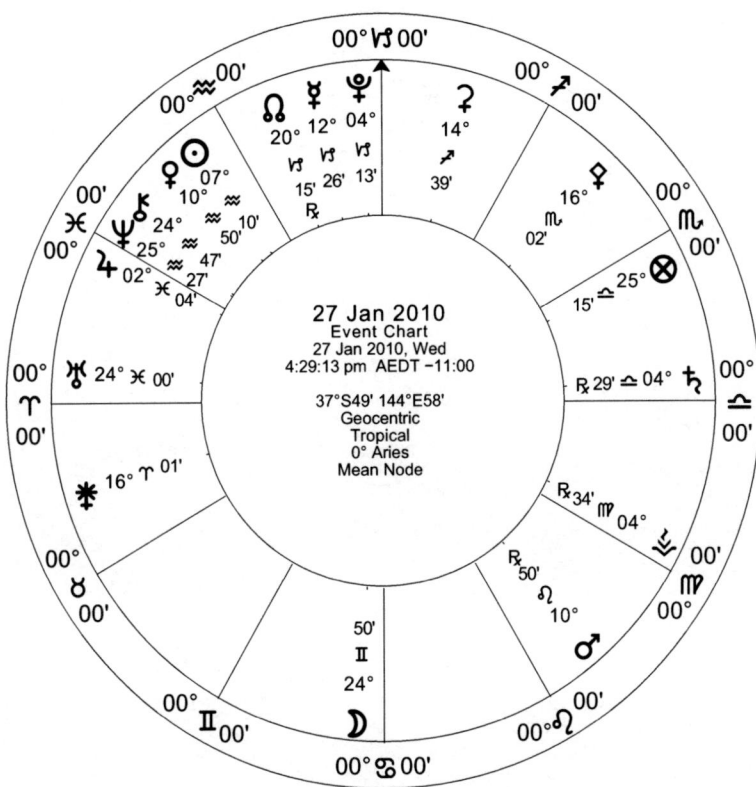

27 January 2010.
Venus-Mars opposition.

By the time Mars stations direct in March, he will already be in trine with Venus. Less than a month later they are in square aspect and by May they are sextile. They quickly get closer and by August they are side by side in the evening sky with Venus at her greatest elongation from the Sun, just as Mars is re-entering the 'Venus zone'.

As we shall see in Part Four, when a conjunction like this occurs, it is late in Venus' solar cycle. This marks the beginning of the end of her association with Mars, for the time being at least. The faster the initial courtship, the less durable their association may be over the long term. This celestial arrangement suggests that in synastry if Mars in one person's chart is retrograde and it is opposing a conjunction of the Sun and Venus in the other chart, the intensity of the passion is likely to be irresistible, but the union may not endure.

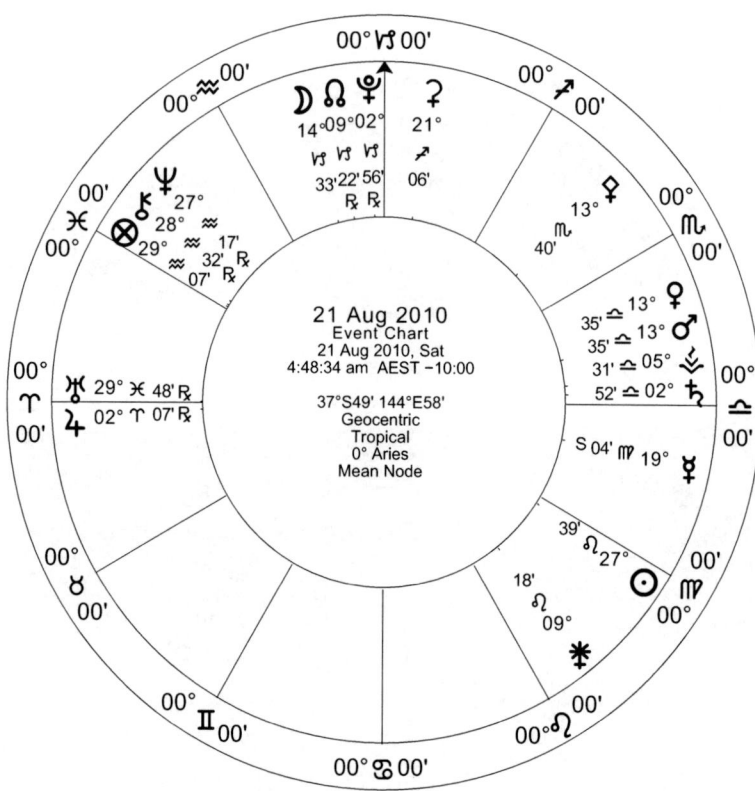

21 August 2010.
Venus-Mars conjunction.

Venus-Mars Phase

Venus and Mars do not always head directly from opposition to conjunction and back again. They can make up to four intervening squares, trines, quintiles and other aspects in between. It's worth noting which half of the cycle you were born into. The Venus-Mars 'phase' says a great deal about our perspective and underpins many of our personal preferences, choices, decisions and actions.

The easiest way is to check is by animating your birth chart using a software program. Check whether you were born after the conjunction and before the opposition, and hence in the waxing half, or between the opposition and the conjunction, in the waning half.

Alexander Ruperti writes; 'The feeling of what is good or bad is established at the Venus-Mars level of experience; and, from these essential feeling-judgements, one acts. Venus, however, not only establishes the individual character and needs of a person but also decides whether or not a particular life-experience really corresponds to one's organic and psychological needs.'[14]

Venusian values and the judgements we place upon things and people are therefore present organically, before the fact, (waxing half) as well as after the fact (waning half). They are present before we have encountered life and after we have experienced relationship and the world around us. We then decide whether these external encounters and people have merit and if we should modify our preconceived notions. Some people are less likely to modify their opinions. Once formed and decided on, they tend to adhere to their standards (waxing half) while others are more given to modify their opinions by seeking consensus (waning half).

In the first half of the cycle, the waxing phase, Venus and Mars are heading from conjunction towards opposition. Venus is inwardly felt, and Mars is expressed outwardly. Venus is more organic and immutable, Mars is more external. If we are born in the first half of the Venus-Mars cycle, Mars takes action based on our Venusian standards and judgements, on how we feel. Do we feel love, or loathing? Are we attracted or repulsed? Alexander Ruperti describes this waxing half of the Venus-Mars cycle as being spontaneous and instinctual. This is the person who approaches life subjectively according to innate values.

The waning half of the cycle differs in that Mars is the inner driving force which is propelled to seek out Venusian experiences. Venus and Mars have been in opposition and are heading towards conjunction. The individual born in this phase places a higher value on the external world of objects, relationships and other people. They are influenced by others' standards, opinions and principles. Mars seeks out Venus for her guidance and judgement. She makes his journey and experiences worthwhile and meaningful. She motivates him.

While the waxing type is motivated by core immutable values which tend not to change once established and propel the individual on their journey out into the world, the waning type is governed more by external circumstances and influenced by others. Rather than having specific opinions and values that are organic as we see in the waxing type, the waning type tends to wait until feedback is received. The waning type is more willing to revise their position in order to gain acceptance and approval.

In an interesting exercise I examined the charts of a number of politicians to see in which of the two phases they were born.

The first group, the waxing group, are those politicians who are motivated by their core values. This group includes Pauline Hanson, Richard Nixon, Robert Mugabe, John Howard, Hillary Clinton, Benjamin Netanyahu, Al Gore, Winston Churchill, JFK, Indira Gandhi, Margaret Thatcher, Kevin Rudd, Bob Brown and Arnold Schwarzenegger. Good, bad or ugly, all these individuals were and are known for their powerful leadership and adherence to core principles and standards. They stand their ground, speak their mind and do not easily change their views. When action is called for, they act without much hesitation. Venus is within, Mars external.

The second group of politicians, those born in the waning half of the Venus-Mars cycle are those who are inwardly motivated by Mars' desire for action, but seek the approval of others. This group is more willing to listen to advice and modify their position if need be. They are perhaps more given to indecision, but are more willing to seek consensus. They are motivated by external circumstances more than by core values. This group includes; Gough Whitlam, George W. Bush, Barack Obama, Julia Gillard and Nelson Mandela.

There is also a third type of Venus-Mars phase. Sometimes Venus and Mars make two conjunctions without having reached an opposition aspect. Those born between successive conjunctions seem to possess both the inner and outer attributes of Venus and Mars. Two politicians who were born in this group are Bill Clinton and Tony Blair.

Aspects of Love

Oppositions

In synastry, the Venus-Mars opposition is said to be one of the most, if not the most passionate and electrifying of all their aspects. This opposition magnifies the attraction between two people, stimulating the expression of feelings and desires.

Opposites do attract, and yet if two people have nothing in common, how on earth can they ever get along? People can have opposing political views or spiritual values. Personality differences too can be highly problematic. If there are no common interests or values, there is no basis upon which to establish or sustain a relationship. Obviously it helps if there is some common ground.

Traditionally, opposite signs of the zodiac are said to be in conflict, for these signs have the same quality, be it cardinal, fixed or mutable, and this can cause problems.

Cardinal signs want to take the initiative and lead. Difficulties arise when planets oppose one another in cardinal signs because we can only have one leader at one time, but both want to lead. In cardinal conflicts such as we find in the Aries-Libra and Cancer-Capricorn oppositions, we often see issues about give and take. Who is the leader and who is the follower? Which path in life do we take? Both parties want to be number one and make the decisions. Ultimately, partners with cardinal issues may discover that they have quite different goals and can end up travelling different paths in life.

Fixed signs are determined, intense, and loyal, but they can be very stubborn and inflexible. These signs don't find compromise easy. Taurus-Scorpio and Leo-Aquarius oppositions can develop into a stalemate if neither party is willing to adapt, or give ground.

Mutable signs are adaptable, amenable and more easily able to compromise, but in Gemini-Sagittarius and Virgo-Pisces relationships things can get confusing. Mutable relationship problems often come about because of a lack of stability. Changes can occur suddenly and when they do we may discover we are partnered with a total stranger. Cardinal conflicts, fixed feuds and mutable misunderstandings tend to be even more problematic when there are square aspects involved.

The good news is that opposite signs of the zodiac have a few things in common. They share the same polarity and are compatible in terms of their elements. Fire and Air are traditional allies. Air allows Fire to burn, so Fire needs Air. Air finds expression and purpose when dealing with Fire. Earth and Water are likewise comfortable with one another. Water nourishes Earth while Earth gives form and structure which supports Water.

'Because Venus and Mars rule opposite signs of the zodiac, the opposition need not necessarily denote disharmony.'[15]

The Venus-Mars opposition helps us to see every facet of another person and relate to them completely, openly and honestly. Mars is always stationary or retrograde when opposing Venus, which serves to intensify Mars' desire. Venus is almost always direct, indicating her willingness to relate. In synastry, their opposition generally brings out the best in both parties and makes each individual more conscious.

The opposition works slightly differently in the natal chart, but still indicates a high degree of passion and intensity. We see this aspect in the chart of tennis champion Rafael Nadal who has a tremendous capacity to focus and enormous energy reserves, no doubt bolstered by Pluto rising in Scorpio. In his chart Mars is exalted and about to station retrograde.

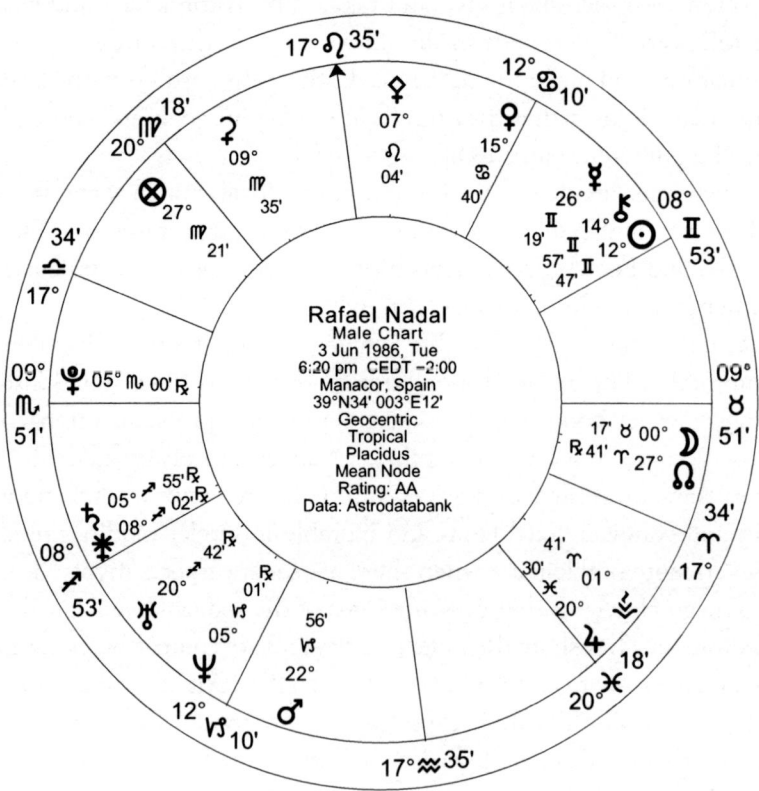

During the 20th century, there were a total of 47 Venus-Mars oppositions. Mars was retrograde in almost all of these oppositions; in the other few he was stationary with Venus at her greatest elongation. In all 47 of these oppositions Venus was direct. In fact Venus and Mars are hardly ever in opposition aspect and retrograde at the same time. The only time Venus and Mars have been in opposition and both retrograde was during a two week period in July and August 1860.[16] During that time three exact oppositions of Venus and Mars took place. After scanning more than 600 years of planetary data, I could find no other time when this occurred. This is highly significant, because it means that when Venus and Mars oppose one another, Mars is *almost always retrograde*, but Venus is *almost never retrograde*.

Oppositions of Venus and Mars occur approximately once every two years.

Well-known people born with Venus Mars in opposition aspect include: Truman Capote, Carrie Fisher, Pauline Hanson, John F. Kennedy Jr, Jay Leno, Alan Leo, Spike Milligan, Rafael Nadal, Martina Navratilova, Dolly Parton, Dame Joan Sutherland, Jimmy Swaggart.

All have Mars retrograde or close to a station.

Quincunxes

Quincunxes are similar to semi-sextiles. As part of the 12th harmonic, the quincunx links signs without polarity, quality, nor element in common. In the natal chart and in synastry the interpretation of this aspect depends to some extent on the elements and qualities involved.

Apart from the harmonious Air-Fire and Water-Earth links between the elements, there are other ways in which the elements combine and interact. For example, Fire and Water both have an imaginative and creative focus. Fire and Water signs tend be naturally spontaneous and creative, more in tune with instinct and intuition. Essentially, these are 'right brain' elements and they tend to see the 'big picture'.

Similarly, Air and Earth share some common ground. Although Air is an extroverted and social element and Earth is more introverted and cautious, they share a rational and logical approach to life. Air and Earth signs prefer to rely on measurable facts and data than on instinct and intuition, and are more adept at managing details than Fire or Water signs. Hence Air and Earth are 'left brain' elements.

The most challenging quincunxes (and other hard aspects) tend to involve those elements which have no common ground. These are quincunxes between planets in Earth and Fire signs, which correspond to the psychological types 'sensation' and 'intuition' respectively. These psychological types are natural opposites and tend to be mutually exclusive.[17] Fire has a very different way of perceiving the world than Earth. Water-Air quincunxes, between 'feeling' and 'thinking' are perhaps even more problematic as these elements and types are associated with judging and evaluating.

Mars rules both Aries and Scorpio; signs that are 150 degrees apart. Venus likewise rules Taurus and Libra. Perhaps Mars-Mars and Venus-Venus quincunxes may be easier to manage because they are naturally aligned this way in rulership.

The quincunx is also related to health matters because Virgo, the sign of health is quincunx the natural Ascendant 0 Aries. Secondarily, the sign Scorpio is also connected with this aspect. Bil Tierney says that quincunxes, 'urge us to undergo major or minor adjustments' before the planets involved can be 'synthesised'.[18]

Those with the natal aspect may enter into relationships in order to heal their partner, or seek out partners who can heal them. In the birth chart this aspect can create an imbalance between the two planets involved. Such imbalances can literally make a person ill.

A Venus-Mars quincunx can be seen in the chart of Judy Garland, whose retrograde Mars in the 6th house exactly opposes her Gemini Sun. Garland's drug and alcohol problems were legendary. Early in life, she and other young performers at MGM were given amphetamines and other drugs by studio executives so they could keep up with the relentless production schedule.[19]

Over the years, she suffered emotional instability and drug dependence. Her sensitive evening star in Cancer endured a succession of relationship and financial difficulties. The talented star died of an accidental overdose at the age of 47.

Despite the difficulties suggested by this aspect, the potential exists for ultimate healing through the power of love which can transform the lives of those with this aspect. In synastry it can also heal. In 1945, Lauren Bacall married Humphrey Bogart after his tumultuous marriage to Mayo Methot.[20] Later, when Bogart was diagnosed with cancer of the oesophagus, Bacall took care of him at home.[21] He died at the age of 57. Bacall's natal Venus in Leo is quincunx Bogart's Mars in Capricorn.

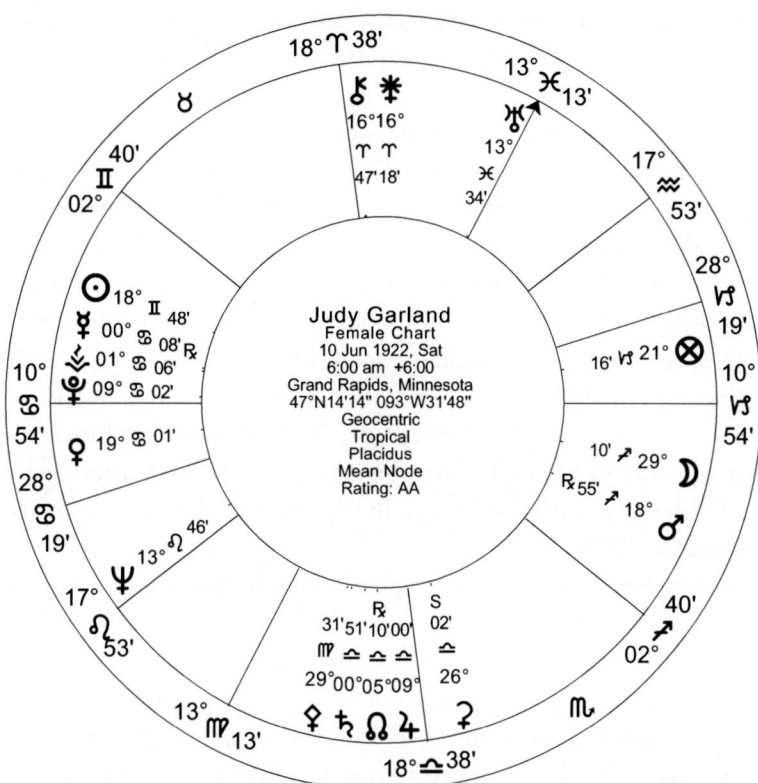

Well-known people with Venus and Mars in quincunx include: Chuck Berry, William Blake, James Dean, Judy Garland, Steffi Graf, Rodney King, Lindsay Lohan, Yoko Ono, Charlotte Rampling.

All have Mars retrograde except William Blake.

Sesquiquadrates

The sesquiquadrate is another potent link between Venus and Mars. As measured from the Ascendant, this angle highlights the middle of fixed signs Leo and Scorpio. Extremes of light and dark are suggested by this Leo/Scorpio influence.

This makes the Venus-Mars sesquiquadrate an emotional, imaginative, and creative aspect, as it is associated with right-brain elements. Because of its fixity it enhances loyalty and determination, but it has an inflexible quality to it too, which can be fraught with problems if not handled with awareness.

The fixity and determination of this aspect suggests loyalty in relationship, but it can also be explosive and volatile. Because Mars stations happen around 135 degrees from the Sun, sesquiquadrates involving Mars remind him of his on-going battle to prove himself. When Venus and Mars are involved in this aspect Mars may feel that his power and autonomy are under threat from Venus. He is liable to become angry and frustrated if he is pushed too far. In synastry, two people who are linked by this aspect will stick together through thick and thin, for better or worse, for richer or poorer, in sickness and in health, but the relationship can also change dramatically and unexpectedly especially if the Mars individual feels ignored, criticised or is being dictated to.

Those with this natal aspect can get themselves into tight spots and find it difficult to get themselves out again. They have a tendency to meet life head on. This is especially the case if Mars is stationary or retrograde.

An extreme example of this aspect is seen in the chart of noted poet of the Romantic Era, Lord Byron. Byron's Mars is retrograde and in its fall in Cancer while his Venus is uncomfortably sandwiched between a stern Saturn, ruling planet of his 7th and 8th houses, and potent Pluto in fixed air sign Aquarius adding to the tension of the sesquiquadrate.

Lord Byron was known for his countless love affairs and was at one time accused of incest and sodomy. He was described by one of his lovers, Lady Caroline Lamb, as 'mad, bad, and dangerous to know.'

In 1824 he died of fever, a Mars ailment, while preparing to fight on the side of the Greeks during their struggle for independence.[22] It is thought that blood-letting aggravated his condition and may have contributed to his death.[23]

Up to four sesquiquadrates can occur between Venus-Mars conjunctions.

Well-known people with Venus and Mars in sesquiquadrate aspect include: Lord Byron, Saddam Hussein, Tim Robbins, Paul Simon, Frank Sinatra, Lily Tomlin, Maria von Trapp, Prince William (Duke of Cambridge).

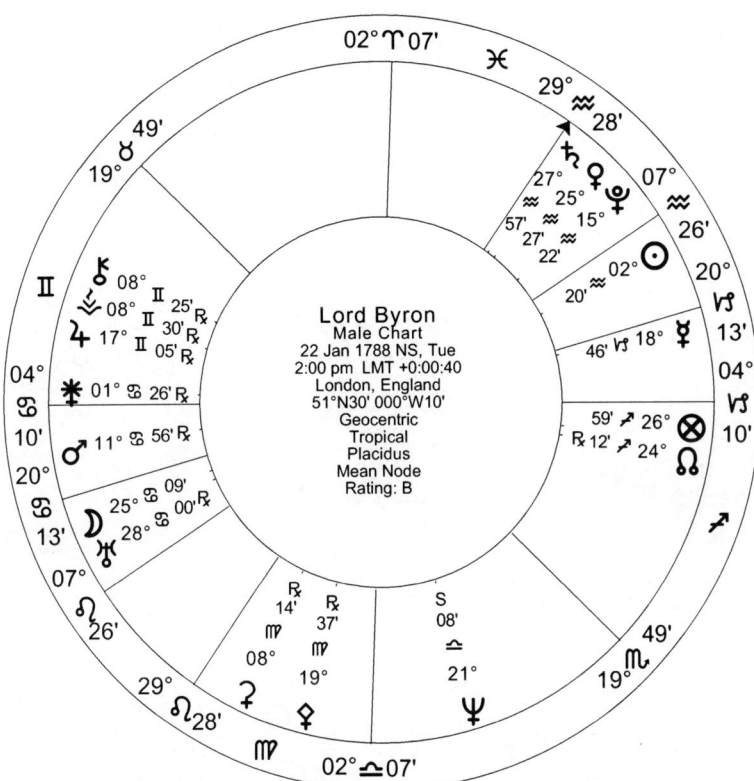

Trines

We tend to think of trines as comfortable aspects. The trine implies an ease of expression, but when it comes to interpreting trines, the jury is still out. A Sun-Mars trine for example, generally indicates abundant confidence. Those with many trines in their charts seem to have more than their fair share of good luck and opportunities, though there can be a tendency to waste these gifts in the pursuit of fun and excitement or through laziness or apathy. In her book *Retrograde Planets*, Erin Sullivan points out that a Sun-Mars trine is a 'most deceptive aspect' and that it 'produces a stubbornness which is not usually associated with trine aspects.'[24] This is because Mars is slow when trine the Sun and not far from stationary.

Nor is it clear how Venus-Mars trines operate. There appears to be a wide spectrum of responses to this aspect. For instance, in this group we find screen legend Greta Garbo, who for many years lived a virtual

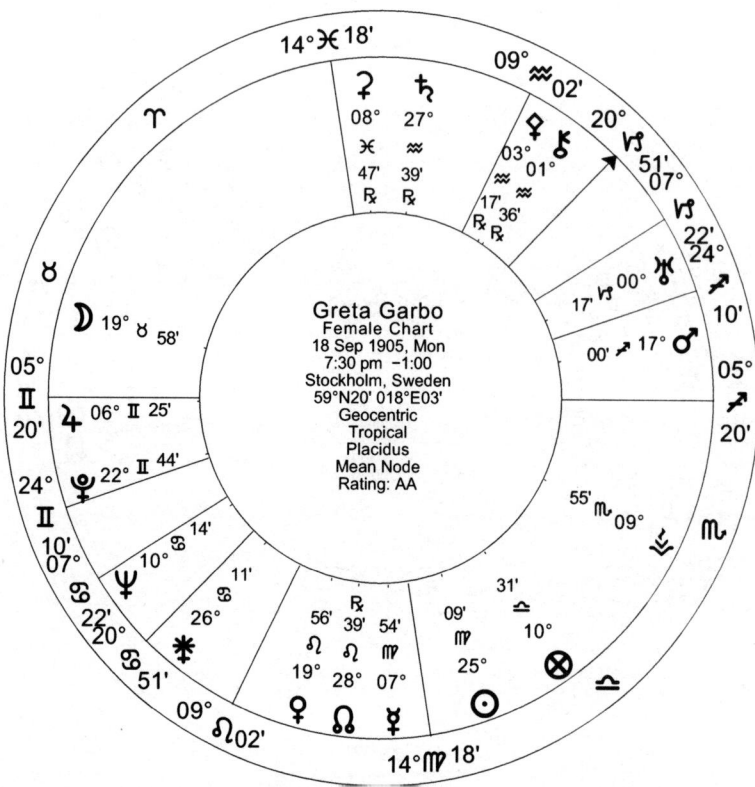

Greta Garbo
Female Chart
18 Sep 1905, Mon
7:30 pm −1:00
Stockholm, Sweden
59°N20' 018°E03'
Geocentric
Tropical
Placidus
Mean Node
Rating: AA

hermit's existence, yet we also find Errol Flynn, who was married three times and had a reputation for wild living and numerous sexual conquests. In 1942 two under-age girls accused Flynn of statutory rape. Flynn was acquitted, but the incident boosted his playboy reputation, leading to the expression 'in like Flynn.'[25]

The interpretation of the trine may depend upon whether it is in the waxing, or the waning half of the cycle. Garbo was born with a waning trine, while Flynn had the waxing trine.

While it is generally assumed that this trine confers good luck in matters of the heart, looking at a list of well-known people who have a Venus-Mars trine, somehow there seems to be a sense of aloneness, a tangible feeling of isolation. Perhaps those with a Venus-Mars trine view relationships too idealistically, so that when disappointments occur they have no way of coping. Insulated from difficulties early in life, they may later find they have trouble coming to terms with relationship problems that invariably crop up at some point.

Trines are not as sturdy, or resilient as hard angles. Too many trines in a chart can lead to apathy, boredom, laziness and complacency. Since Venus and Mars seem to have a natural affinity with the eighth harmonic and hard angles, the trine may actually weaken their relationship.

Traditionally in synastry this aspect denotes a high degree of compatibility, common values and shared interests. Partners are likely to feel comfortable and relaxed in one another's company and express their affection and love generously. Even so, further investigation of some of these anomalies is needed before we can arrive at a verdict.

Up to four Venus-Mars trines can occur between their conjunctions.

Well-known people with Venus and Mars in trine aspect include: Julian Assange, Karen Carpenter, Judith Durham, F. Scott Fitzgerald, Errol Flynn, Greta Garbo, Billie Jean King, Jayne Mansfield, Mozart, Helen Reddy.

Approximately half this group has Mars retrograde.

Squares

This is a powerhouse aspect. It can be intensely creative and equally it can be very destructive, and sometimes both at once.

Because Venus' greatest elongations from the Sun are exactly 90 degrees from Mars' stationary points, the square aspect between Venus and Mars activates these points in their solar journeys. These are the places where both planets alter their course. Venus cannot stray beyond her greatest elongation. She is not as free as Mars and is compelled to stay tethered to the Sun. When Mars stations he faces his greatest tests and must also change course. This suggests that when they are squaring one another Venus and Mars are reminded of their respective limitations.

Square aspects challenge us. They can frustrate, block and inhibit, but they can also lead to opportunities. Bil Tierney describes the square aspect as 'uncompromising'. He says that the faster moving planet, in this case Venus, can feel 'boxed in' and 'resentful' of the demands placed on it by the slower moving planet, in this instance, Mars.

In a natal context, this aspect is often seen in dynamic and highly creative individuals. It is found in the charts of a number of well-known

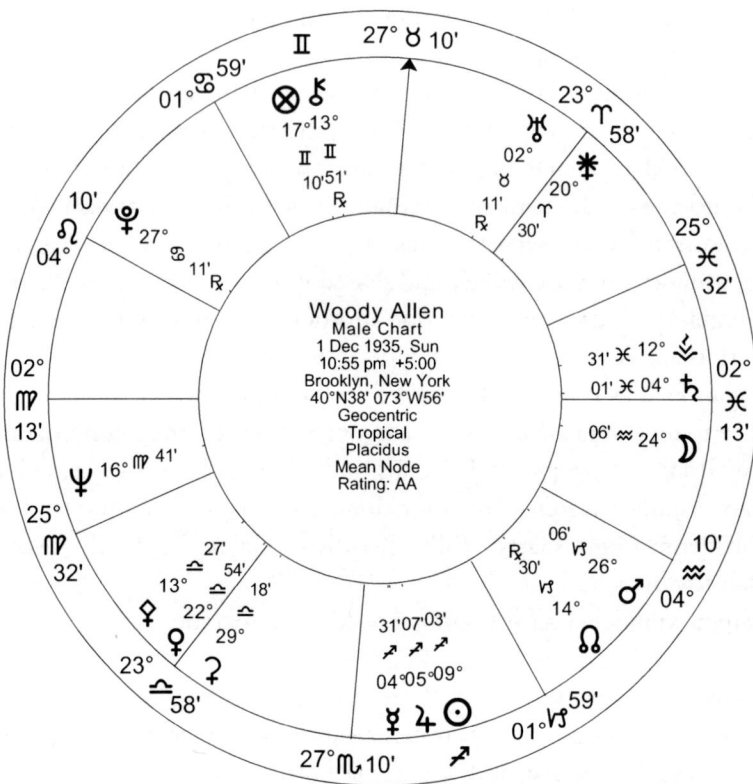

comedians including Woody Allen, John Cleese, Peter Cook, Benny
Hill, and Magda Szubanski. It may provide the edginess and black
humour we see in their work.

In synastry Venus-Mars squares generate a lot of heat. Love and hate,
passion and desire, all emotions are heightened. These can be pressure-
cooker relationships. The intense emotions generated need to find
release and this can lead to frequent arguments and explosive episodes.
Partners with this aspect seem to thrive on the love-hate nature of their
union, and the relationship can survive this volatility for a long time,
though the pain and tension can eventually become too much and lead
to separation.

The square aspect links qualities that are the same. The cardinal
square can result in a tug-of-war for supremacy as both parties want
to lead. When cardinal conflicts escalate, the two parties are likely to
end up heading in different directions. Fixed squares are probably the

most difficult, for neither party is willing to adapt. Compromise becomes impossible. Fixed feuds can degenerate into power struggles that end up going nowhere. Mutable squares are perhaps not so fraught, though mutable misunderstandings can become blown out of all proportion.

The volatility of this union can be seen in a number of well-known partnerships that developed significant issues. For example Mia Farrow's Mars in Capricorn squares Woody Allen's Venus in Libra. Allen has a Venus-Mars cardinal square in his natal chart. They share a Mars-Mars conjunction. They were together for many years but the relationship ended bitterly.

Another example is seen in the charts of Sarah Ferguson and Prince Andrew. He was born with a Venus-Mars conjunction in Capricorn; she has a Sun-Mars conjunction in Libra. Her Mars-Sun squares his Venus-Mars.

On the other side of the ledger, some relationships with a Venus-Mars square will endure. Sophia Loren and Carlo Ponti were married for fifty years until his death. Her Venus in Virgo squares his Mars in Sagittarius. Perhaps the mutability helped.

Whatever transpires, there is both tension and a magnetic attraction in this combination. It glues people together and creates a powerful, but volatile bond. There can be up to four exact squares between conjunctions.

Well-known people with Venus and Mars in square aspect include: Woody Allen, Princess Anne, John Cleese, Aleister Crowley, Peter Cook, Michael Faraday, Jodie Foster, Patty Hearst, Katharine Hepburn, Benny Hill, Lee Harvey Oswald, Magda Szubanski, Nikola Tesla.

Quintiles

Quintiles are unique aspects which deserve more attention. These are highly productive and prolific aspects. Because there is a natural affinity between the quintile aspect and the Golden Mean and Fibonacci series, the quintile aspect is naturally fertile. Venus quintiles are especially creative and are often seen in charts of talented artists, poets and musicians.

Individuals with a natal Venus-Mars quintile seem to be imbued with style and grace. They do not rest on their laurels, but work hard at their craft. They are also interested in encouraging and fostering creativity in

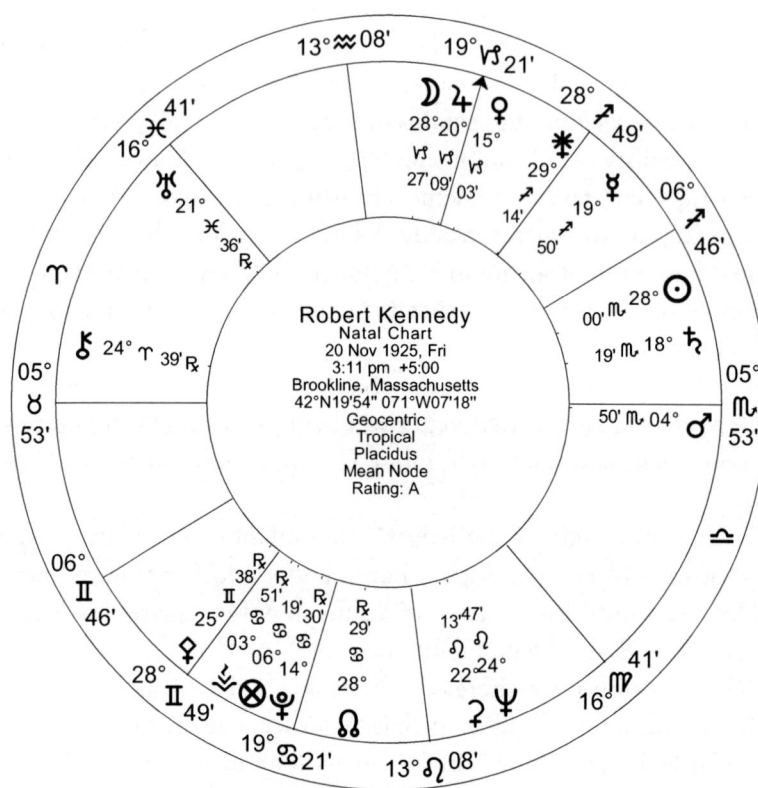

others, helping less talented souls get their projects off the ground and out into the public arena. Together Venus and Mars can produce things of great beauty and value.

The immense output of Sir Isaac Newton filled volumes. His areas of interest encompassed optics, astronomy, alchemy, physics, religion and philosophy to name a few.

Prolific actor and film director Clint Eastwood, now in his eighties, is also a producer, composer and musician.

As well as enhancing creative output this highly productive aspect suggests a high degree of organic fertility and in the natal chart or in synastry, can produce many offspring. The natal aspect is seen in the chart of Robert Kennedy. While supporting his brother's political campaigns and serving as US Attorney General, he also fathered eleven children.[26]

Venus-Venus quintiles and Mars-Mars quintiles seem to be associated with exceptional levels of creativity too, and in synastry quintile links are often seen in couples who work together in the arts or related fields. Not only are they capable of working in partnership together, but seem to enjoy encouraging one another to express their ideas and creativity independently. Mars and Venus seem to bring out the best in one another when in quintile.

In the charts of Katharine Hepburn and Spencer Tracy we see an exact (to the minute) quintile between their respective Mars positions. Another example of a working relationship is seen in the charts of Steve and Terri Irwin; her Mars is quintile his Venus.

Comedian/musician/presenter and playwright Billy Connelly and his wife actor/comedian/therapist Pamela Stephenson have a double whammy quintile. Her Venus in Capricorn is quintile his Mars in Scorpio and his Venus in Sagittarius is quintile her Mars in Virgo. In both cases, the orbs are less than one degree.

Venus-Mars quintiles can occur up to four times between conjunctions.

Well-known people born with Venus and Mars in quintile aspect include: Muhammad Ali, Clint Eastwood, Jane Fonda, Cary Grant, Sir Robert Helpman, Robert Kennedy, George Lucas, Paul McCartney, Sir Isaac Newton, Gregory Peck, Giacomo Puccini, Dmitri Shostakovich, Percy Bysshe Shelley, Patrick Swayze, Brian Wilson.

Sextiles

The sextile has a friendly quality to it. Signs linked by this aspect complement one another. Bil Tierney says that the sextile has an air-like nature, courtesy of its natural links to Gemini and Aquarius. He describes the sextile as being 'eager for new experiences'.[27]

This makes the active, outgoing and social sextile helpful in facilitating communication and establishing relationships. It suggests an air of confidence. The 'yang' qualities of a sextile make it useful for learning new skills, sharing information and relating to others.

As in all areas of astrological interpretation, no single factor ever works in isolation, but should always be assessed in the context of other factors in the chart. I was reminded of this when I looked at the list of notable people below who have a natal Venus-Mars sextile. Some of these people possess an intensity of expression more in keeping with say a Venus-Mars square, than the sextile. This prompted me to look more closely at their charts.

Actor and comedian Robin Williams has a waxing Mars in Cancer in the action hero first phase, in sextile to evening star Venus in Virgo. With his Mars in its first phase he has a full-throttle Mars, but on its own this does not fully account for the high adrenaline we have come to associate with his rapid-fire performances. In looking at his chart however, you quickly see his Mars is conjunct Uranus which makes him much more excitable than would otherwise be the case.

Similarly, in the chart of notorious Australian underworld figure, Carl Williams we see Mars in Virgo, also in the action hero first phase, in sextile aspect to evening star Venus in Scorpio. Although there is

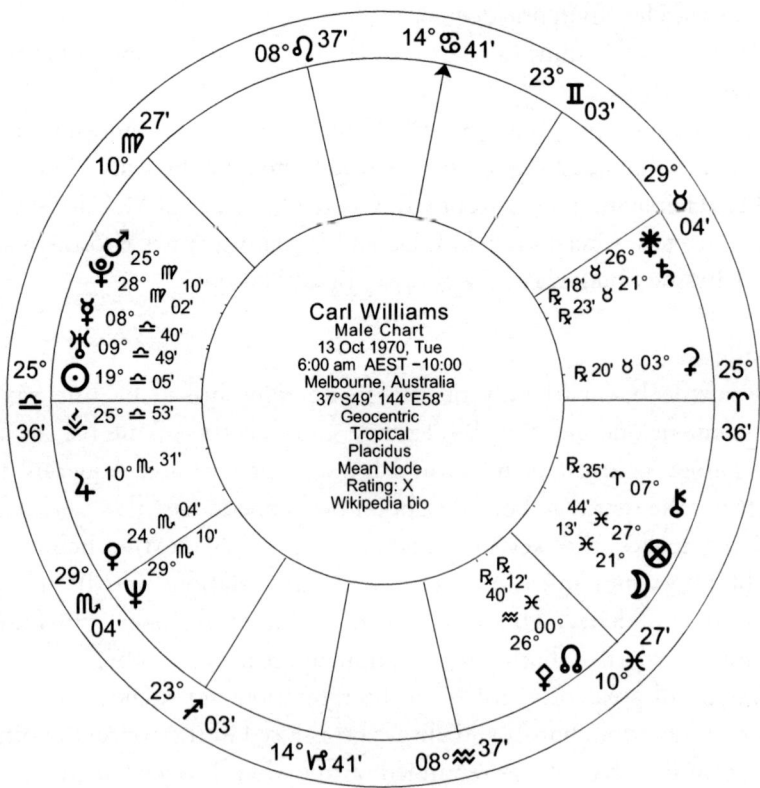

no birth time available for Carl Williams, his Mars is conjunct Pluto which added considerably to his potential for violence. Even without a time of birth, there is a good chance that these planets oppose a Pisces Moon. This seems like a reasonable assumption, given he had the ability to emotionally isolate himself from his violent actions. The outward expression of this sextile is also fuelled by an intense Venus in Scorpio which is conjunct Neptune and opposing a hard-line Saturn in Taurus.

Under normal circumstances a Venus-Mars sextile provides an ease of expression and a friendly, easy-going approach to life and relationships. Despite his violent nature Carl Williams had a rather cheerful demeanour, which was partly why he was not initially suspected of violence.

In terms of synastry the sextile between Venus and Mars is not as commonly seen as one might suspect. In fact, I was surprised by how infrequently Venus-Mars sextiles, Mars-Mars sextiles and Venus-Venus sextiles show up in the charts of lovers and partners. It's possible that these aspects may be more often found between friends rather than in romantic attachments.

Relationships, be they intimate, friendly or professional, build bridges between people and connect communities. These networks have been mapped and show that any two people on Earth are only six steps away, by introduction, from anyone else on Earth.[28] The modern-day concept of 'six degrees of separation' may have a mathematical connection to the sextile as the aspect is associated with the number six, and has an 'air-like' nature. It is quite possible that this friendly, outgoing aspect is primarily used in building these social networks.

Venus-Mars sextiles happen up to four times as the planets move from conjunction to opposition and back again.

Well-known people who have Venus-Mars sextile aspect include: Pamela Anderson, Russell Crowe, Harrison Ford, Angelica Huston, Joanna Lumley, Rene Rivkin, Wallis Simpson, Brett Whiteley, Patrick White, Carl Williams, Robin Williams.

Semi-Squares
This is another intense aspect for Venus and Mars which rivals the square in its potency. Venus reaches her greatest elongation around 45 degrees from the Sun which makes the semi-square a significant aspect for Venus. At this point in her solar journey, morning or evening, she

stops separating from the Sun and begins applying to it. Her perspective changes as she begins moving in a new direction.

Like the sesquiquadrate, the semi-square has a fixed quality to it. Forty-five degrees from the Ascendant takes us to the middle of fixed signs Taurus and Aquarius. In the natal chart, or in synastry, this makes the semi-square an intense, determined and passionate aspect. It is sensual, devoted and loyal and intensifies relationship chemistry.

In terms of Mars' solar journey, the semi-square defines the perimeters outside which he cannot unite with Venus. The 45 degree marker is where Mars leaves the Venus zone, and also where he reunites with his love after his worldly adventures, giving this aspect an 'all or nothing' flavour. With the Venus-Mars semi-square the fairy tale romance can quickly deteriorate.

Prince Charles' Venus is in a tight semi-square (orb 0.16) with the late Princess Diana's Mars. This is the only synastry aspect formed

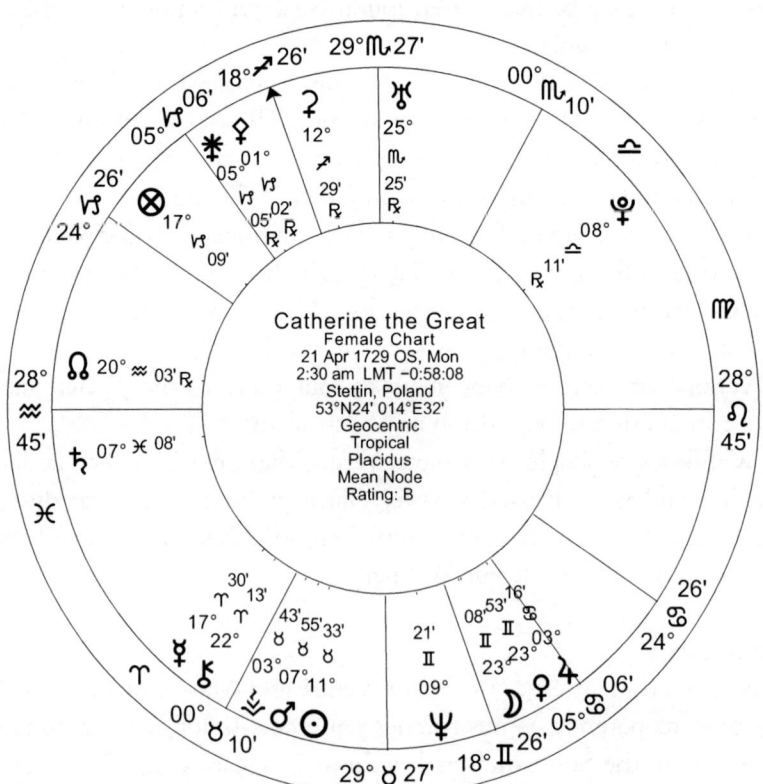

between Venus and Mars in their charts. Nor do we see any Mars-Mars or Venus-Venus links. Throughout their tumultuous marriage her Mars grew stronger and she became a more independent and wilful individual. Her self-sufficient Virgo Mars, which is conjunct Pluto, began to be expressed more consciously.

Charles' Venus in Libra is conjunct Neptune. After their turbulent marriage ended, he married Camilla Parker-Bowles, whose Mars in Gemini is in a comfortable trine with his Venus-Neptune in Libra.

We see the natal aspect in the chart of Catherine the Great, who ruled the vast Russian Empire. Her Mars is conjunct the Sun in Taurus. Her Venus is an evening star alongside the Moon in Gemini. Catherine came to power in her own right in 1762 after taking an active role in a coup against her husband, Peter III. Despite this she was a popular and successful leader. She was passionate about the arts and reformed and modernised Russian society. After her husband's death, Catherine took many lovers, often promoting her young men to positions of authority within her administration and bestowing them with many gifts. Later in life, one of her young lovers was forty years her junior.[29] She was known for her openness and independent approach to relationships

There can be up to four semi-squares between conjunctions.

Well-known people with a Venus-Mars semi-sextile aspect include: Sandra Bernhard, David Bowie, Cher, Agatha Christie, Catherine the Great, T.S. Eliot, Uri Geller, Billy Graham, Lena Horne, Shirley MacLaine, Dane Rudhyar, Elizabeth Taylor.

Semi-Sextiles

The semi-sextile aspect connects signs which are adjacent to each another. These signs have neither polarity, nor quality, nor element in common. Despite the fact that this aspect is considered to be a minor aspect, these differences suggest that the semi-sextile might actually be one of the most challenging of all aspects, especially in relationships.

Signs in semi-sextile share a common boundary, but they can't really see one another clearly. Like neighbours who share a common fence line, planets in semi-sextile may live next door to one another, but probably know nothing about the activities that go on behind closed doors. In many ways they are strangers.

Venus stations occur when she is semi-sextile the Sun. This gives us additional clues as to how a Venus semi-sextile operates.

Edward VIII and Wallis Simpson had a tight Venus-Venus semi-sextile in their synastry. Her Venus in Gemini sought the security that his Venus is Taurus provided. His Venus aspired to the freedom and sociability of her Venus. He was by all accounts besotted with Wallis and in order to marry her, chose to abdicate the English crown.[30]

Semi-sextiles are not commonly seen in synastry comparison, but they may indicate that some kind of sacrifice is required by one of the people involved.

Unlike the sextile that evokes the energy of the Air signs Gemini and Aquarius, the semi-sextile resonates with Pisces and Taurus, signs that are adjacent to the natural Ascendant. This Pisces-Taurus flavour suggests that this love sacrifice is most often made by the person whose planet is earlier in the zodiac, while the latter sign may benefit financially. This was the case with Edward VIII and Wallis with their Venus-Venus semi-sextile.

My feeling is that semi-sextiles on the whole take us out of our comfort zone. In the natal chart one of the planets often represents a seemingly undesirable or unconscious part of the personality that is often projected onto others. Those with this natal aspect seem to actively promote certain traits of their personality contrary to their underlying nature, or their persona can be in stark contrast to their real character. This can result in a great deal of confusion in relationships when the hidden part of the personality is revealed.

Venus and Mars rule signs that are semi-sextile one another as well as opposite signs. Unlike the opposition aspect which provides scope for Venus and Mars to see one another, the semi-sextile can be a real blind spot. Others can usually see these unconscious traits very clearly, but the native cannot. This blind spot is more often represented by the planet in a latter sign of the zodiac. In the natural sequence of the signs of the zodiac, the later sign represents a future time which has yet to occur and hence is not yet conscious.[31]

Operatic star Dame Nellie Melba's chart reveals Venus in Gemini in semi-sextile to Mars in Cancer in its fall in the 7th house. She has been described as having a 'tenacity of purpose allied with exceptional powers

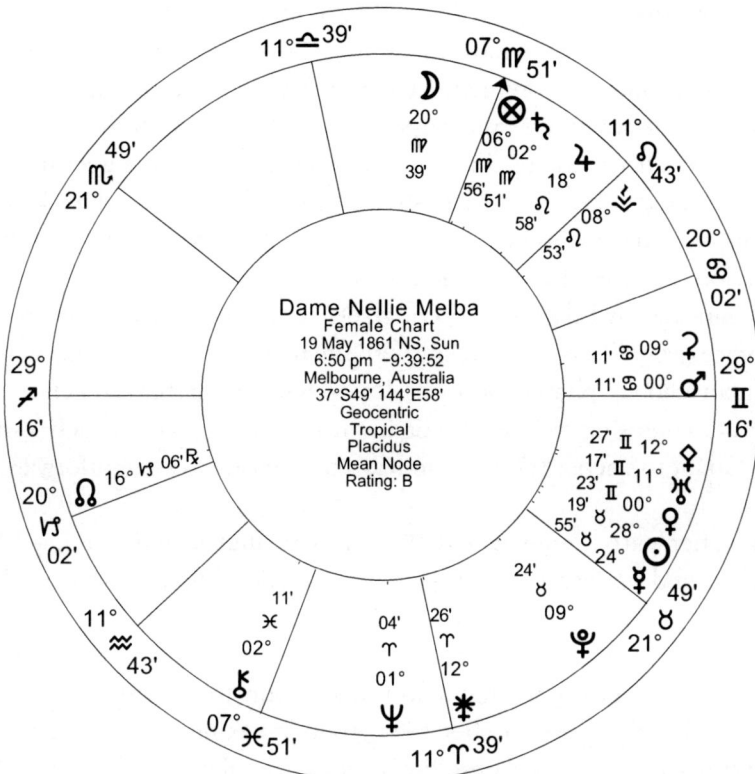

Dame Nellie Melba
Female Chart
19 May 1861 NS, Sun
6:50 pm −9:39:52
Melbourne, Australia
37°S49' 144°E58'
Geocentric
Tropical
Placidus
Mean Node
Rating: B

of concentration'. In a less flattering assessment of her personality, Sir Thomas Beecham once described Melba as 'wanting in genuine spiritual refinement'. Others have spoken of her coldness. George Bernard Shaw thought she was 'hard, shallow, self-sufficient and altogether unsympathetic.'[32] This is not to say that everyone with this semi-sextile will behave like a 'prima donna'. The native may engage in behaviour which is contrary to their real nature, or their true nature may be hidden from view. The person with this aspect can be difficult to get to know and is easily misunderstood.

There are only two semi-sextiles between conjunctions.

Well-known people with Venus-Mars in semi-sextile aspect include: John Belushi, Larry Hagman, Barry Humphries, JFK, John Lennon, Henri Matisse, Dame Nellie Melba, Roy Orbison, Camilla Parker-Bowles, Albert Schweitzer, Donald Trump.

Conjunctions

Sometimes the most obvious things are overlooked. For example, when Venus and Mars are conjunct, Mars is always in direct motion. This is because their conjunctions always occur in the 'Venus Zone' or within 48 degrees either side of the Sun, and Mars is always in direct motion when located here. That Mars should always be 'direct' when kissing Venus, should come as no surprise. After all, this is Mars! Mars is a man of action. He goes after what he wants, when he wants it.

Venus meanwhile, can be retrograde, stationary, or direct when she embraces Mars. This is in keeping with the nature of the feminine, which has many moods, phases and styles. It stands to reason that her behaviour is rather confusing to Mars, for he has no way of knowing which Venus he is about to encounter. He wonders why she isn't as straightforward as he is.

For her part, Venus would like Mars to understand her need for subtlety and variety. On the whole our gender differences mean that men tend to be more conscious of Mars and women more connected to Venus. As a result women are able to multi-task more easily than men, while men tend to apply their efforts and energy to one thing at a time.

Jean Shinoda Bolen, in her 1985 groundbreaking book, *Goddesses in Everywoman*, describes Aphrodite/Venus as an alchemical goddess, for she embodies many different aspects of the feminine. At times she is self-sufficient, autonomous and empowered, not needing or wanting a relationship, a virgin goddess. At other times she is a passionate sexual love goddess, she is also a creative artistic woman, as well as a mother.[33]

How confusing for Mars! When Mars embraces Venus, he is always direct, so what you see is what you get, but when Venus embraces Mars, she can be anything! Mars is never quite sure which Venus he will encounter. He has to get used to it.

Venus-Mars conjunctions cannot happen in the 'Mars zone' because Venus cannot go where Mars goes. Venus is compelled to stay within her designated area. She must wait here for her lover to return from his worldly adventures. Mars will always leave her. She should get used to it. The good news is that Mars will always come back.

While these traditional and stereotypical gender roles of men and women are reflected in the heavenly dance of Venus and Mars, it is important to remember that men have a Venus and woman have a Mars, and the more in touch we are with both planets, the better our relationships will be. Whether male or female, heterosexual or homosexual, all personal relationships are enhanced.

In synastry the Venus-Mars conjunction is a potent indicator of a committed union, though it does not necessarily mean the relationship will be long-lived or harmonious, nor that we will live happily ever after. Ultimately, any relationship comes down to the level of consciousness of each individual which is always unfolding, growing and developing.

After their conjunction, Venus and Mars don't always move directly towards an opposition aspect. They may only move as far apart as the semi-sextile, the semi-square, the sextile, the square, the quintile or the trine before the gap between them closes again. When this occurs, it is always after an *evening star* conjunction.

What has happened is that Venus retrograde has intervened and prevented the planets from reaching an opposition. Therefore, although

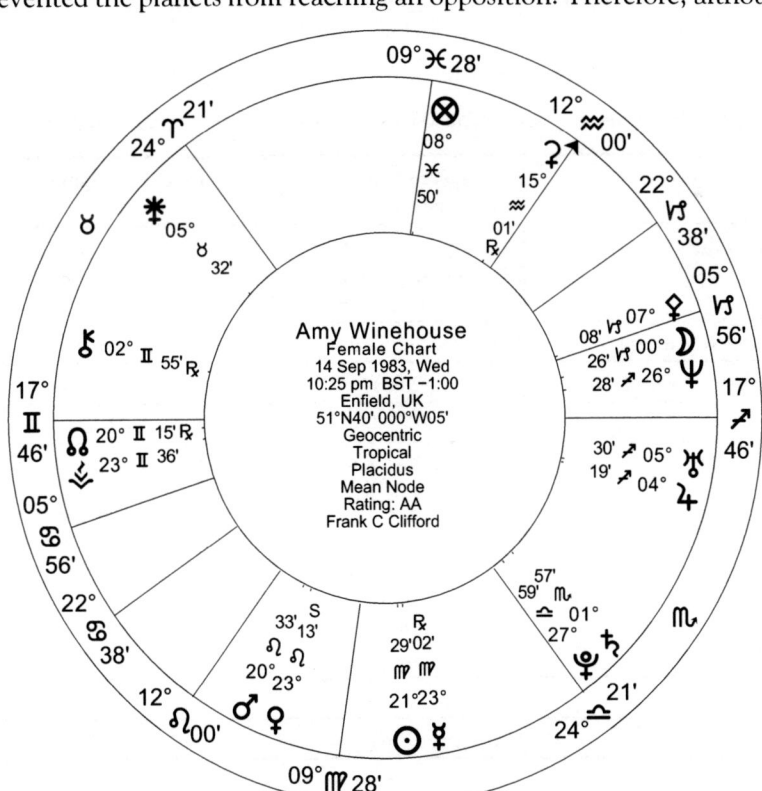

Venus retrograde is a time of evaluation, and can sometimes signal the end of a relationship, she is nevertheless reluctant to let go of Mars. She does so because her core standards and values are in conflict with her outer circumstances.

Although Venus withdraws into herself while retrograde in order to reflect and evaluate, her reasons for doing so are to establish a more perfect bond with Mars. After their late night coupling, as evening stars, they will embrace one another again in the morning.

Those born under a Venus-Mars conjunction are passionate people in every sense of the word. Troubled singer, Amy Winehouse who was known for her soulful performances was born a few days before a Venus Mars conjunction in Leo. Her chart reveals a fragile, yet powerful Venus that was stationary direct. After a long history of drug and alcohol abuse she was sadly found dead at the age of 27.

Well-known people with Venus-Mars conjunction include: Andrew Agassi, Prince Andrew, Jim Carrey, Bill Clinton, Sally Field, Heidi Fleiss, David Helfgott, Adolf Hitler, Tom Jones, Bruce Lee, Al Pacino, Keanu Reeves, Greta Scacchi, Orson Welles, Amy Winehouse.

Table B: Venus and Mars synastry aspects in well known relationships[34]

Sarah Ferguson	Mars square Mars Mars square Venus	Prince Andrew
Lauren Bacall	Venus quincunx Mars Mars semi-square Mars Venus opposite Venus	Humphrey Bogart
Joanne Woodward	Venus sextile Venus	Paul Newman
Elizabeth Taylor	Mars trine Mars	Richard Burton
Katharine Hepburn	Mars quintile Mars	Spencer Tracy
Terri Irwin	Mars quintile Venus Venus opposite Mars	Steve Irwin
Gillian Helfgott	Mars trine Mars Mars trine Venus	David Helfgott
Steffi Graf	Mars opposite Mars Mars opposite Venus Venus semi-sextile Mars	Andre Agassi
Liza Minnelli	Mars opposite Venus	Peter Allen
Susan Sarandon	Venus opposite Mars	Tim Robbins

Chris Evert	Venus quincunx Mars Venus semi-square Venus	Greg Norman
Catherine Zeta-Jones	Venus semi-square Mars	Michael Douglas
Farrah Fawcett	Mars square Venus Mars conjunct Mars Venus trine Venus Venus semi-square Mars	Ryan O'Neal
Princess Diana	Mars semi-square Venus	Prince Charles
Camilla Parker-Bowles	Venus square Venus Mars trine Venus Mars opposite Mars	Prince Charles
Mia Farrow	Venus quintile Mars Mars conjunct Mars Mars square Venus	Woody Allen
Jane Fonda	Mars square Venus Mars sesquiquadrate Mars	Ted Turner
Margaret Whitlam	Mars conjunct Mars Venus square Venus	Gough Whitlam
Angelica Huston	Venus trine Venus Mars sesquiquadrate Mars Mars quincunx Mars	Jack Nicholson
Audrey Hepburn	Venus square Mars Mars conjunct Mars	Mel Ferrer
Elizabeth Hurley	Mars square Mars Venus semi-square Venus	Shane Warne
Sophia Loren	Venus sesquiquadrate Venus Venus square Mars Mars trine Mars	Carlo Ponti
Jennifer Aniston	Venus square Mars Mars semi-square Mars Mars sextile Venus	Brad Pitt
Angelina Jolie	Venus opposite Venus Mars square Mars	Brad Pitt
Demi Moore	Venus square Venus Venus trine Mars Mars opposite Venus	Ashton Kutcher
Katie Holmes	Venus square Venus Mars sesquiquadrate Venus	Tom Cruise
Nicole Kidman	Mars sextile Venus Venus conjunct Venus	Tom Cruise

Ava Gardner	Venus square Mars Venus semi-square Venus Mars sextile Venus	Frank Sinatra
Marilyn Monroe	Mars sesquiquadrate Mars Venus opposite Venus	Arthur Miller
Marilyn Monroe	Mars square Venus Mars sextile Mars	JFK
Marilyn Monroe	Venus opposite Mars Mars sesquiquadrate Mars	Robert Kennedy
Jacqueline Kennedy Onassis	Venus conjunct Venus Mars square Venus Mars trine Mars	JFK
Jacqueline Kennedy Onassis	Venus square Mars Mars opposite Mars Venus quincunx Venus	Aristotle Onassis
Maria Callas	Mars square Venus	Aristotle Onassis
Nancy Reagan	Mars opposite Mars Venus square Venus	Ronald Reagan
Britt Ekland	Mars conjunct Venus	Peter Sellers
Chrissie Hynde	Venus conjunct Venus	Jim Kerr
Nicole Brown-Simpson	Venus conjunct Venus Mars semi-square Mars	O.J. Simpson
Kate Middleton Duchess of Cambridge	Mars conjunct Mars Venus trine Mars Mars sesquiquadrate Venus	Prince William Duke of Cambridge
Frida Kahlo	Mars conjunct Mars Venus opposite Venus	Diego Rivera
Vivien Leigh	Venus square Mars Mars opposite Mars	Laurence Olivier
Tina Turner	Mars square Mars	Ike Turner
Priscilla Presley	Mars opposite Mars Venus opposite Mars	Elvis Presley
Dottie West	Mars square Venus Venus quintile Venus Venus sesquiquadrate Mars	Fred West
Julie Andrews	Venus conjunct Venus Venus square Mars Mars conjunct Mars Mars square Venus	Blake Edwards

Princess Margaret	Mars square Venus Mars trine Mars	Anthony Armstrong Jones
Callista Flockhart	Venus trine Venus	Harrison Ford
Pamela Stephenson	Mars quintile Venus Venus quintile Mars	Billy Connelly
Elizabeth Barrett Browning	Venus square Venus Venus quintile Mars Mars square Mars	Robert Browning

Return to Love

Mars and Venus Returns

Venus-Mars aspects are being formed all the time. Each moment contains infinite possibilities. Love will blossom when the time is right for it to bloom. One way to pinpoint when love is likely to find us, is by looking at Venus and Mars Returns.

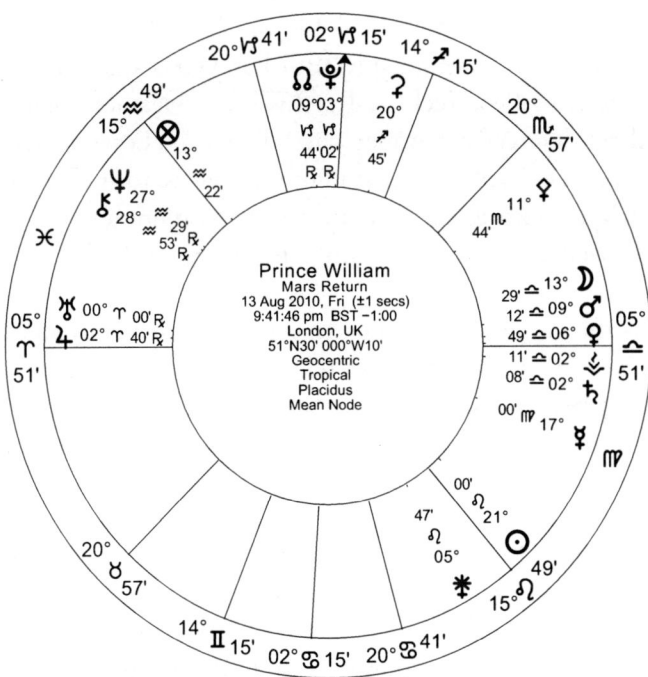

While one might think the Venus Return should take precedence over the Venus Return, Mars is a planet of action and if we are looking for some relationship action, his relationship with Venus in these charts can be crucial. When Venus holds a special position in a Mars Return the scene is set for romantic developments. Every so often Venus and Mars will make a conjunction in a Mars Return chart and this will often signify the start of a committed union.

Prince William and Kate Middleton, the Duke and Duchess of Cambridge, have a Mars-Mars conjunction in their synastry. They were born six months apart. She was born just prior to a Mars station in Libra, and he was born just after Mars stationed direct. They announced their engagement in November 2010, just as Venus stationed direct in Libra.

Their Mars Return charts for 2010 show Venus right alongside Mars. In William's case for whom we have an exact time of birth, this conjunction is in the 7th house, very close to the Descendant.

Another example is seen in the relationship of Sophia Loren and Carlo Ponti. They met when she was just 15 years of age. The couple married in September 1957 when she was 22 and he was 44. Sophia Loren's Mars Return chart for July 1957 has Venus and Mars in a tight conjunction at 13 Leo. Technically, this was a bigamous marriage, for Ponti had not divorced his former wife.[35] Ponti and Loren married again in 1966, this time legally. In Carlo Ponti's Mars Return chart for 1965, Mars and Venus are again seen in a close conjunction. The couple remained together for fifty years until his death in 2007 at the age of 94.

Besides the conjunction, other aspects between Venus and Mars in the Mars Return can signify major relationship developments.

Poet Elizabeth Barrett Browning eloped with Robert Browning in September 1846, when her Mars Return had Venus and Mars in a tight sextile. Though there is some uncertainty about his birth time, in this chart Mars is on the cusp of the 7th house. Prior to their elopement, Robert Browning's Mars Return shows Mars and Venus in a tight square. In this chart, set for April 1846, Venus is located at 10 Pisces 23, which is tightly conjunct Elizabeth's natal Mars at 9 Pisces 45.

Similar themes can be seen in relation to the position of Mars in the Venus Return.

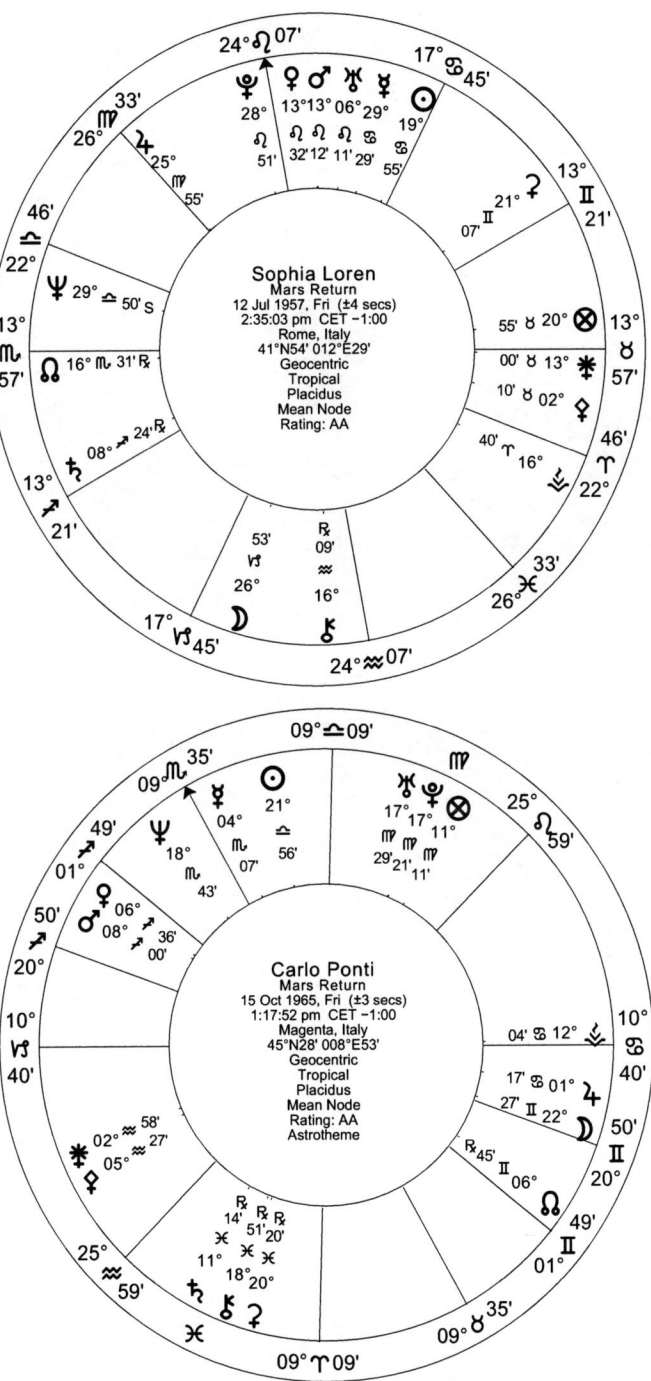

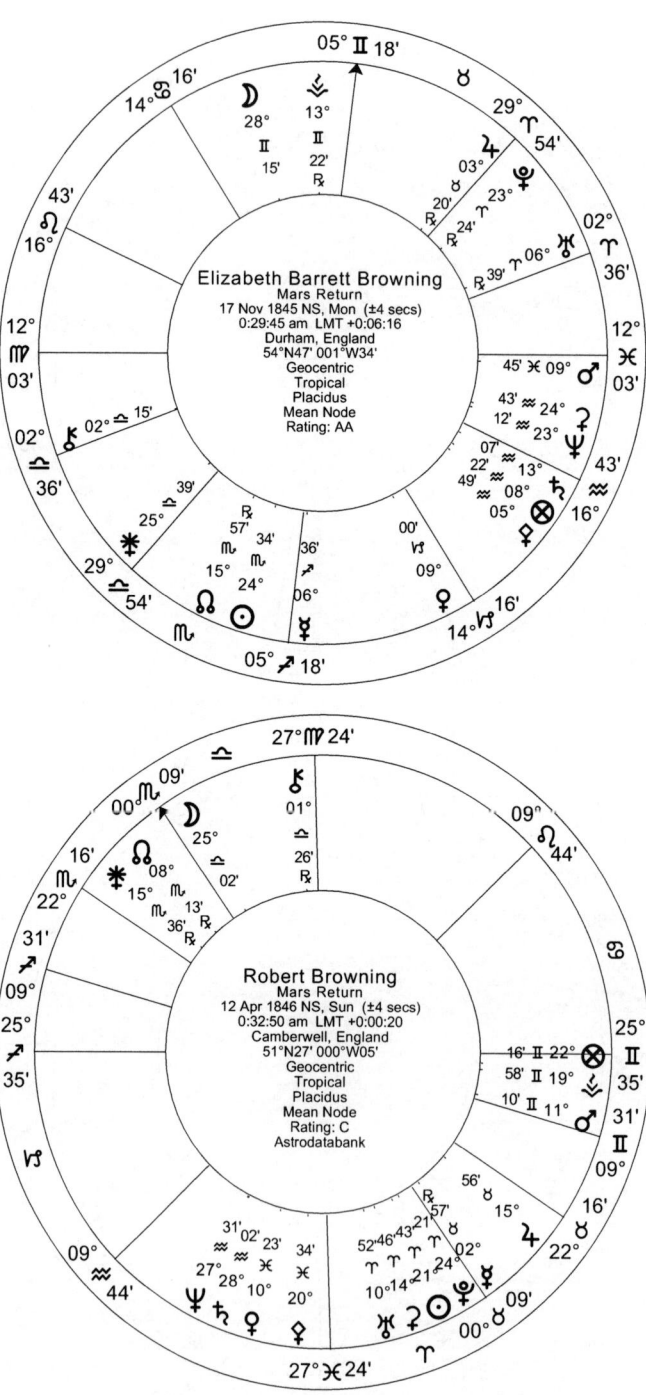

But Venus does not need to be joined to Mars in the Venus Return for love to occur, though when she is, this is a strong signal that a passionate union will ensue. Venus might be tied in aspect to another planet and this can reveal the kind of love and attraction that will develop. Venus is sometimes conjunct Saturn when a committed relationship comes along especially when Venus is in the 5th or 7th house of the return chart. On the other hand squares and opposition between Venus and Saturn do not augur so well.

When Venus and Pluto are squaring, and this will generally be seen in a couple of subsequent Venus return charts, owing to the slow motion of Pluto, it often indicates the end of a relationship. It can also herald the beginning of a new partnership.

When Venus is in hard aspect with Chiron this generally brings a painful relationship experience. The individual is likely to enter into a relationship with someone who is very wounded, either emotionally, psychologically or physically, or experience pain throughout the relationship.

For reasons that are difficult to fathom, I have often seen Venus and Ceres in tight aspect when an individual becomes involved in an extra-marital affair. In Bill Clinton's 1995 Venus Return just before his fling with Monica Lewinsky, we see Venus and Ceres conjunct. While in Lewinsky's Venus Return for August 1995, her Venus at 28 Leo 27 was just reaching superior conjunction and was squaring powerful Pluto in Scorpio.

Venus-Uranus tends to bring surprising and completely unexpected developments that alter the nature of one's relationships. When it is the conjunction, the native is the one likely to initiate these changes.

Venus with Neptune can herald a fairy-tale romance, especially when the 5th house is involved. Though it must be said that one is apt to be disillusioned or disappointed when reality finally dawns. An example of this is seen in the Venus Return chart for Grace Kelly in the lead up to her marriage to Prince Rainier. Neptune moved across her natal Venus at 28 Libra 51 in 1955 and 1956. The middle hit of this transit took place on 27 April 1956 two weeks after her marriage. For her handsome prince she willingly gave up the Hollywood fairy tale.[36]

Another feature of Venus and Mars Returns worth noting is when a Venus Return and a Mars Return occur at the same time.

These synchronised returns can foreshadow truly amazing events in relationships and in other areas of life. Somehow everything effortlessly falls into place. Dreams can come true under these circumstances, so be careful what you wish for if you are having a synchronised return.

Not all people will experience synchronised Venus-Mars returns, while some individuals will have several happen in a lifetime. To check, calculate all your Mars Return charts and then check these charts to see if Venus is close to its natal position. This gives you fewer charts to look at than calculating all your Venus Returns.

Wallis Simpson had an amazing run of these synchronised returns in the lead up to her marriage to Edward. Her natal Mars at 21 Aries 43, is in a sociable sextile with her natal Venus at 23 Gemini 54.

In her Mars Return for 1926 Venus was at 22 Gemini 46. In her Mars Return for 1928 Venus was at 19 Gemini 03. In her next Mars Return in 1930 Venus was again in Gemini, at 27 Gemini 28. Venus was again close to returning in her next Mars return in 1932 when it was located at 25 Gemini 54. In her 1934 Mars Return chart, Venus was not returning, but Mars and the Sun were conjunct within 40 minutes of arc. Then

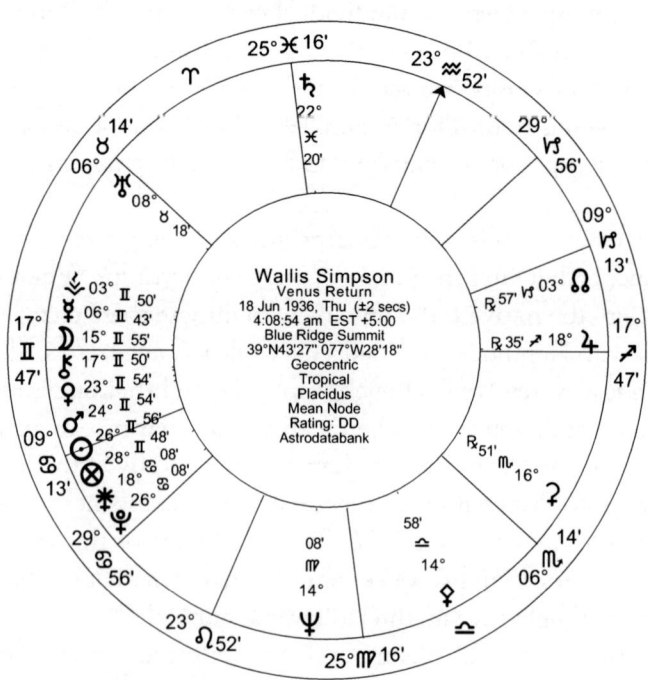

in 1936 six months after Edward ascended the throne and six months before he abdicated to marry Wallis, Wallis' *Venus Return* has Mars at 24 Gemini 54 making a conjunction to Venus and also the Sun.[37]

Footnotes

1. The associations between the planets and metals are explored in *Metal Power* by Alison Davidson and *The Metal-Planet Relationship* by Nick Kollerstrom.
2. Nick Kollerstrom, *The Metal-Planet Relationship*, Borderland Sciences Research Foundation, California, 1993, p.127
3. http://en.wikipedia.org/wiki/Intrauterine_device [May 2011]
4. Eileen Nauman, *The American Book of Nutrition and Medical Astrology*, Astro Computing Services, San Diego, 1982, p.207
5. Eileen Nauman, *The American Book of Nutrition and Medical Astrology*, Astro Computing Services, San Diego, 1982, p.202
6. Kelly Lambert, 'A Tale of Two Rodents', published in *The Scientific American Mind*, September/October 2011 edition, pp.37-43. This fun and informative article provides many insights into sexuality in rats and in humans.
7. http://www.theoi.com This site is a comprehensive and easy to access reference for Greek mythology.
8. Mars' two small moons are named Phobos and Deimos. Their proximity to Mars aligns these emotions, fear and terror, with the red planet. There are asteroids named after Eros, Anteros and Harmonia and it can be useful to locate these bodies in the natal chart and look at their synastry aspects. For example, if one person's Eros sits on another's personal planets, nodal axis, or has links to Venus or Mars, or if it is adjacent to an angle, especially the descendant, it suggests the presence of a powerful magnetising force that will pull two people together, for better or worse. I have briefly looked at the asteroid Harmonia. As one would expect her 'harmonious' aspects in synastry appear to help create harmony on the domestic front.
9. http://www.independent.co.uk/news/science/scientists-prove-it-really-is-a-thin-line-between-love-and-hate-976901.html [May 2011]
10. http://mathworld.wolfram.com/PlatonicSolid.html
11. John D. Barrow, *Cosmic Imagery*, The Bodley Head, 2008, p.268
12. David Berlinski, *The Secrets of the Vaulted Sky*, p.181
13. See Part Two.
14. Alexander Ruperti, *Cycles of Becoming*, Earthwalk School of Astrology Publishing, Santa Monica, USA, Second Edition, 2005, p.82
15. Ronald Davison, *Synastry*, Aurora Press, New York, 1983, p.129
16. See Case history Alan Leo.
17. Liz Greene, *Relating*, Samuel Weiser Inc., York Beach, Maine, 1984, Chapter III.
18. Bil Tierney, *Dynamics of Aspect Analysis*, CRCS Publications, California, 1983, pp.35-6

19. http://en.wikipedia.org/wiki/Judy_Garland [October 2011]

20. http://www.humphreybogart.com/index.php/biography [May 2011]

21. ibid

22. Solar Fire Literature data base.

23. http://en.wikipedia.org/wiki/Lord_Byron#Death [May 2011]

24. Erin Sullivan, *Retrograde Planets*, Samuel Weiser, York Beach, Maine, 2000, pp.171-2

25. http://en.wikipedia.org/wiki/Errol_Flynn [June 2011]

26. His widow Ethel, now in her eighties, has Venus in late Pisces, conjunct Mercury and Uranus in early Aries. Venus and Mercury are in quintile aspect to her North Node in Gemini. Ethel Kennedy 11 April 1928 at 3.30 am, Chicago, Illinois. Data from Astrotheme.

27. Bil Tierney, *Dynamics of Aspect Analysis*, CRCS Publications, California, 1983, p.18

28. Six degrees of separation refers to the idea that everyone is on average approximately six steps away, by way of introduction, from any other person on Earth, so that a chain of, "a friend of a friend" statements can be made, on average, to connect any two people in six steps or fewer.

29. http://www.saint-petersburg.com/history/catherine2nd.asp [July 2011]

30. See also Case History section.

31. The idea that we consciously evolve through the natural sequence of the signs of the zodiac, is explored in the author's first book, *Secrets of the Zodiac*, Allen and Unwin, Sydney, 2009

32. http://adb.anu.edu.au/biography/melba-dame-nellie-7551 [July 2011]

33. Jean Shinoda Bolen, *Goddesses in Everywoman*, Harper Collins, New York, 1985, p.17

34. Ten degree orbs for conjunctions and oppositions have been allowed in this table.

35. http://en.wikipedia.org/wiki/Sophia_Loren [May 2011]

36. http://www.imdb.com/name/nm0000038/bio [February 2012]

37. See also Case History Part Five.

Part Four
The Venus-Mars Saros

Love Makes the World Go Around

The Venus-Mars 32-year Synodic Cycle

My interest in the Venus-Mars cycle began one day when I happened to ask myself a simple question; how often do Venus-Mars conjunctions take place? As it turns out there is no simple answer to that question. Like relationships, the Venus-Mars cycle is rather complex.

When viewed from Earth, successive conjunctions of Venus and Mars can happen a few weeks apart, or a few months apart, up to a maximum of 23 months apart. Like love itself, the Venus-Mars cycle is seemingly random and unpredictable, yet there is a pattern to it. Before we can see the beauty of this pattern clearly we have to get up close and personal.

Although conjunctions of Venus and Mars skip back and forth across the zodiac randomly, each conjunction is part of a series of conjunctions that step along the zodiac in a predictable way; every 32 years Venus and Mars rendezvous. When Venus and Mars renew their vows every 32 years, their meeting point moves a few degrees along the zodiac. After another 32 years have passed, the point of conjunction will have shifted along again by a few degrees, and so on. Some of these conjunction cycles advance through the zodiac in direct motion, and some move backwards, or in retrograde motion, through the zodiac.

In Table C you will see a list of sequential Venus-Mars conjunctions spanning the years 1964-78. When viewed this way, in time sequence, conjunctions occur randomly. The conjunction on 17 July 1964 was located at 21 Gemini and was followed a few weeks later by another conjunction on 27 August 1964 at 17 Cancer. The pattern to their cycle is only seen when you look ahead 32 years.

In 1996, 32 years after 1964, another pair of Venus-Mars conjunctions took place. The first was on 29 June, at 12 Gemini. This was a retrograde cycle because the point of conjunction had moved backwards from 21 Gemini in 1964 to 12 Gemini in 1996. See Table D. The second conjunction happened on 3 September 1996 at 25 Cancer. This being a direct cycle as the point of conjunction had moved forward from 17

DATE	Degree
17 July 1964	21°Ge01'
27 Aug 1964	17°Cn44'
19 Oct 1965	10°Sg33'
9 Jan 1966	13°Aq32'
4 Aug 1966	15°Cn50'
21 June 1968	29°Ge54'
9 May 1970	14°Ge02'
21 April 1972	16°Ge24'
17 May 1972	02°Cn52'
5 Dec 1972	12°Sc26'
25 Oct 1974	27°Li32'
11 Sept 1976	11°Li36'
16 May 1977	14°Ar09'
7 June 1977	00°Ta37'
13 Aug 1978	05°Li41'

Table C: Sequential
Venus-Mars conjunctions
1964-1978

17 July 1964	21°Ge01'
27 Aug 1964	17°Cn44'
29 June 1996	12°Ge02'
3 Sept 1996	25°Cn55'
14 June 2028	04°Ge51'
8 Sept 2028	02°Le03'

Table D: The 32-year
cycle Venus-Mars
cycle. Initial retrograde
cycle followed by a
direct cycle.

Cancer in 1964 to 25 Cancer. In 2028, after another 32 years have passed, the point of conjunction will have moved along again by a few degrees.

In this way every Venus-Mars conjunction is part of a series of conjunctions that shift backwards or forwards through the zodiac by small increments every 32 years.

I began listing conjunctions, their dates and degrees, on a spreadsheet. In the first column I listed the first 31 years, then in the next column the next 31 years, and so on, so that the 32 year cycle could be seen to move across the page by degree increments. I was able to see how the point of conjunction had moved a few degrees backwards, or forwards, from its previous position. I continued plotting conjunctions and watched as a beautiful pattern began to emerge.

Over any given 32-year period, there will be 25 Venus-Mars conjunctions and each is one of a series that is unfolding.[1] Of these 25 conjunctions, 5 will be retrograde and 20 will be direct. Every fifth conjunction is a retrograde cycle. Once again we see the significance of the number five in relation to Venus. This confirms that when it comes to relationships, Venus is in charge.

To the best of my knowledge this cycle has only been investigated by a handful of astrologers.[2] In a posthumous interview published in *The Mountain Astrologer* in 2011, Robert P. Blaschke said how he had examined over 500 years of the Venus-Mars cycle.[3] Previously, Alexander Ruperti talked about the Venus-Mars synod in his book, *Cycles of Becoming*,[4] but the full extent of the Venus-Mars cycle only emerged after I had examined 1500 years of conjunctions.

After making fruitless enquiries in astrological and astronomical circles to try to ascertain if there was a name for this 32 year cycle, I decided to call it: 'The Venus-Mars Saros'. Although technically it is not an eclipse cycle, it is in many ways similar to the Saros cycle in its scope and pattern.

> 'The use of the word saros to mean a 223 lunar month eclipse cycle was erroneously introduced in 1691 by Edmund Halley when he applied it to the Babylonian eclipse cycle on the basis of a corrupt manuscript by the Roman naturalist Pliny. The Babylonian sign SAR has meaning both as a word and a number. As a word it means (among other things) universe. As a number it means 3600, signifying a large number. There is no evidence that the Babylonians ever applied saros to the 18 year eclipse cycle.'[5]

While searching for information about the Venus-Mars cycle I came across this information in relation to the origins of the term 'Saros' and its usage. Since the word 'sar' means 'universe', and 'large number', and appears to have been mistakenly applied to the Sun-Moon eclipse cycle in the first place, I feel comfortable in adopting the term and applying it to the Venus-Mars 'Saros'.

New Cycles

As I continued to plot conjunctions on my spreadsheet, I noticed that every so often the zodiacal degree did not fit this pattern. I soon realised this meant that a particular cycle had just ended, or a new one has just commenced.

When new Venus-Mars cycles start, they do so in pairs – holding hands if you like. The *retrograde* cycle always comes first. This first conjunction in a new series will be followed a few weeks later by another conjunction, its partner, which is the first conjunction of a *direct* cycle.

Each retrograde series of Venus-Mars conjunctions spans approximately 250-350 years and during that time there will be between 9 and 12 conjunctions, each spaced at 32 year intervals, back-tracking through the zodiac. Direct cycles take much longer to unfold. They span more than 1200 years from start to finish and there are around 40 conjunctions in these long direct cycles.

Roughly ten conjunctions before a long direct cycle is due to finish, a new retrograde cycle will be born, along with a new direct cycle – its partner. This new retrograde cycle of 300 years will make its usual ten or so conjunctions, and then finish *immediately after the preceding direct cycle*, which is now at an end. The new direct cycle which began at the same time as its retrograde partner, will continue on for about 1200 years. Then once again, 300 years before this direct cycle ends, another pair of new conjunctions will commence, and so on. In this way the cycles are interlinked. This is more clearly seen in Diagram 11. Two Venus-Mars conjunction cycles start out together hand-in hand, but as time progresses a new retrograde cycle – new love interest if you will – arrives on the scene and establishes a connection to the previous long direct series.

Over long periods of time, the partnership that started out dissolves. Each new retrograde cycle is accompanied by its partner, a new long direct cycle, but the former ends up becoming the partner of an earlier series, bringing that cycle to a close. The initial commitment between the pair is broken. In this way each old long cycle eventually ends up married to a new younger partner! Similarly, in loving relationships we can fall in and out of love. When a new love interest arrives on the scene it can signal the end of a long standing prior commitment.

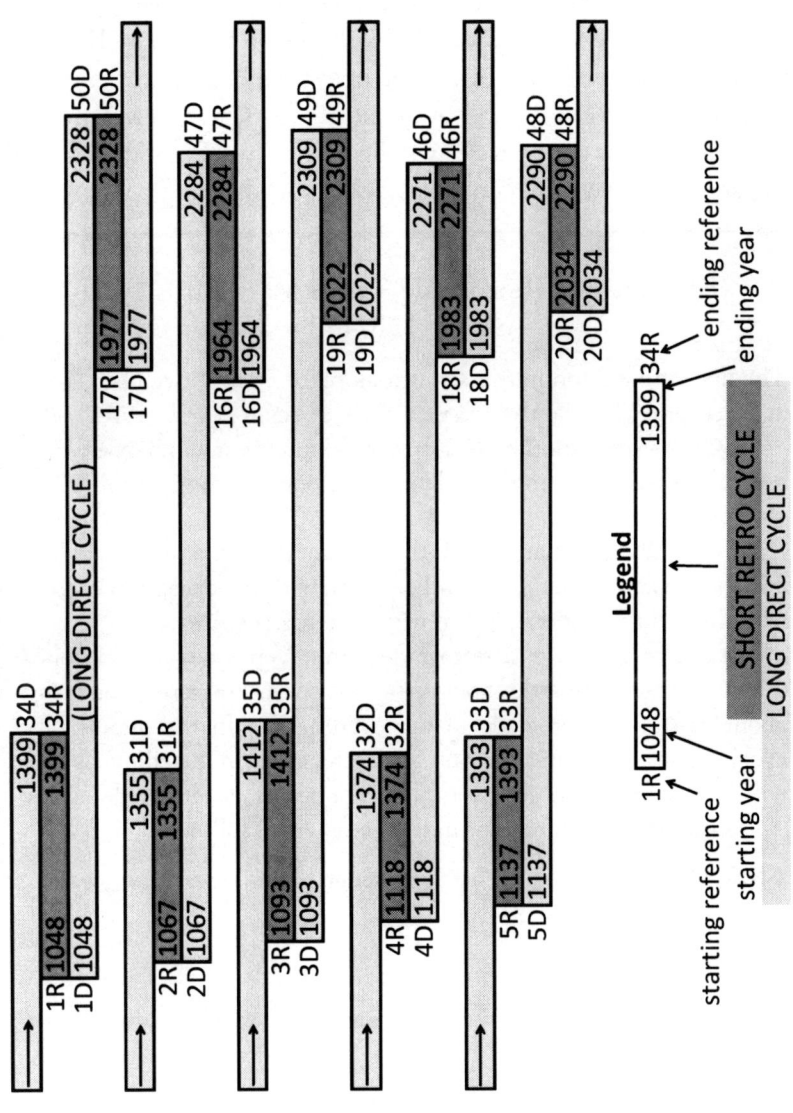

Diagram 11: The five retrograde cycles and their partners, the five direct cycles which began in the 11th century. Note how they are linked to the new cycles that started in 1964.

The whole pattern of the Venus-Mars Saros is driven by Venus. This is as it should be. Venus is the goddess of love so naturally she is the one that initiates relationship and plans how it unfolds. Venus retrograde and her stations are the fuel that drives the Venus-Mars Saros engine.

Both retrograde and direct cycles continue on for hundreds of years without any new cycles starting, or old ones stopping. Then, beautifully, in pairs of five, over a period of about 80 years, five new retrograde cycles and five new direct cycles will be born, while five old ones, both retrograde and direct, will conclude. [See Appendix]

Example of a Retrograde Venus Mars Saros cycle
Cycle 15R/43R

The first conjunction in this series took place on 29 November 1735 at 5 Scorpio. This was the last new cycle to begin prior to 1964.

Every 32 years another Venus-Mars conjunction will happen several degrees *earlier* in the zodiac, as the point of conjunction is *retrograding*.

If you calculate charts for all the conjunctions in a retrograde cycle you will discover that in all of them, with the exception of the first one and the last one, Venus will be retrograde.

In the first chart of a retrograde series, Venus has just stationed direct in the morning sky, and in the last one in the series, she is just about to station retrograde in the evening sky. In the middle of a cycle, Venus, Mars and the Sun are all together in a stellium. Venus will be at inferior conjunction. This applies to *all* retrograde cycles.

Venus-Mars conjunctions in this series are as follows:

29 Nov 1735	**5 Scorpio**	**First conjunction in this series. Morning sky.**
11 Nov 1767	26 Libra	
26 Oct 1799	18 Libra	
12 Oct 1831	12 Libra	
28 Sept 1863	**5 Libra**	**Venus, Mars and Sun together. Venus inferior**
13 Sept 1895	29 Virgo	**conjunction.**
31 Aug 1927	22 Virgo	
15 Sept 1959	15 Virgo	
26 July 1991	**6 Virgo**	**Last conjunction in this series. Evening sky.**

Cycle New Direct 3D/49D

Direct cycles are much longer than retrograde cycles. There will be around 40 conjunctions in all. Direct cycle 3D/49D commenced on 1 May 1093 at 10 Aries and will not conclude until 10 August 2309 at 2 Libra. I have not listed all 39 conjunctions in this series, but those mentioned below will give you an idea of the scope of a direct cycle. The central conjunction in a direct cycle also occurs when Venus, Mars and the Sun are in conjunction, but Venus will be at superior conjunction, and therefore direct.

11 May 1093 10 Aries   **First conjunction in this series. Morning sky.**
21 May 1125   21 Aries   2nd conjunction.

Followed every 32 years by another conjunction moving direct through the zodiac until…

4 July 1669   12 Cancer 19th and middle conjunction. Sun Venus and
Mars together.

Followed every 32 years by another conjunction moving direct through the zodiac until…

1 Aug 2277   24 Virgo   38th conjunction
10 Aug 2309 2 Libra   Last conjunction in series. Evening sky.

During these periods, when new cycles are starting and old ones concluding, human relationships and social customs undergo dramatic changes. The social fabric seems to be woven with different threads and new materials. The introduction of these new styles and textures affects us all. Old standards of behaviour are no longer the norm. These new trends can make relationships more transient and short lived, but at the same time these new ways of relating breathe new life into outmoded concepts and traditions. And on a personal level they help new relationships get off the ground. These 70-80 year periods of radical social change don't happen very often, but we are living through one of them now.

From these lists of conjunctions you will see that any conjunction of Venus and Mars can be quickly categorised. Simply by looking in the ephemeris, or calculating a chart for a conjunction and noting where Venus and Mars are positioned in relation to the Sun, you will know right away whether it is a new, or newish Venus-Mars Saros conjunction, which will be in the morning sky and hence earlier in the zodiac than the Sun, or one that is in the middle of its cycle, which will be conjunct the Sun, or whether the series is nearing its end, in which case Venus and Mars will be evening stars.

Note that all cycles start, and end, with wide orbs of about 10 degrees or so between conjunctions spaced 32 years apart, but the orb between subsequent conjunctions in a series diminishes towards the middle of each cycle, where they are spaced much closer together, perhaps less than one degree apart.

The first, the middle and the last conjunctions in each series appear to be the most significant. These special conjunctions are discussed later in this section.

The Relationship Revolution 1964-2034

The 1964 conjunctions of Venus and Mars were the first new cycles to commence since the year 1735. These conjunctions ushered in an era of radical social change and creative influences which had a dramatic impact on personal relationships and society as a whole.

The strict moral codes of the 1950s, along with the tight fitting underwear, were gone. Mini-skirts and rock and roll were in. Sex before marriage was now okay.

These 1964 conjunctions kicked off the first new group series to commence since 1665, being the first pair of conjunctions in the current group of five that are now unfolding.[6] Tables E and F list the dates of this group series which spans the years 1964-2034. A more comprehensive list of these Venus-Mars cycles can be found in the Appendix.

The new retrograde cycle that began in 1964 saw Venus and Mars positioned at 21 Gemini 01. Fascinatingly, the Sabian symbol for the 22nd degree of Gemini is 'Dancing Couples in a Harvest Festival', which clearly resonates with the atmosphere of the 1960s. Totally new values in interpersonal and social relationships were emerging. People were having fun, relating naturally together and enjoying life as they would at a festival.

Occurring in Mercury-ruled Gemini everyone was now openly discussing sexuality. Taboos were no longer taboo. Gays were liberated. Men and women were free to be themselves.

Living together before marriage was unheard of in the conservative 50s. In the 60s all that changed. Divorce became more commonplace too. Pretty soon a sexual revolution was underway. The free-love era of the 1970s culminated with the advent of nudist colonies, wife-swapping and open marriages when the second pair of cycles commenced in 1977.

In the 1960s the contraceptive pill was first made available, paving the way for the sexual revolution which ensued. Women no longer had to worry so much about falling pregnant. But it wasn't just the advent of the Pill that was responsible for the new sexual freedom, for women were taking to the streets demanding the right to an abortion as well as equal pay.

Collectively we are in the process of evolving beyond gender stereotypes, moving towards integration and wholeness. Since 1964 increasing numbers of men have become more conscious of sensuality and feeling and other qualities normally classified as 'feminine'. Similarly, women from all walks of life are far more independent than they used to be and continue to move into positions of authority and power that were once the exclusive domain of men. Across the world more and more we are witnessing the legalisation of same-sex marriage. This revolution is still unfolding.

The astrological glyphs for Venus ♀ and Mars ♂ are identical to those used in biology to identify the sexes. And to some extent they still function in terms of their traditional gender associations in women and men. By and large men are more conscious of Mars, just as women are more in tune with Venus, but their symbolic meaning is no longer as gender specific it once was. Gender roles, along with the times, have altered dramatically. Like Venus, who leads Mars in this sacred dance, it is women who have led this revolution.

The dramatic social changes that swept the world during in the 1960s and 1970s continue to be felt. This current cluster of change spans the years 1964 to 2034, a period of just 70 years.

The next new retrograde cycle will start on 17 February, 2022. This is the fourth new retrograde cycle in the current group series. When this conjunction arrives we may see further breakthroughs in women's rights in those regions of the world where women continue to suffer oppression. Occurring at 16 Capricorn 55, the Sabian Symbol for this degree is; 'A Repressed Woman Finds Psychological Release in Nudism'.

Astrologers will be aware that in the 1960s Uranus and Pluto formed a conjunction. These two outer planets are well-known as symbols of revolution and their hard aspects herald widespread political and social change. The 1960s saw waves of demonstrations and protests. The civil rights movement emerged as people called for social reforms. The political landscape underwent a dramatic shift across the globe. While the wide sweeping changes of the 1960s can be explained solely by the Uranus-Pluto conjunction, the rapid pace of change in gender roles, relationships and sexuality that occurred is equally consistent with the advent of this new Venus-Mars era.

Fascinatingly, there is a fundamental link between these two diverse planetary cycles that converged in the mid 1960s. In his book, *The Little Book of Coincidence in the Solar System*, John Martineau presents a number of beautiful spiral patterns that illustrate the way pairs of planets interact. Like the familiar flower Venus-Earth pattern we saw in Part Two, each of these planetary pairings is unique.

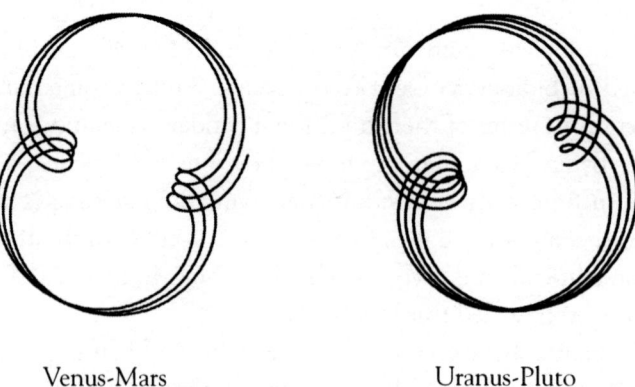

Venus-Mars   Uranus-Pluto

Diagram 12: The Venus-Mars relationship and the Uranus-Pluto relationship. By permission John Martineau.

When I first came across these diagrams I was struck by the fact that the Venus-Mars pattern and the Uranus-Pluto pattern are virtually identical. The book contains numerous planetary combinations, but these are the only two which look so similar. They also differ markedly from the other patterns. This suggests that as catalysts for change, the dynamic energy exchanged between Venus and Mars is just as potent as the combination of Uranus and Pluto. Since Venus and Mars aspects happen more frequently they will be felt more personally.

That Venus and Mars are as dynamic and forceful as Uranus and Pluto is not so far fetched, especially when we consider the powerful electromagnetic interaction that Venus and Mars generate as the metals copper and iron. They are opposites that work in tandem.

We also know that Mars and Pluto are similar because of their association with Scorpio. Pluto is said to be the 'higher octave' of Mars and since its discovery Pluto has taken on some of the more destructive aspects of the Mars archetype, becoming the modern-day ruler of Scorpio.

Venus and Uranus are linked too because of their mythic association; Venus is a child of Uranus. She was spawned by Uranus in the foaming ocean. This makes her highly creative and unique.

We can think of the combination of Venus and Mars as being akin to the energy of Uranus-Pluto, except that its revolutionary and creative power is more personally accessible. Being personal planets, Venus and Mars function more consciously than the outer planets.

We are individually synchronised to the Venus-Mars cycle through our likes and dislikes, our personal preferences, choices and actions. They influence our decisions and experiences in myriad ways across the fabric of everyday life. As an underlying causal factor Venus and Mars generate our passions, priorities and principles. They spur us to act. Their sacred love dance affects our relationships, sexuality, creativity, reproduction, family, friendships, actions, ambitions and even our finances. They are in our blood.

Mundane Implications of the Venus-Mars Saros
Sabian Symbols

It appears that the initial conjunction in a Venus-Mars cycle is incredibly potent and just as electrifying as the early stages of a new relationship.

Group Four New Cycles	Start Date	First conjunction
16R	17 Jul 1964	21°Ge01'
16D	27 Aug 1964	17°Cn44'
17R	16 May 1977	14°Ar09'
17D	7 Jun 1977	00°Ta37'
18R	19 Sep 1983	23°Le42'
18D	26 Oct 1983	16°Vi19'
19R	17 Feb 2022	16°Cp55'
19D	6 Mar 2022	00°Aq04'
20R	12 Nov 2034	20°Li37'
20D	31 Dec 2034	22°Sc19'

Group Four Cycles End	End Date	Last conjunction
41D	21 Apr 1972	16°Ge24'
41R	17 May 1972	02°Cn52'
42D	1 Feb 1985	28°Pi31'
41R	28 Feb 1985	18°Ar39'
43D	24 Jun 1991	16°Le43'
43R	26 Jul 1991	06°Vi34'
44D	21 Aug 2010	13°Li35'
44R	4 Oct 2010	12°Sc40'
45D	14 Nov 2029	07°Cp50'

Tables E and F: The five new Venus-Mars conjunction cycles and five ending conjunction cycles of our current era. When cycles begin and end they do so in pairs and in groups of five, clustered together over roughly 80 years. See also Appendix 4.

The intensity of their first embrace ignites powerful feelings and starts a chain reaction. Given that together Venus and Mars seem to have a similar potency to Uranus and Pluto, their cycle imprints itself powerfully.

The first conjunction sets in motion a five-fold pattern that spans countless generations and which has links to other eras. As such the Venus-Mars Saros has implications in terms of our most intimate soul connections that potentially span many lifetimes.

Although they are personal planets, in a collective sense the Venus-Mars Saros describes commonly held values, social themes and customs which many people engage in. Conceivably, Venus and Mars may resonate with a similar intensity to that of Uranus-Pluto. If so, the combination is at the same time highly creative and potentially destructive.

Exactly how powerful are Venus-Mars conjunctions? Before we explore how this cycle operates in the natal chart and in synastry, further exploration of the mundane implications of the Venus-Mars Saros seems warranted.

World War II

The Venus-Mars conjunction that occurred immediately prior to the outbreak of World War II took place on 8 May 1938 at 9 Gemini 38, or the tenth degree of Gemini. The Sabian Symbol for this degree is, 'An Airplane Performing a Nosedive' which hardly needs further interpretation. This degree sits in Adolf Hitler's 8th house conjunct his natal Pluto. By transiting over his Pluto, this conjunction appears to have awakened some deeply disturbing and destructive elements within his already twisted psyche.

Adolf Hitler was himself born on the day of a Venus-Mars conjunction, just hours before the aspect was exact.[7] Hitler's Venus-Mars sits in his 7th house, with Mars in detriment, by house and by sign, and with Venus dignified, though retrograde. The 7th house is the house of 'others' the house of relationship where Hitler projected his debilitated Mars and dissatisfied Venus onto the world.

The Sabian Symbol for 17 Taurus is, 'A Symbolic Battle Between Swords and Torches'. Dane Rudhyar explains this image as, 'refusing to depend upon the past, the seeker turns warrior, fighting anew the eternal "Great War."'[8]

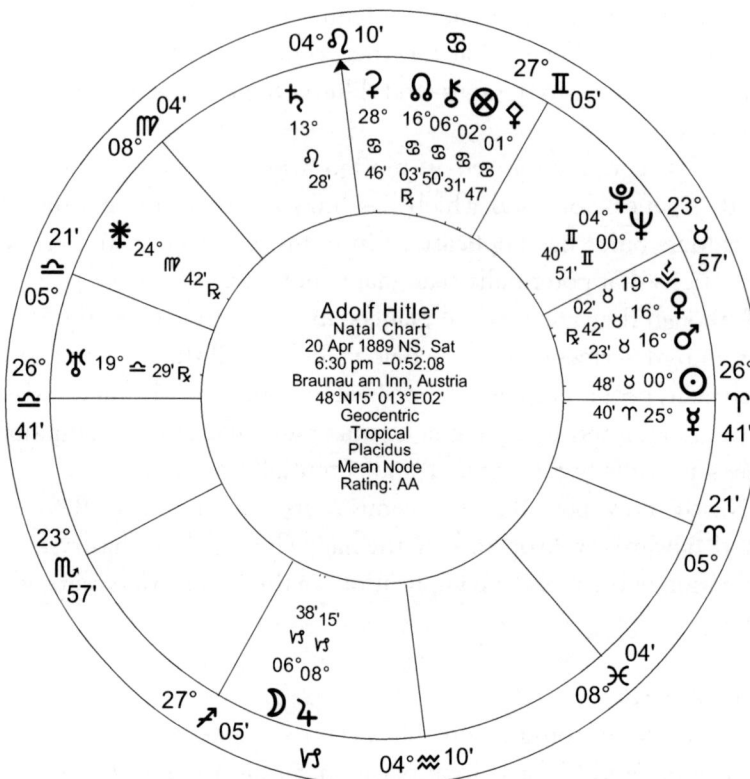

Tracking Hitler's natal Venus-Mars conjunction back to the first in its series (11R), a retrograde cycle, we find that this particular cycle started in 1665 and it was, as in 1964, the very first one in a new group series. This makes the 1665 conjunction highly significant, for it heralded the dawn of a new era. The degree where this 1665 conjunction took place was 3 Cancer 23, or the 4th degree of Cancer. The Sabian Symbol for this degree is, 'A Cat Arguing with a Mouse', which Rudhyar describes as 'an attempt at self justification'.[9]

Placing this degree 3 Cancer 23 in Hitler's chart we find it is prominently located between his Part of Fortune and Chiron in his 9th house. His personal wounds wrought by a brutal father and an over protective mother were projected onto the world at large, especially onto those who he deemed as 'foreigners'.

The chart for this initial Venus-Mars conjunction of cycle 11R, set for 29 July 1665, the cycle under which Hitler was born, shows Venus

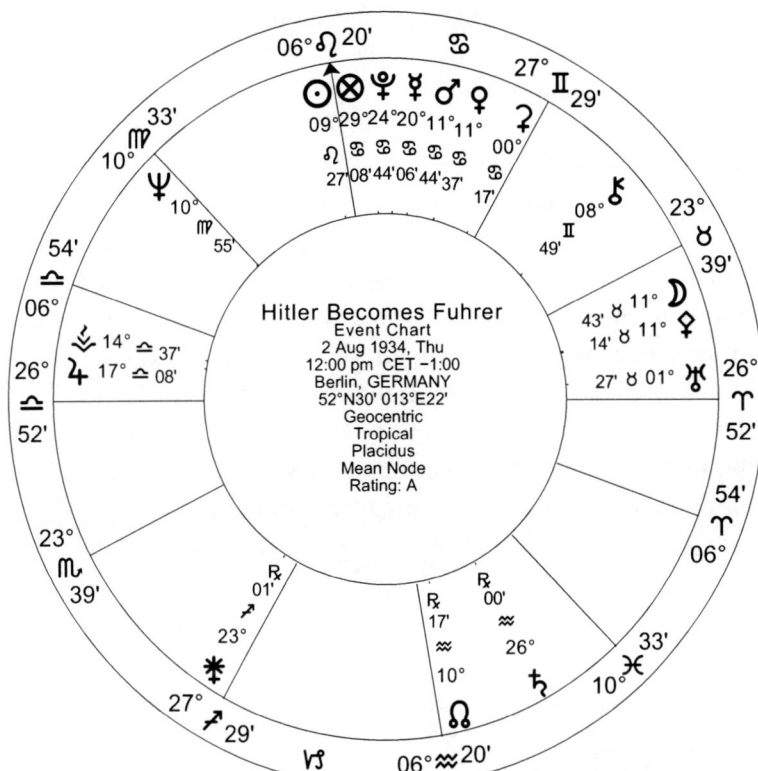

Hitler Becomes Führer.
Data from *Book of World Horoscopes* by Nicholas Campion

and Mars in a very tight opposition to Saturn in Capricorn.

The tight opposition from Venus-Mars to a dignified Saturn suggests that the passionate values and desires of this conjunction are pent up and frustrated. They struggle to find an outlet and fight against the reality of the world upon which they are projected.

This opposition aspect has been transmuted into Hitler's natal chart amplified by his own Venus-Mars conjunction, which squares his tenth house Saturn, manifesting with a similar degree of frustration and rage.

Hitler became President and Chief of the Armed Forces at 12.00 noon on 2 August 1934 upon the death of President Hindenburg at 9am that same day.[10] The consolidation of Hitler's power happened under a Venus-Mars conjunction too – once again in Cancer and within orb of his North Node and Chiron.

This is an extreme example of the destructive side of Venus and Mars, yet they can also be incredibly creative. Sometimes destruction and creativity go hand-in-hand.

1665 – Age of Enlightenment

The chart for the first Venus-Mars conjunction of the 17th century has some interesting features. There is a tight Jupiter, Chiron, Uranus conjunction in Aquarius, signifying the birth of the Enlightenment and the powerful paradigm shift towards a more rational and scientific world view that ensued. The Moon, the dispositor of the Venus-Mars conjunction, is also located in this futuristic and inventive sign.

Naturally enough just one Venus-Mars conjunction cannot account for the many events to take place under its watch. And yet, this 1665 conjunction did usher in a dramatic period in human history.

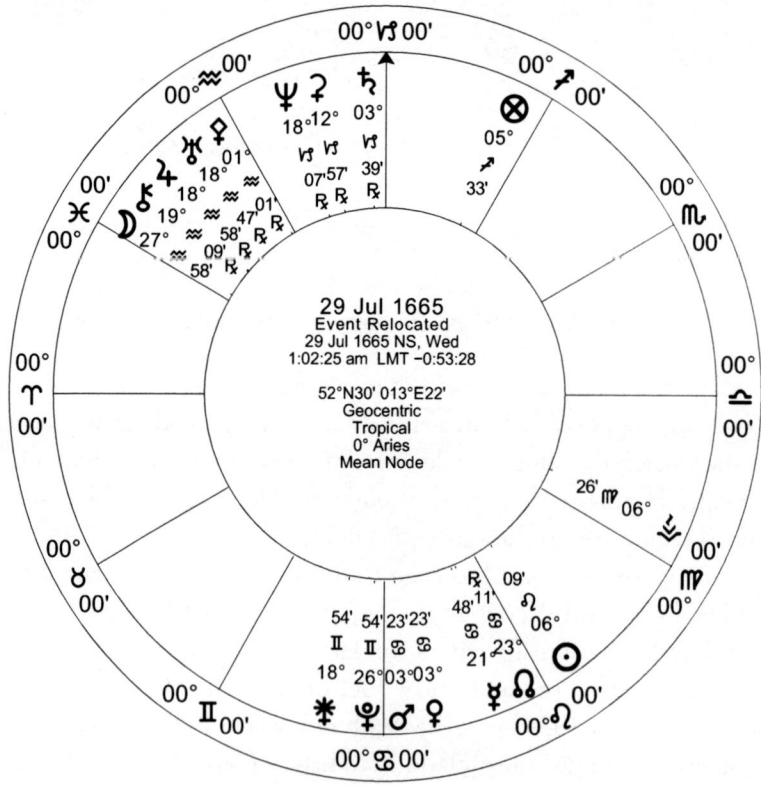

Venus-Mars Saros 11R.
The first conjunction of Group Series Three

This particular conjunction occurring as it did in tight opposition to Saturn, brought with it elements of hardship which seems to have specifically impacted on the city of London.

In the summer of 1665 plague broke out. By mid-July over 1,000 deaths were being reported in the city every week. This increased to over 6,000 per week in August. It was rumoured that dogs and cats were spreading the disease, so the Lord Mayor ordered all the dogs and cats destroyed. Author Daniel Defoe in his *Journal of the Plague Years* estimates that 40,000 dogs and 200,000 cats were put to death. This of course made matters far worse, since it meant that there were fewer natural enemies of the rats who were carrying the plague fleas.[11] This is particularly interesting in light of the Sabian symbol for the 4th degree of Cancer, where this conjunction occurred, is a 'Cat Arguing with a Mouse'.

One year later in September 1666 the Great Fire of London destroyed about 80 per cent of the city.[12] Obviously these events had a dramatic impact on living conditions and personal relationships. When

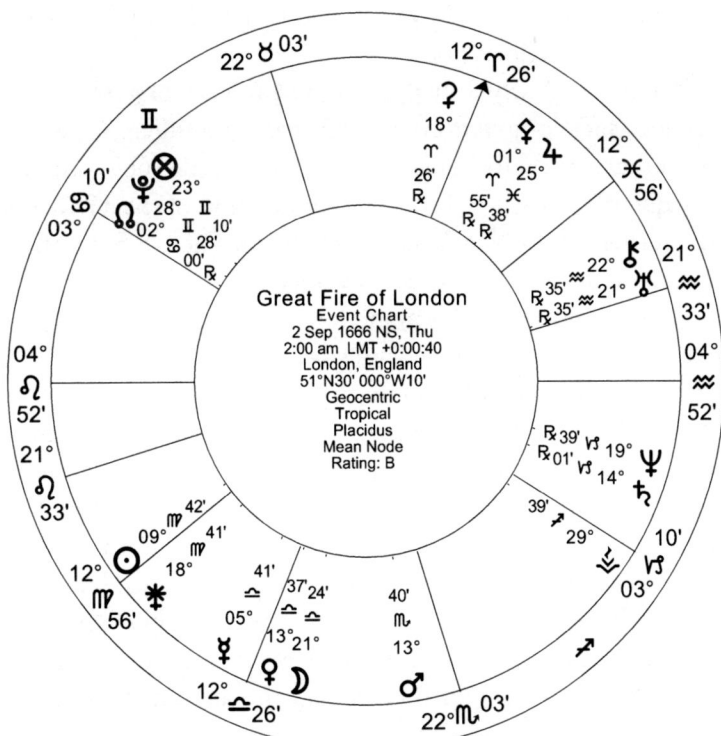

fire broke out, the transiting North Node had reached the same degree of Cancer where the new Venus-Mars conjunction had taken place the year before.

This initial 1665 conjunction was followed by its partner, new long direct cycle 11D, which commenced on 8 September 1665 at 29 Cancer 50 reinforcing the emphasis on home and family. With over 100,000 people homeless, one sixth of the population of London,[13] the creative focus shifted to rebuilding.

With the plague and then the fire, many people left the city and chose to settle in the new colonies. Some relocated to New York, formerly called New Amsterdam; the city had been renamed in June 1665 after it was acquired from the Dutch.

The US Sibly Chart and Major Events
September 11

When the degree of the first conjunction in a Venus-Mars cycle falls on a planet, or sensitive chart point, or when is later triggered by a transiting planet or point, it appears to have a dramatic impact, either creative, or destructive, and sometimes both.

On 21 June 2000, which happened to be the day of a solstice, there was a Venus-Mars conjunction. Though part of a different cycle, this conjunction occurred at the same zodiacal degree as the 1665 conjunction and consequently it triggered the first conjunction of the 17th century when the settlement of New York was renamed. The US Sibly chart for 1776 has Venus at the same degree of Cancer.

The 2000 Venus-Mars conjunction at 3 Cancer 33 was the conjunction that occurred immediately prior to the September 11, 2001 terrorist attacks. Two months before that fateful September day, Venus and Mars reached an opposition aspect. This happened just as Mars was stationing direct. This turbo charged Mars was making a conjunction to Pluto. Meanwhile, Venus was in a conjunction with Saturn, further intensifying the destructive capabilities of the Pluto-Saturn opposition. This intense energy exchange unleashed tremendous forces as it straddled the Ascendant/Descendant axis of the US chart. By the time the terrorist attacks of 9/11 occurred a few weeks after this Venus-Mars opposition, the transiting North Node had also arrived at 3 Cancer 06, the exact degree, and minute, of the US Venus.

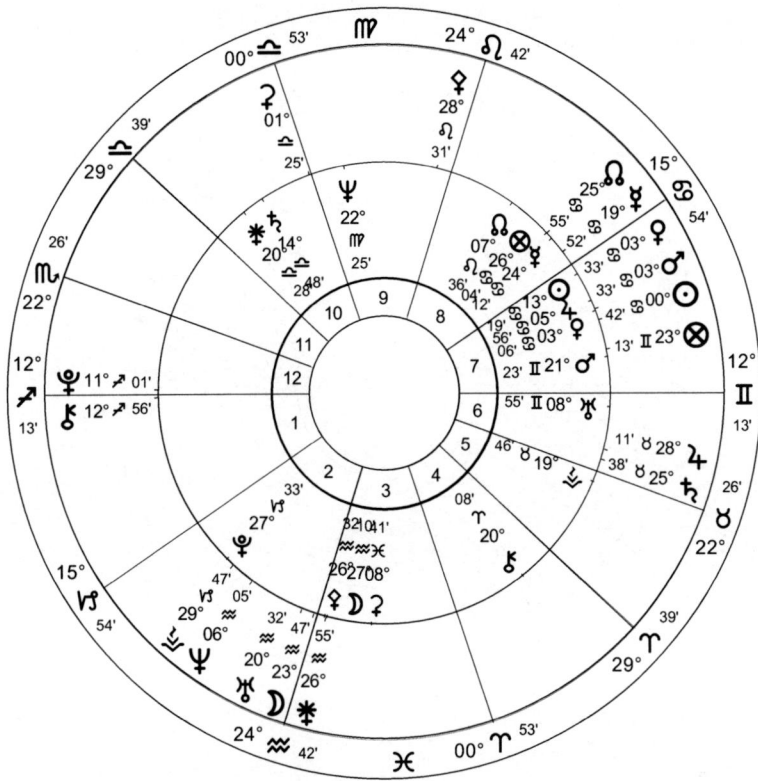

Inner Wheel: USA Sibly Chart.
(4 July 1776, 5.10pm, Philadelphia, USA. 39N57 75W10)
Outer Wheel: The Venus-Mars Conjunction of 21 June 2000.

If we trace the pre-9/11 Venus-Mars conjunction of 2000 back through time we discover that this karmic thread commenced in 1392 at 7 Pisces 03 or the 8th degree of Pisces. The Sabian Symbol for this degree is, 'A Girl Blowing a Bugle' which Rudhyar describes as, 'a call to participation in the service of (one's) race, as an evolutionary crisis approaches'.[14]

Incredibly, this is the same Venus-Mars cycle under which the United States was founded! One would be hard pressed to find a more apt description of the national psyche of the United States. This degree is located in the Sibly chart third house conjunct Ceres. It describes the patriotic love of homeland, family values, free speech and democracy.

Inner Wheel: USA Sibly Chart.
Outer Wheel: The Venus-Mars Opposition of 19 July 2001

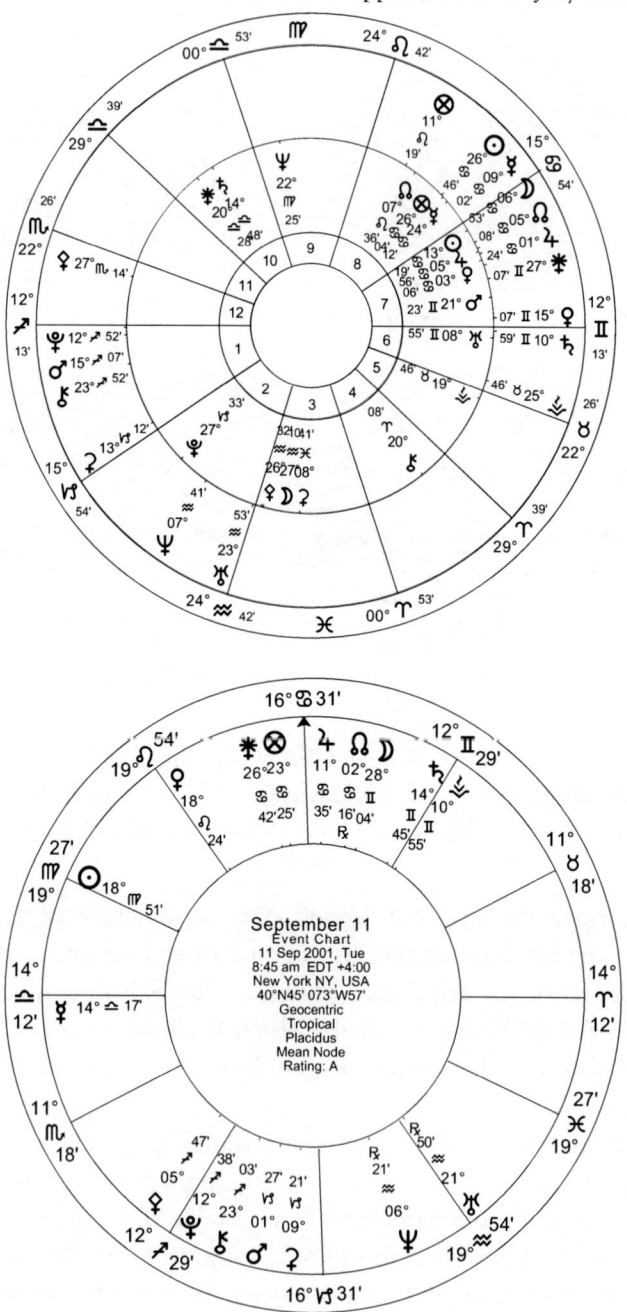

The sign of Pisces says something too about the evangelical religious heart of the country, as well as the concept of the American 'dream' that the nation holds so dear.

Kennedy Assassination

We again see the destructive power of the Venus-Mars Saros in action in the assassination of President Kennedy in Dallas in 1963. The assassination took place just a couple of days after a conjunction of Venus and Mars at 19 Sagittarius 09, with Venus and Mars then at 20 and 21 Sagittarius. Venus and Mars were opposing Mars in the US chart which

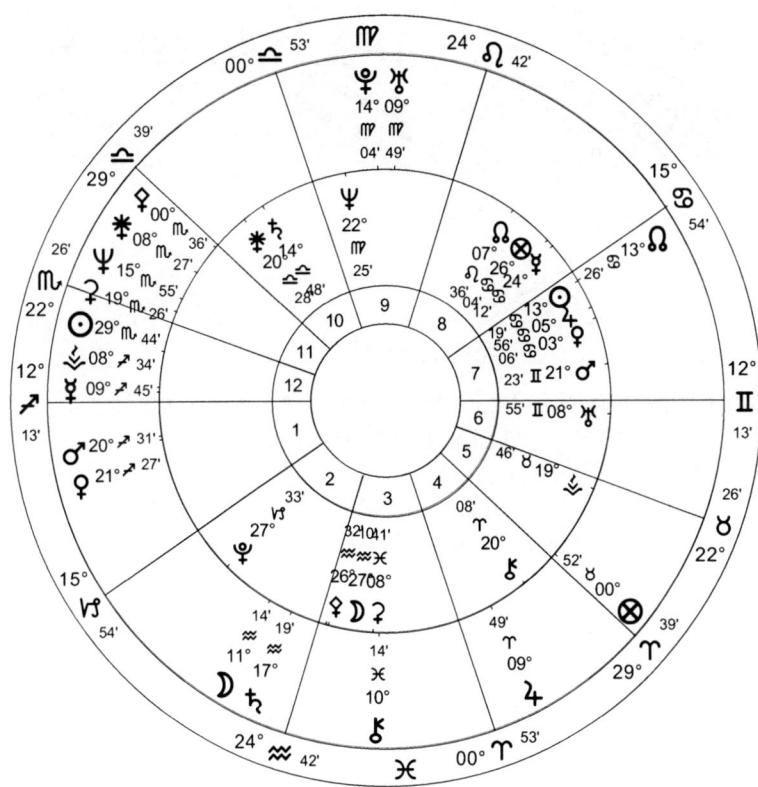

Inner Wheel: USA Sibly Chart.
Outer Wheel: JFK Assassination. 22 November 1963, 12.30pm, Dallas, USA. 32N47 96W48.

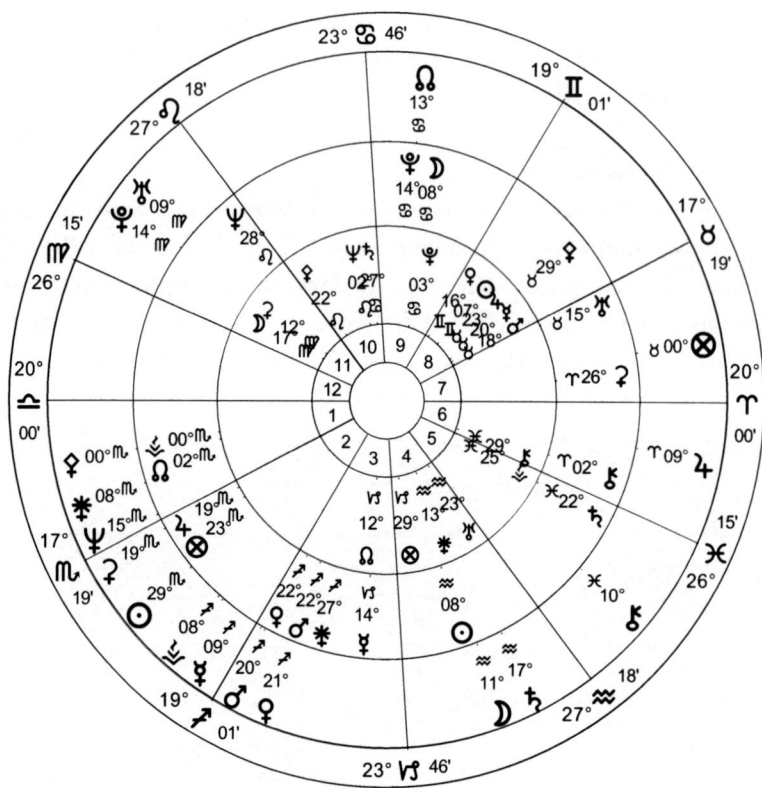

Inner Wheel: JFK. 29 May 1917, 3.00pm, Brookline, Massachusetts, USA. 42N20 71W07.
Middle Wheel: Venus-Mars Saros 10D. 19 January 1437.
(The initial conjunction in which Kennedy was born.)
Outer Wheel: JFK Assassination.

is at 21 Gemini 23 in the US 7th house. Tracing this 1963 conjunction back to its original source conjunction, cycle 2D/47D, we find that it commenced at 19 Leo 50. This degree sits exactly on the Descendant at the moment that the assassination took place.

JFK was born in 1917. If we trace his pre-natal Venus-Mars conjunction back to its original source conjunction we find that this cycle – 10D – commenced in the year 1437. The degree of this original conjunction was 22 Sagittarius 10, virtually the same position as Venus and Mars were located at the time of Kennedy's assassination.

The original 1437 conjunction under which Kennedy was born – 22 Sagittarius 10 – and the 1963 conjunction under which he was assassinated – 19 Sagittarius 09 – oppose JFK's natal Venus at 16 Gemini 45, as well as the US Mars at 21 Gemini 23.

It is generally thought that Kennedy's assassination, by whoever was responsible, came about because of intense opposition to his values and policies by those who had the most to lose.

Destructive acts like this tend to happen when one's passions and values are in direct conflict with another's. Similarly, Venus and Mars manifest in positive ways when parties are in agreement. For better or worse the opposing forces of Venus-Mars together generate a lot of heat and energy.

It seems that the original source conjunction in each cycle has tremendous energy. Its intense impulse operates in a similar way to the revolutionary forces we see when Uranus and Pluto combine.

The first conjunction in a cycle describes deeply embedded drives and our most passionate urges. These originate from ancient cultural values imprinted upon us through our family heritage, through long standing social customs and traditions and may even be inherited biologically through our genes and family blood lines.

Similarly, our values and standards are handed down to the next generation and influence their personal preferences and choices. The Venus-Mars Saros, and especially the first degree of each new cycle, can be seen to represent this intensely dynamic and creative impulse. It is a deeply embedded influence and a fundamental part of our psyche.

The initial conjunction in a cycle describes what we love and are most passionate about. It shows what we are driven to create, to conquer, or to destroy and it has a powerful magnetic and energising force. Just as when copper and iron first connect in a circuit and copper stimulates iron creating a surge of energy, this first meeting of Venus and Mars is a powerhouse conjunction that sets off a chain reaction and fuels their ongoing relationship. The zodiacal position where this initial connection takes place must therefore be highly charged. I chose to call this degree: 'The Degree of Passion'.

The Degree of Passion

The location of the 'Degree of Passion' in our natal chart describes our personal preferences, values, passions and drives. The intensity of these feelings gives rise to our choices, decisions and actions. Though it can function unconsciously, we can see it operating in others, just as others can generally see it clearly in us.

To determine the nature of a specific 'Degree of Passion' and how it functions, clues can be found in examining the conditions of the original conjunction chart, the Sabian Symbol of its degree, and the aspects this degree makes to the chart in question. Destructive tendencies are seen when the degree of passion is making a hard aspect to Pluto or Saturn, or when it is otherwise negatively aspected, while creative and positive tendencies result from beneficial aspects. As with all threads of astrology, there are positive and negative layers of meaning woven within the fabric of its symbolism.

When placing the degree of passion in the natal chart special attention should be given to transits across this degree, especially by the Nodal axis, or by another Venus-Mars conjunction. Eclipses and even New Moons can trigger the Degree of Passion too, heralding significant developments.

Just as our choices and actions can impact on others, and other's decisions affect us, many people will have the same 'Degree of Passion'. It is therefore not surprising that it operates in a mundane context as well as personally. However, this means that in the natal chart its house position and aspects are likely to be more important that its sign.

While many people belong to the same Venus-Mars soul group it appears to resonate individually too.

Since this initial source conjunction reverberates through time at 32 year intervals, it echoes in each subsequent conjunction as the cycle unfolds opening a window to our past, and a door to our future.

When I speak with clients and colleagues about this point in the chart there is widespread confirmation that the Degree of Passion has a very familiar feel to it – similar to the recognition we experience when we meet someone who we feel we have always known, but are meeting for the first time. It represents soul themes that are deeply rooted within us.

The Degree of Passion will often describe the type of partner we seek and the qualities we want in a relationship. More than this, it symbolises our creative expression and talents. It describes who and what we are attracted to and the qualities we admire. It is both part of us, and what we seek in others. In short, it is the 'degree of passion' we feel.

One may or may not be born into the same soul group as one's partner, though two people who are born close together in time may indeed be born with the same Degree of Passion.

Synastry aspects will always be important when assessing compatibility. The degree of passion can be examined in this way too. One individual may have their Degree of Passion in the 8th house, while their partner may have it located in Scorpio, indicating a similar level of intensity, depth and sensitivity. Similarly, one person may have their Degree of Passion conjunct Saturn while their life-partner may have it on the midheaven. This kind of link is often seen in committed relationships. Likewise, it can be activated when it aligns with our partner's planets, in particular the Sun, Venus or Mars.

When the Degree of Passion is positioned next to a natal planet this planet becomes especially significant. This may explain why some people are so driven about their particular interests or creative pursuits.

Even though many people will share the same Degree of Passion, it appears to function with great intensity in the birth chart, and is responsive to transits and other astrological triggers.

How to find your Degree of Passion
To find your 'Degree of Passion', look up your date of birth in Table G. This table lists all currently active Venus-Mars cycles for dates between 1914 and 2041.

Find the conjunction that took place *immediately before* your birth. This is your pre-natal Venus-Mars conjunction. If you were born shortly before a Venus-Mars conjunction was exact, and therefore have this conjunction as an applying aspect in your chart, then the conjunction *immediately after* your birth, the closer one, may be the better one to consider.

Then look across the table to the column marked 'Degree of Passion' to see when this cycle commenced and note where this degree falls in

Cycle	First Date	Degree of Passion	1914-1946	Pre-natal	1946-1978	Pre-natal	1978-2010	Pre-natal	2010-2041	Pre-natal
14R/44R	25 Feb 1723	28°Cp23'	22-Nov-14	07°Sg51'	07-Nov-46	00°Sg26'	22-Oct-78	22°Sc15'	04-Oct-10	12°Sc40'
14D	6 Apr 1723	29°Aq33'	15-May-15	21°Ar53'	18-May-47	27°Ar52'	21-May-79	03°Ta37'	23-May-11	09°Ta01'
10D	19 Jan 1437	22°Sg10'	01-Apr-17	04°Ar01'	03-Apr-49	09°Ar26'	05-Apr-81	14°Ar44'	07-Apr-13	19°Ar58'
4D/46D	27 Nov 1118	24°Li42'	14-Feb-19	13°Pi50'	17-Feb-51	19°Pi42'	19-Feb-83	25°Pi38'	22-Feb-15	01°Ar42'
18R/46R	19 Sep1983	23°Le42'					19-Sep-83	23°Le42'	01-Sep-15	15°Le10'
18D	26 Oct 1983	16°Vi19'					26-Oct-83	16°Vi19'	03-Nov-15	24°Vi05'
42D	*	28°Le11'	10-Jan-21	03°Pi38'	18-Jan-53	13°Pi48'	01-Feb-85	28°Pi31'		
11R/42R	29 Jul 1665	03°Cn23'	07-Apr-21	09°Ta34'	22-Mar-53	01°Ta19'	28-Feb-85	18°Ar39'	06-Oct-17	19°Vi13'
11D	8 Sep 1665	29°Cn49'	03-Oct-21	08°Vi43'	04-Oct-53	12°Vi17'	05-Oct-85	15°Vi47'	25-Aug-19	04°Vi08'
6D	29 Jun 1347	29°Ta35'	24-Aug-23	24°Le43'	24-Aug-55	27°Le51'	24-Aug-87	00°Vi59'	13-Jul-21	19°Le49'
3D/49D	11 May 1093	10°Ar32'	11-Jul-25	09°Le25'	12-Jul-57	12°Le51'	13-Jul-89	16°Le17'		
43D	*	17°Cp47'	10-Jun-27	02°Le16'	15-Jun-59	08°Le22'	24-Jun-91	16°Le43'		
15R/43R	29 Nov 1735	05°Sc26'	31-Aug-27	22°Vi58'	15-Aug-59	15°Vi50'	26-Jul-91	06°Vi34'		
19R/49R	17 Feb 2022	16°Cp55'							17-Feb-22	16°Cp55'
19D	6 Mar 2022	00°Aq04'							06-Mar-22	00°Aq04'
15D	13 Jan 1736	05°Sg45'	14-Feb-28	19°Cp01'	17-Feb-60	25°Cp04'	19-Feb-92	01°Aq01'	22-Feb-24	06°Aq58'
8D	30 Oct 1385	01°Li19'	03-Jan-30	03°Cp11'	04-Jan-62	08°Cp04'	06-Jan-94	13°Cp03'	08-Jan-26	18°Cp09'

Table G. Venus-Mars conjunctions 1915-2041 and corresponding 'Degree of Passion' where the first conjunction in each series occurred. Note that if you are born under a Venus-Mars

Cycle	First Date	Degree of Passion	1914-1946	Pre-natal	1946-1978	Pre-natal	1978-2010	Pre-natal	2010-2041	Pre-natal
2D/47D	23 Sep 1067	19°Le50'	19-Nov-31	14°Sg17'	21-Nov-63	19°Sg09'	23-Nov-95	24°Sg12'	25-Nov-27	29°Sg28'
16R/47R	17 Jul 1964	21°Ge01'			17-Jul-64	21°Ge01'	29-Jun-96	12°Ge02'	14-Jun-28	04°Ge51'
16D	27 Aug 1964	17°Cn44'			27-Aug-64	17°Cn44'	03-Sep-96	25°Cn55'	08-Sep-28	02°Le03'
45D	*	01°Cn48'	14-Oct-33	03°Sg11'	19-Oct-65	10°Sg33'	06-Oct-97	19°Sg45'	14-Nov-29	07°Cp50'
12R/45R	19 May 1678	22°Ar57'	25-Jan-34	21°Aq49'	09-Jan-66	13°Aq32'	03-Dec-97	03°Aq24'	24-Nov-29	15°Cp08'
12D	3 Jul 1678	25°Ta19'	03-Aug-34	11°Cn53'	04-Aug-66	15°Cn50'	01-Aug-98	19°Cn40'	06-Aug-30	23°Cn22'
9D	3 Apr 1392	07°Pi03'	20-Jun-36	26°Ge09'	21-Jun-68	29°Ge54'	02-Jun-00	03°Cn33'	22-Jun-32	07°Cn10'
5D/48D	11 Feb 1138	12°Cp40'	08-May-38	09°Ge45'	09-May-70	14°Ge02'	01-May-02	18°Ge17'	12-May-34	22°Ge37'
20R/48R	12 Nov 2034	20°Li37'							12-Nov-34	20°Li37'
20D	31 Dec 2034	22°Sc19'							31-Dec-34	22°Sc19'
41D	*	06°Sc48'	10-Apr-40	05°Ge25'	21-Apr-72	16°Ge24'				
13R/41R	5 Oct 1684	07°Vi38'	07-Jun-40	13°Cn15'	17-May-72	02°Cn52'				
13D	2 Nov 1684	24°Vi43'	03-Dec-40	08°Sc16'	05-Dec-72	12°Sc26'	01-Dec-04	16°Sc34'	07-Dec-36	20°Sc40'
7D	11 Sep 1366	10°Le23'	24-Oct-42	24°Li01'	25-Oct-74	27°Li32'	05-Oct-06	01°Sc03'	26-Oct-38	04°Sc37'
1D/50D	21 Jul 1048	18°Ge04'	10-Sep-44	08°Li00'	11-Sep-76	11°Li36'	02-Sep-08	15°Li17'	03-Sep-40	19°Li06'
17R/50R	16 May 1977	14°Ar09'			16-May-77	14°Ar09'	22-Apr-09	29°Pi45'	01-Apr-41	20°Pi18'
17D	7 Jun 1977	00°Ta37'			07-Jun-77	00°Ta37'	21-Jun-09	15°Ta17'	09-Jun-41	24°Ta08'
44D	*	20°Ar01'	09-Aug-46	29°Vi43'	13-Aug-78	05°Li41'	21-Aug-10	13°Li35'		

retrograde cycle, your natal Venus can still be direct. Similarly, if you are born in a direct cycle, your natal Venus can still be retrograde.

your birth chart. You might be surprised to find how accurately it describes your inner longings, creative interests, passions and relationship needs. Check its house position and aspects. Look at how this point connects with your partner's chart and how their Degree of Passion reflects back to your chart. For additional insights, look at the Sabian Symbol for this degree, or calculate the chart for this initial conjunction.

The pre-natal conjunction itself may prove to be important, although it does not seem to have the same potency and power of the initial source conjunction. Transiting conjunctions however, can stimulate the natal chart throughout life. Consider these transits in light of important life events, decisions and relationship encounters. When a conjunction transits across a personal planet, angles or the Moon's nodes, this can open our hearts to love and success. Equally they can bring events to a head in other dramatic ways.

When operating at its most positive, Venus-Mars conjunctions can help us get relationship timing just right. As well as the first one in a series, the middle conjunction of each cycle and the last one seem to be especially important. More on relationship timing later.

Because new retrograde cycles are always followed a few weeks later by direct cycles, fewer people are born in retrograde cycles. Yet these individuals may be naturally more intense and passionate than those born in direct cycles. They seem to be more inclined to follow their passions wherever they may lead, despite opposition – similar indeed to having natal Venus retrograde.

Passion is not always a positive thing. It can be a double-edged sword. We see this in the chart of the highly talented, but equally self-destructive singer-songwriter Amy Winehouse who was born a few days before cycle 18R/46R commenced.

The Sabian Symbol for her Degree of Passion, the 24th degree of Leo is, 'A Yogi with Transcendent Powers Yet Untidy and Unkempt'. This degree is described by Sabian Symbol expert Linda Hill as 'not paying enough attention to (one's) body and physical needs'.[15]

Winehouse was born with Venus stationary direct. Mars joined Venus on the 19th September, not having moved from this degree.

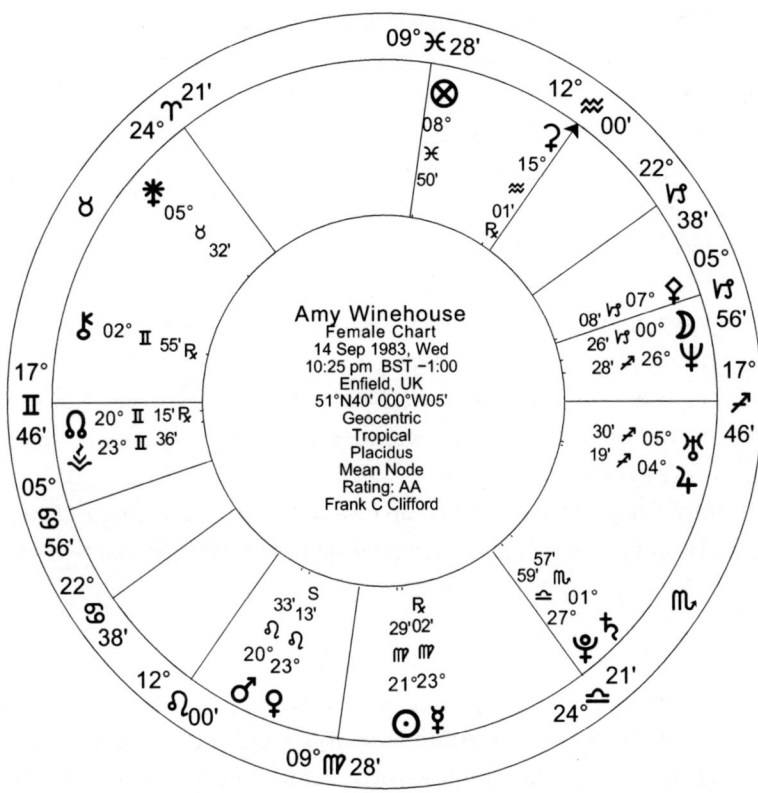

Amy Winehouse.
Born a few days before the start of cycle 18R/46R.

Interpreting the Degree of Passion in the Natal Chart
In Aries, the First house, or with Mars

The Degree of Passion in Aries, the first house, or in aspect to Mars, suggests a liking for independent and creative types. It indicates a high level of leadership potential that is valued in others as well. The influence of Aries-Mars brings with it a great deal of self sufficiency and an admiration for entrepreneurial types and self-starters. If the first house or Ascendant is involved the native may enter into relationships with those who are well-known or prominent in some way.

This Degree of Passion appreciates people who are honest and forthright. It is important that partners are able to manage on their own. Independence is admired.

The Mars-Aries influence makes for a romantic and passionate lover. Spontaneous, energetic and impulsive, this type wears their heart on their sleeve and has no hesitation in taking the initiative in relationships, seldom taking no for an answer. They know that affections can be won with chivalrous and romantic gestures.

This Degree of Passion is generous and eagerly goes after what it wants. When a relationship isn't working, this individual is willing to cuts ties and does so with seeming ease.

If operating negatively, this Degree of Passion can lead to destructive or hostile behaviour. There may be anger issues which can lead to violence, especially if a dysfunctional Mars is involved. Emotional outbursts and displays of temper can occur when this degree is triggered by transits or eclipses.

A helpful aspect from Saturn can be a stabilising influence and anchor creativity and passions so they are channelled towards productive results over the long term.

In Taurus, the Second House, or with Venus

Since Venus is the ruling planet of Taurus, love and relationships are an essential part of life for those with this Degree of Passion. It makes for a tactile and affectionate lover who adores all things that stimulate the senses including the feel and texture of luxurious fabrics, the smell of essential oils and flowers, and the taste of sumptuous food. If operating negatively, too much of a good thing can lead to excesses and overindulgence.

Blessed with style and good taste this Taurus influence appreciates quality in all things. As a patient and sensual lover this native takes time to enjoy all the pleasures of love making and feels it is important to share similar values and areas of interest with loved ones.

If operating negatively, this Degree of Passion can result in a 'gold-digger' mentality, where potential partners are only interesting and valued if they possess material wealth.

Good fortune and financial success are implied by this placement especially if Venus is involved. Benefits can come from investments or inheritance as well as from a high earning capacity.

Actor Marlon Brando had his Degree of Passion within a degree of his natal Venus in Taurus. Brando was once paid 3.7 million dollars for two weeks work on *Superman*. A passionate man in every sense of the word, he fathered eleven children to several different women.[16] So passionate was he about the plight of indigenous Americans that he refused to accept an Oscar for his role in *The Godfather* citing Hollywood's erroneous portrayal of the American Indian in film and television.

In Gemini, the Third House, or with Mercury

Those with the Degree of Passion in Gemini, the third house or in aspect to Mercury have a love of words and language. This is a passionate communicator of ideas, who likes to keep busy and enjoys exchanging information and sharing knowledge. Whether it's creative writing, nonfiction, or poetry, all written and spoken communication is likely to be powerfully expressed and have a great impact.

This Degree of Passion values social interaction and stimulating conversation more than the physical, emotional and spiritual aspects of love which are perhaps secondary to the need to connect on a head level. Variety and mental stimulation is vital. The Gemini influence indicates the desire to maintain friendships and activities outside the main relationship. It may be difficult to settle down and commit to one stable relationship because of a tendency to become bored easily.

As with the 1964 conjunction in Gemini when we witnessed so many profound changes throughout society, the Gemini Degree of Passion is restless and highly animated.

The Mercury-Gemini-Third House influence appears to provide many and varied talents that can find expression in diverse areas such as media, teaching and public relations. If operating negatively it can result in manic behaviour because passions are so diverse and sporadic and cover so many different areas of life, it can be difficult to prioritise and focus on one thing at a time.

In Cancer, the Fourth House, or with the Moon

This Degree of Passion indicates a caring and sensitive soul who is nurturing and giving. It is important this individual feels wanted and needed, but they also like to be taken care of and appreciated in return. This is an instinctual Degree of Passion and suggests someone who is very much aware of their partner's moods and feelings and highly responsive to expressions of love. This person needs a lover who is equally attuned to these subtleties; someone they can connect with emotionally and intimately. It is important that they feel comfortable and secure in their primary relationship.

Mother and mothering often play a powerful role in the lives of these people and it suggests a deep love of one's home and homeland. There can be a very subjective perspective and a tendency to place too high a value on mother, ancestry, or family values. This can result in an insular kind of fanaticism if operating negatively, where traditions and routines must be upheld, otherwise the person may become insecure and moody.

The acute sensitivity of this type can mean it takes a long time for them to heal from emotional pain and relationship breakups.

Actor Keanu Reeves has been single for many years and has never married. For a long time he chose to live in a hotel rather than buy his own home.[17] Reeves moved around a great deal as a child and his mother married several times. Sadly, in 2001 his girlfriend Jennifer Syme died in a car accident. Two years earlier she had given birth to a stillborn child.[18]

His chart features a Venus, Mars, Moon conjunction in Cancer in his seventh house. He was born in 1964 just a week after cycle 16D commenced. Syme was born on 7 December 1972 and she too had a Venus-Mars conjunction.

In Leo, the Fifth House, or with the Sun

This Degree of Passion makes for a dynamic and generous lover who enjoys providing for their partner and showering them with gifts and romantic gestures. Commitment and loyalty, ritual and ceremony are very important to this type, who generally places a high value on children and probably desires a large family.

The Leo influence suggests they are attracted to the limelight and to people who stand out from the crowd. Associating with successful people can bring out the best in this individual, but it can also be a means to an end. Indeed, this type may seek a partner who can help them gain public recognition. If negatively aspected, this Degree of Passion can indicate someone who is overly focused on themselves. There may be a streak of vanity, or narcissism which can manifest as a domineering tendency or feelings of superiority. If so, this type can treat lovers and partners as personal servants which can have a detrimental impact on personal relationships.

On the whole this is a highly creative Degree of Passion and it is often seen in artists and performers. This type is enthusiastic about sharing creative ideas and projects with loved ones. If highly evolved the Leo-Sun influence can create a high degree of conscious awareness.

In Virgo, the Sixth House, or with Mercury

Virgo is a sign known for its earthy sensuality as well as for its clear thinking and ability to work hard. With this Degree of Passion you often see a love nature that is a combination of mind and body. Unlike the Gemini type who operates mostly on a head level, the Virgo influence is more sensual and enjoys physical contact as well as sharing ideas. Physical, verbal and written expressions of love are equally important.

The Virgo theme can make this type rather choosey. They strive for high standards and ideals in relationships that few people can match. They can be rather critical and picky. This tendency can have a detrimental impact on personal relationships if taken to extremes.

This type can be very particular in their personal preferences, likes and dislikes. Creatively and in matters of the heart they like to have things just right. If others do not measure up, this type will go their own way. They are generally self sufficient and can manage on their own effectively.

Virgo is the sign of health and work showing a passion for these matters and high standards around work and ethics. It is vital that this type enjoys their work, if not, their health can suffer. This Degree of Passion has a high sense of duty and obligation which when taken too far can become an obsession, preventing a heart union from taking place. Work can be so all consuming that it can lead to a hermit-like existence and a failure to develop effective social and relationship skills.

In Libra, the Seventh House, or with Venus

Libra and Taurus are the two signs where Venus is most comfortable. Being part of this soul group means that to these people personal relationships are as important as the air they breathe. Highly social, this type enjoys flirting and romance, but also places a high value on exclusive partnership.

Keen to make a good impression on others this type functions best when in a committed relationship. In many ways they can feel incomplete without a special person to love. It is vital they share their ideas, interests, and life with another.

This Degree of Passion is passionate about style, décor, fashion, and good manners. When Venus is involved with this Degree of Passion it can indicate special artistic talents.

Equality and fairness are especially valued leading this native to become a passionate advocate for social justice issues. The Libra influence can lead to an interest in politics or law. Gay rights activist Harvey Milk had his Degree of Passion in Libra and in his 7th house. He used his people skills and political nous to seek acceptance, equality and justice for the gay community.

When this Degree of Passion is operating negatively there can be a tendency to place too much credence in the opinions and values of others. This individual can find it extremely difficult to cope on their own. When conflict occurs in relationships, decision making can become impossible. When relationships fail, it can send them into a tail spin. A strong natal Mars and/or Sun will go a long way to boosting self confidence.

In Scorpio, the Eighth House, or with Pluto

This is a passionate and intense person who also values these qualities in others. When entering into a relationship they do so wholeheartedly, with all their soul, mind and body. There are no half measures. It's all or nothing.

When the right person comes along there is a deep sense of connection, a feeling of recognition; a soul connection is the only kind of relationship that matters. They want a partner who understands them totally and who has hidden depths – a true soul union.

This Degree of Passion can be incredibly intense when it comes to expressing feelings and affections. The physical and spiritual aspects of love are equally important. This type can be possessive, but their loyalty is beyond reproach. Once in love, it is forever. If betrayed, they will walk away without looking back.

There is often a deep interest in psychology, or related fields. This person wants to know what makes people tick. They want to understand the underlying causes that operate in hidden dimensions. Research of one kind or another is likely to be another intense area of interest.

Intimacy is a key ingredient in the lives of this type and yet there may be lengthy periods spent alone. This aloneness can lead towards a rare depth of understanding and insight.

If operating negatively resentment can brew and lead to vindictive acts, fanatical behaviour, jealousy, possessiveness and potentially to violence.

Financially, this position augurs well for business and other dealings and can indicate a substantial inheritance if the 8th house is involved.

In Sagittarius, the Ninth House, or with Jupiter

With the Degree of Passion in Sagittarius, the ninth house, or in aspect to Jupiter, there is an adventurous streak. This is an energetic lover and a seeker of truth. Physical affection is perhaps not as important as a spiritual connection.

This type does not like to be tied down and may prefer to keep partnership options open. Sagittarius is known for its love of freedom and the outdoors, wide open spaces, travel, and different cultures. These are also qualities they admire in potential partners.

This type is likely to aspire to a relationship with someone who shares their worldview and overall life philosophy. When the right person comes along they will be happy to stay in a committed relationship, feeling a sense of total freedom that is not altered by their loyalty and commitment to another. They appreciate that absence makes the heart grow fonder, and when separated from loved ones, still feel secure.

Sometimes this native can seek to attain a higher standing through marriage, or try to escape restrictive circumstances through an alliance with a Jupiter type.

It's intriguing to note that Wallis Simpson, Grace Kelly and Princess Diana, all of whom married royalty, were born in cycle 15D. With 32 years separating their births, they all had the Degree of Passion at 5 Sagittarius 45. Kate Middleton was born in cycle 10D also with the Degree of Passion in Sagittarius, at 22 Sagittarius 10.

This Sagittarian link to royalty may be due to Jupiter's role as the 'king' of the gods suggesting an innate desire to connect with those individuals who are somehow larger than life itself.

In Capricorn, the Tenth House, or with Saturn

This type is not one to put their feelings on display, but nonetheless they are very earthy and passionate. They can seem rather shy and withdrawn to more adventurous types but in those intimate moments when emotions are stirred they can be one of the most sensual lovers in the zodiac.

Once a commitment is made they honour that promise. Where romance is involved this type is pragmatic and naturally cautious. They don't like gushy sentimental displays nor do they like to rush things. They respect the traditions of courtship and will honour their marriage vows. They do not take partnership responsibilities lightly and will tolerate quite a lot of angst before considering breaking ties.

This type generally seeks a partner who is ambitious and successful. As with Virgo, this Degree of Passion is often present in those who are very passionate about their life's work or vocation.

If operating negatively, this Degree of Passion suggests too much emphasis is placed on career matters and personal goals to the detriment of personal relationships. Alternatively, it can suggest that marriage itself is the main goal that is sought. The security others provide makes them feel respected. There can be a compelling drive to marry someone who is highly esteemed, especially if the Midheaven is involved.

The influence of Saturn can bring about relationships with much older partners.

In Aquarius, the Eleventh House or with Uranus

This Degree of Passion values the original and intellectual. Sharing and exchanging ideas and stimulating discussion helps this type connect with others. While connections are important, paradoxically the ideal relationship may be one where they have freedom to come and go.

Under the influence of Uranus there can be some unusual, quirky or unpredictable aspects to the love life of this type. They may even favour an open marriage. On the whole however, friendship is more important than intimacy or a life-long commitment.

The unconventional, original and eccentric qualities associated with Uranus, can make this person feel like an outsider. Often this type feels intrinsically awkward or out of place because they cannot be themselves and in a relationship at the same time. But when the right partner comes along they will know because they will immediately feel accepted and not have to change for the sake of the relationship.

Others can think this type aloof, standoffish, or difficult to pin down. They are easily misunderstood. Self expression and creative freedom are vital to this type. Their ideal relationship will not be restrictive in any way, and should make them feel totally accepted.

If negatively aspected this Degree of Passion can result in chaotic and unpredictable episodes in relationships and a high degree of restlessness or eccentric behaviour that distances and shields them from experiencing emotion.

In other respects it can indicate a real passion for one's community, for science and technology, and other Aquarian fields of endeavour.

In Pisces, the Twelfth House, or with Neptune

This Degree of Passion creates a sensitive and caring soul who will make great sacrifices for love. Highly idealistic about love, a special spiritual and soul connection is what they seek. Romance, dreams and fantasy play a big role too.

Giving and affectionate by nature, Neptune's influence makes this type easily aroused and keenly attuned to subtle expressions of love.

If operating negatively, this Degree of Passion can result in relationships that only exist in some kind of faraway fantasy. These fantasies may be projected onto a public personality who is unattainable. Neptune's influence can also result in relationships where partners mysteriously vanish, either physically or psychologically, or instances where the promised relationship fails to live up to expectations. Deception and misunderstandings can also occur.

This type has a deep need to feel they belong. Such is their level of empathy they may want to rescue or heal those with whom they are involved. Equally they may be looking for a saviour or healer, which can lead to inequality and co-dependency.

Neptune's influence enhances creative and artistic expression. It can generate a compelling interest in the unconscious and lead to a deep understanding of hidden dimensions of experience. Both Carl Jung and Sigmund Freud had their Degrees of Passion in the 12th house.

Relationship Timing

Falling in love is a magical feeling. When we are energised by the magnetic power of Venus and Mars we are transfixed. This is often accompanied by the feeling that we have known one another before, and perhaps we have. The Venus-Mars cycle provides us with a possible astrological explanation about how soul connections can span many lifetimes.

Getting the timing right, especially during the initial stages of relationship can be quite crucial. How do we know if it is right? If we have to ask ourselves this question, it probably isn't. When it is, somehow we just know.

The whole cycle of Venus and Mars is initiated by Venus, and it is her stationary direct position that makes a new relationship possible. The first conjunction of a new cycle takes place in the morning sky about 30 degrees away from the Sun. Note that this first conjunction with Mars takes place *after* Venus stations direct. When this happens she awakens to love. Mars unites with Venus just after she stations direct, but not before. Venus stationing direct is the signal that the time is right for a new relationship. Fresh from her beauty sleep, she is ready for love.

It is now that new partnerships and connections are sought. We are more confident and willing to express our feelings. While we are vulnerable, with Venus now waxing we are open and willing to express our feelings.

It is interesting too that Venus stations when semi-sextile the Sun. This reinforces her readiness for relationship. Semi-sextiles link two signs which are adjacent to each other. This aspect symbolises our first awareness of another, of someone who is different. As we learn to relate to this 'non-self' we start to understand more about other people and learn from our experiences.

The semi-sextile aspect is reflected in the signs which Venus and Mars rule; Aries and Taurus are semi-sextile, as are Libra and Scorpio, these cusps are the points of connection, and the barriers that exist between ourselves and others. We can learn a great deal from the sign adjacent to our own.[19]

At the first Venus-Mars conjunction in a series, Venus is moving very slowly and while she is eager to relate, she is inexperienced. Over the next few weeks she quickly increases in speed and will make another conjunction with Mars; the conjunction that starts a new long direct cycle.

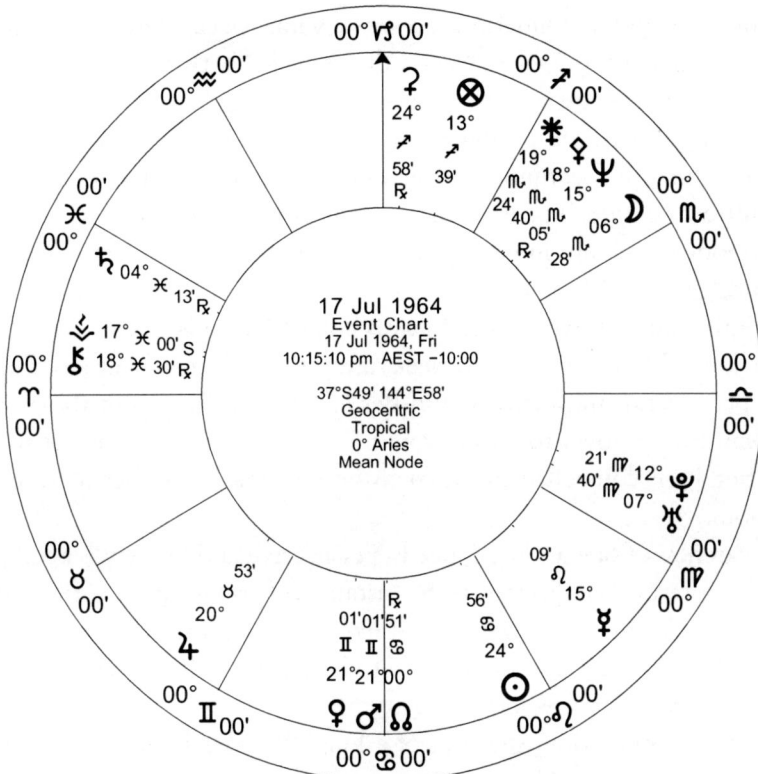

The Relationship Revolution.
New Retrograde Cycle 16R/47R. 17 July 1964.

A new retrograde cycle starts when…

- Venus and Mars are conjunct.
- Venus has recently stationed direct.
- They are morning stars and both waxing.
- Mars is moving faster than Venus.

After their first kiss…

- They will stay close for several weeks.
- She will speed up and start chasing after him.
- She will catch him… but will it last?

After their initial conjunction, Venus and Mars remain very close in the sky. This period symbolises the initial courtship stage of relationship when there is a great deal of passion and intensity.

Their second conjunction occurs several weeks later, and this conjunction marks the start of a new direct cycle. By this time Venus has arrived at her greatest western elongation from the Sun. The potential for making a long-term commitment is perhaps at its strongest now.

But while this conjunction signifies the potential for a lengthy committed relationship, it is also at this point that Mars leaves the Venus zone. Their union may be equally short-lived – new relationships may not get past this point.

Venus cannot travel where Mars is compelled to go. Just when the future looked secure, only a few weeks after their first blissful union, they must part. Venus must stay within her allotted 48 degrees of the Sun, and wait for her lover to return from his hero's quest. Mars cannot stay with her, he is compelled to go. At this point new lovers face a critical decision.

Awareness of one another's needs, perspective and journey is needed for a long term commitment to be sustained. Periods of separation are inevitable. As much as lovers would like to remain united forever in a state of bliss, it is simply not possible to be together all the time. Venus must allow Mars his freedom.

At this conjunction, the start of a long direct cycle, we are offered a choice. Venus and Mars must respect one other's individuality and differences. If this mutual understanding is present this conjunction signifies the start of a long term loving commitment. Although they must part, Mars will always return to his love.

A new direct cycle starts when…
- Venus and Mars are conjunct.
- Venus reaches greatest western elongation as morning star.
- She has caught Mars.

But then…
- Mars leaves the Venus zone.
- Venus changes course and begins applying to the Sun.

The Venus-Mars cycle is the law of attraction in action. The first two conjunctions in a new cycle are generally spaced about six weeks apart and throughout this period Venus and Mars remain close. This is the ideal time for potential partners to get to know one another. This is the

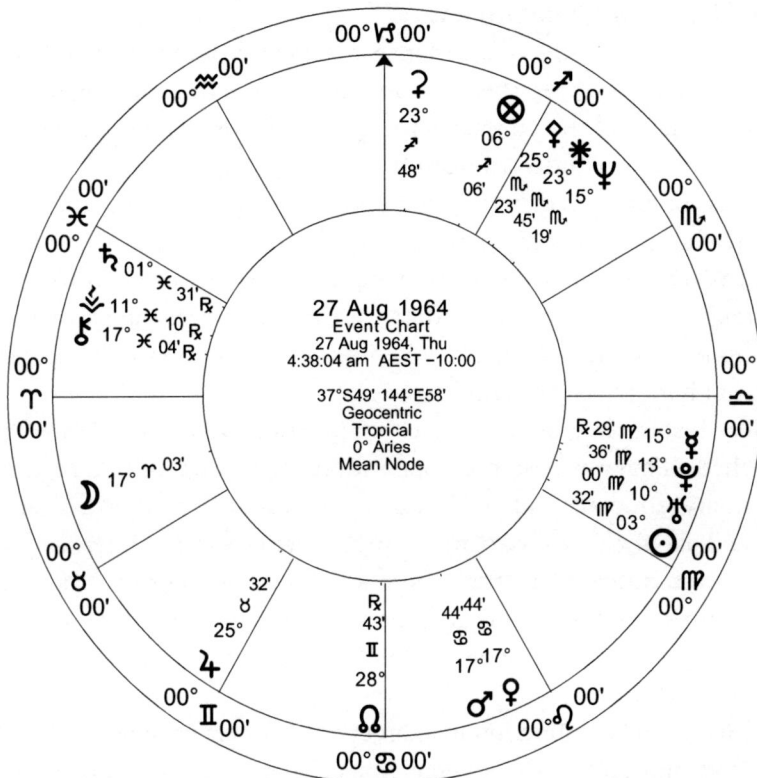

New Direct Cycle 16D. 27 August1964.

cosmic signal that symbolises the initial courtship phase of relationship when the most compelling emotions are felt.

Yet in practise, Venus and Mars do not have to be involved in a conjunction for a new relationship to start. When two people fall in love Mars might be located in the Venus zone, or he might be elsewhere. He might be in aspect to Venus, or he might not.

It is Venus that plays the pivotal role in establishing new relationships. It is when she is waxing and in the morning sky that she is most likely to initiate contact and seek an intimate union. Regardless of exactly where Mars is positioned at any given time – the two most important factors that help us to establish a new relationship are:

- Venus' station direct
- Venus' greatest elongation (morning star)

The Degree of Commitment

At the middle of every Venus-Mars Saros cycle we find that Venus, Mars and the Sun are all together in a stellium. This is the half-way point of their journey and the pinnacle of their association. The bond between Venus and Mars is at its strongest now.

This conjunction of Sun, Venus and Mars implies that consciousness is fully engaged in our relationship choices. In a *direct cycle*, this midway point is reached when Venus is at *superior* conjunction, signifying her marriage to both the Sun and Mars – an idyllic and blissful partnership. At this point in her solar journey Venus transitions into the evening star phase of her cycle. She matures.

Just before they arrive at this conjunction Venus and Mars have travelled a long way from their opposition. At that opposition Mars was stationary retrograde and Venus was at her greatest elongation as evening star and about to turn retrograde. At first Venus was not interested and didn't even notice Mars; then there was a long period when they were caught up in their own journey. When they did start getting closer, there was a time of uncertainty before they arrived at this committed union. (See Part Three)

This central conjunction in a direct cycle occurs in isolation. Unlike the start and end of each Venus-Mars Saros when two conjunctions occur close together in time, in the middle of a cycle there will not be another conjunction for the longest possible time. Prior to and after this central conjunction Venus and Mars will not embrace for about 23 months. This central conjunction is the only conjunction that Venus and Mars will make in over three and a half years.

This tells us that the Sun-Mars-Venus stellium has a sustaining influence on relationships. Literally and symbolically, there are no other unions that 'come close' to this one. Consequently, we might call the middle conjunction in a direct series the 'Degree of Commitment' for it implies that this is as good as it gets.

When a central conjunction triggers personal planets or angles in the natal chart, it can herald a long term commitment. I was amazed to discover that three married friends of mine each entered into their relationships in 1987 around the time of a central Venus-Mars conjunction. All three marriages have endured and are going strong

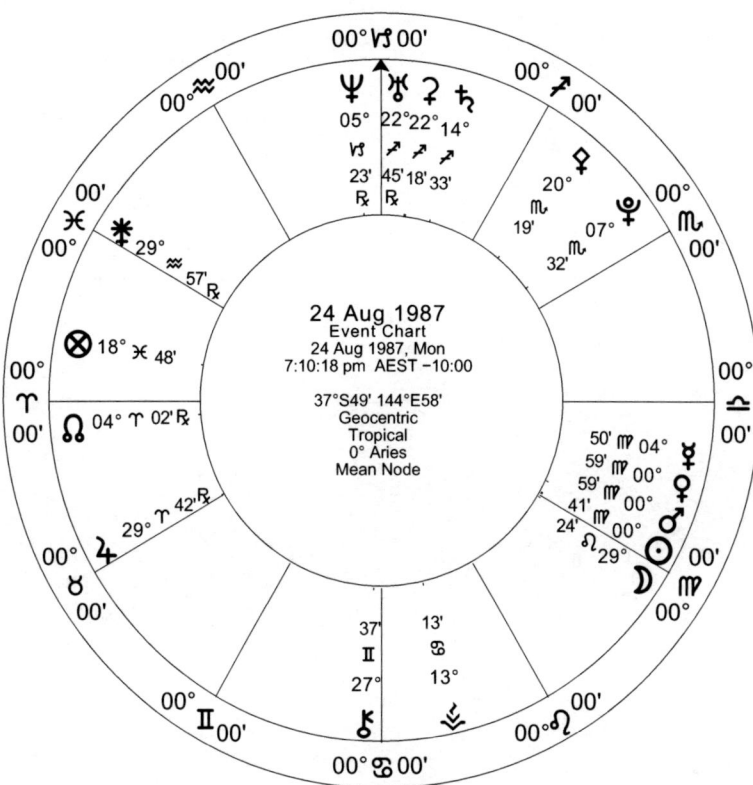

24 August 1987. The Degree of Commitment. The 19th and Central
Conjunction of Direct Cycle 6D that started in 1347.

after 25 years.[20] Several workshop participants have told me that they
too began long term relationships, or were married around this time.

In a *retrograde cycle* the middle of a cycle is reached when Venus,
Mars and Sun are together too, but with Venus retrograde at her *inferior*
conjunction. At this retrograde union with the Sun and Mars, Venus
turns away from others, which is probably not such an ideal time for
relationship. With Venus at inferior conjunction and retrograde, Venus is
more self contained. There are no 23 month gaps between conjunctions
as there is with the middle of a direct series.

The Degree of Separation

Just as when cycles start, when they conclude, they end in pairs. The
direct cycle ends first, followed by the retrograde cycle. Again, at the end

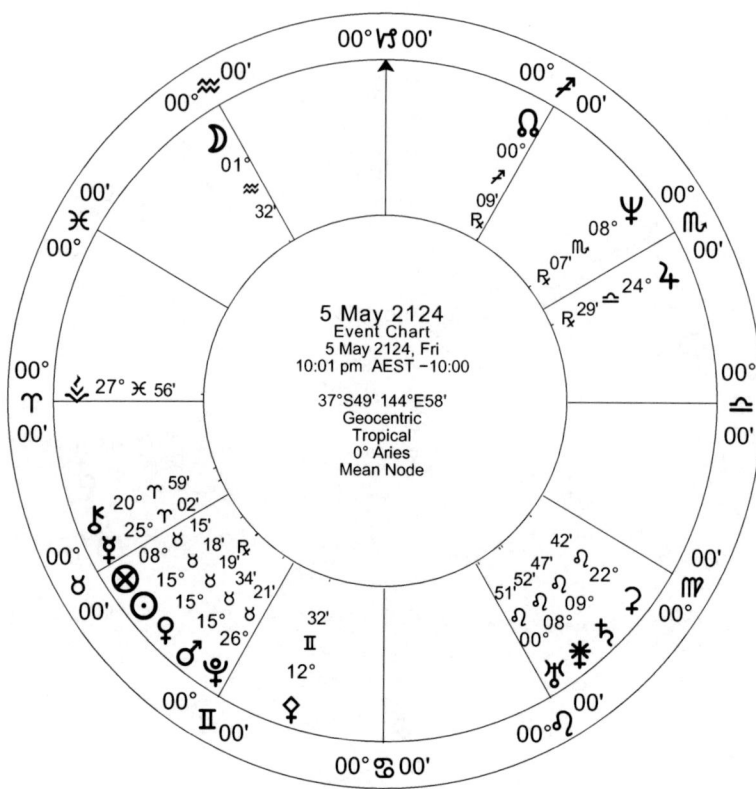

5 May 2124. The Sixth and Central Conjunction of Retrograde Cycle 16R/47R that commenced in 1964.

of a series there will be two Venus-Mars conjunctions spaced just a few weeks apart.

Retrograde cycles start first and finish last. The station direct of Venus starts the whole relationship process and her station retrograde ends it.

The conjunction that marks the end of a direct cycle occurs near Venus's greatest eastern elongation when Venus is the evening star. This is about seven weeks before she stations retrograde.

While all Venus-Mars conjunctions might seem like the perfect time to start a new relationship, conjunctions occurring right at the end of a series are probably not so ideal. My sense is that relationships that commence as a cycle is concluding may not endure like those that start out when the conjunction is near the beginning, or the middle of a cycle.

The opposition immediately prior to this conjunction happened when Mars was opposing the Sun and Venus. This reinforces the notion that the quicker the courtship, the less durable the partnership will be over the long term.

The two triggers which tell us it's time to review, assess, or possibly end a relationship if Venus deems it necessary are:

- Venus' greatest elongation as evening star.
- Venus' station retrograde.

When Venus turns retrograde she retreats from contact in order to evaluate her experiences against her core values and standards.

This is not to say that all relationships are destined to come to an end at this time however, even the best relationships will generally undergo a test as the 'Degree of Separation' approaches. When Venus retrogrades our relationships and commitments generally come under review, regardless of where Mars is located.

If the existing relationship is found to be fundamentally worthwhile, then it will continue and grow stronger for ultimately it fulfils Venusian standards. If however, there is a significant disparity between inner ideals and the outer circumstances Venus will decide to sever contact and end the relationship.

When Venus is retrograde those relationships without a strong foundation will fade, those that are destructive will tend to break down, but those that are truly worthwhile will survive and grow if Venus is content.

OJ and Nicole

An extreme example of the difference between a conjunction at the start of a series and one at the end of a series and its potential effect can be seen in the relationship of O.J. Simpson and Nicole Brown. They first met in late June 1977[21] a few weeks after Venus-Mars Saros 17D commenced, with the Degree of Passion at 00 Taurus 37. Though OJ was still married to his former wife, he and Nicole began dating.

Eight years later, after OJ's divorce, he and Nicole married on 2 February 1985. This was just two days after a Venus-Mars conjunction; however this conjunction was the very last one of direct cycle 42D.

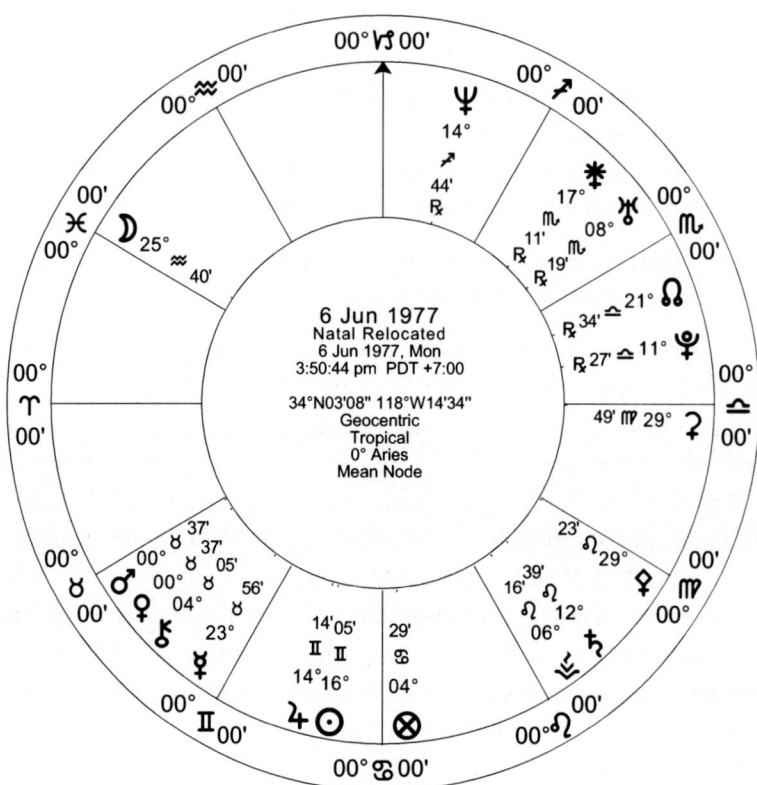

6 June 1977. New Direct Cycle 17D.
Degree of Passion at 00 Taurus 37.
Nicole Brown met O.J. Simpson a few weeks later.

By the time a cycle comes to an end, Venus and Mars have built a long karmic history together. They have been meeting once every 32 years for hundreds of years. The karma can be good, or bad, but at the end of a cycle there will be no more 32-year anniversaries. This means that there are no further opportunities for Venus and Mars to work out their differences. Any issues of long standing will come to a head and seek resolution.

After the birth of two children, their relationship began to deteriorate and they divorced in 1992. Nicole was murdered in 1994.

Though acquitted of her murder and that of her friend Ronald Goldman, O.J. Simpson was found liable of their wrongful deaths in a civil trial.

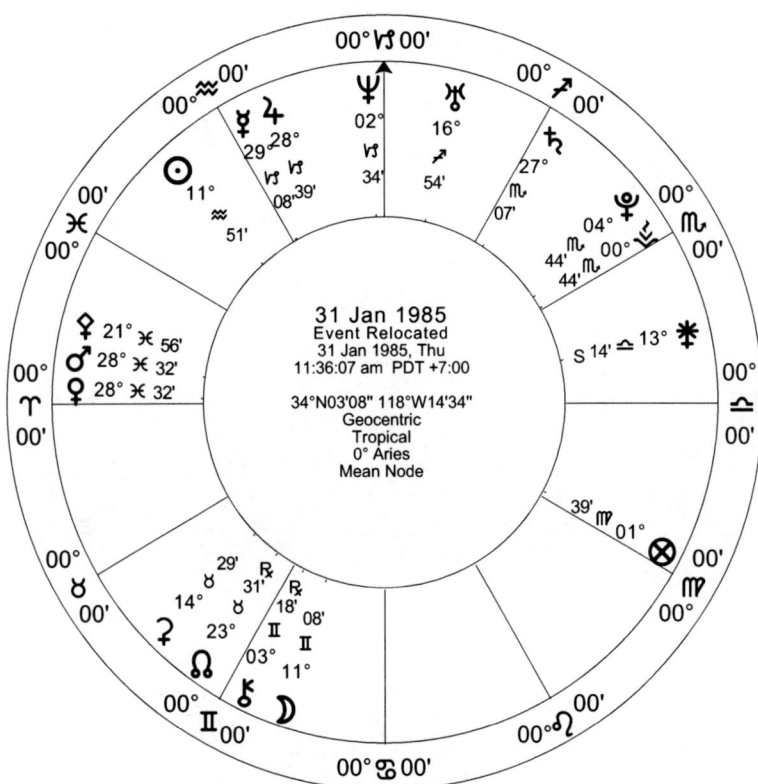

31 January 1985. End of Cycle 42D.
Degree of Separation 28 Pisces 32.
Nicole and OJ married two days later.

OJ Simpson was born in the 'Action Hero' first Mars phase. OJ's Sun in Cancer sits at the midpoint of Nicole's Venus and Mars indicating a potent magnetic attraction.

With Nicole's Degree of Passion at 10 Aries 32 closely aligned with her South Node it suggests a love of Mars types, and the possibility of a past life association that was destined to play out in her current experience. Her Degree of Passion opposes her many planets in Libra in her 7th house, including the Moon, and opposes OJ's Neptune, implying unconscious patterns of behaviour.

In his hypothetical memoir *If I Did It*, O.J. Simpson describes Nicole Brown as having a dual personality; one caring and another abusive. He

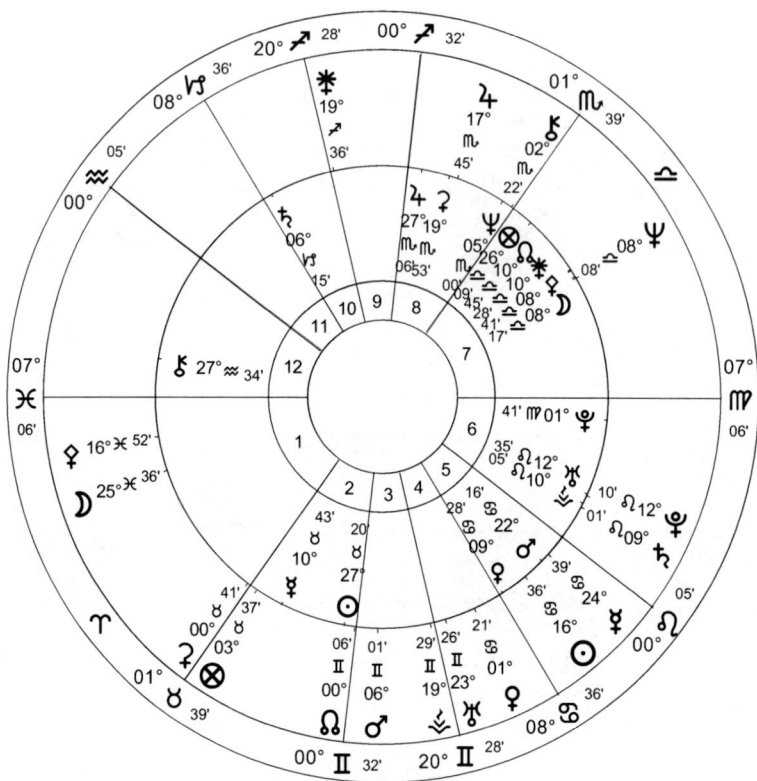

Inner Wheel: Nicole Brown 19 May 1959, 2.00am, Frankfurt am Main, Germany. 50N07 08E40. Rating AA.
Outer Wheel: O.J. Simpson 9 July 1947, 8.08am, San Francisco, California. 37N46 122W25. Rating AA.

also describes Brown as a habitual user of drugs. The book's ghostwriter Pablo Fenjves later said that Simpson's views were self-delusional.[22]

OJ's Degree of Passion at 29 Aquarius 33 falls in his 7th house and aligns with Nicole's 12th house Chiron.

Nicole's brutal death on 12 June 1994, happened shortly before OJ's 47th birthday. In his Solar Return for July 1993, transiting Saturn is located at 29Aquarius 41, right on his Degree of Passion, making for a lot of frustration.

In their synastry they have Venus widely conjunct Venus, and Mars semi-square Mars. Both aspects indicate a high degree of attraction

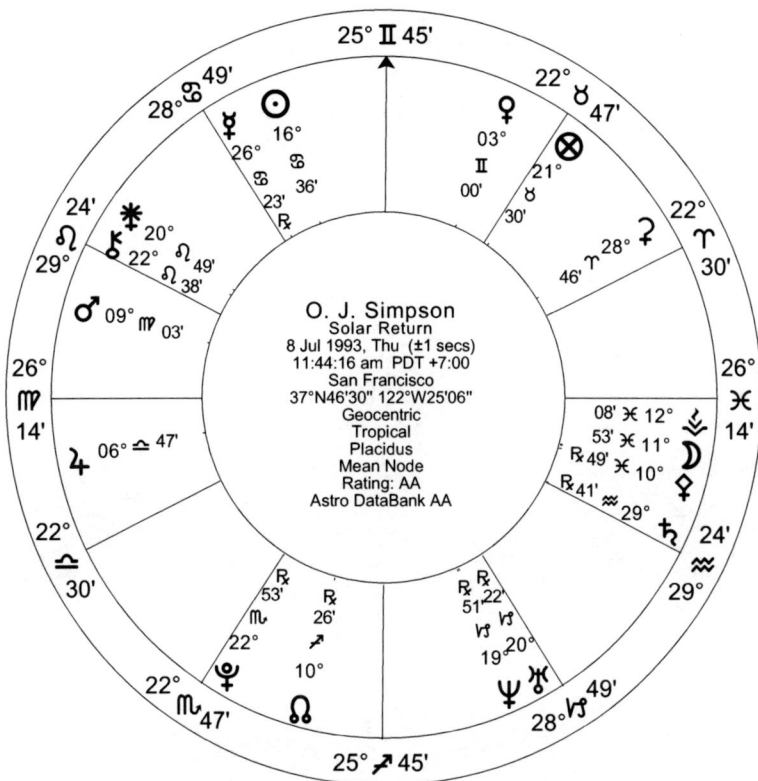

O.J. Simpson's Solar Return for 1993.

and passion. Yet the latter suggests they each wanted space to express themselves freely as individuals within the relationship and indicates a volatile union where violence could easily erupt.

Mundane Implications of the Degree of Separation

The Degree of Separation also appears to function in a mundane context marking the end of an era. A good example of this can be seen in the 1972 conjunction which was the last one in cycle 13R/41R at 2 Cancer 52.

Using the example of the US Sibly chart once more, we can see that this Venus-Mars conjunction again highlighted Venus in the US chart, this time within 14 minutes of arc. This Venus-Mars conjunction occurred exactly one month to the day before the Watergate Break-in that took place on the exact day of Venus's inferior conjunction.

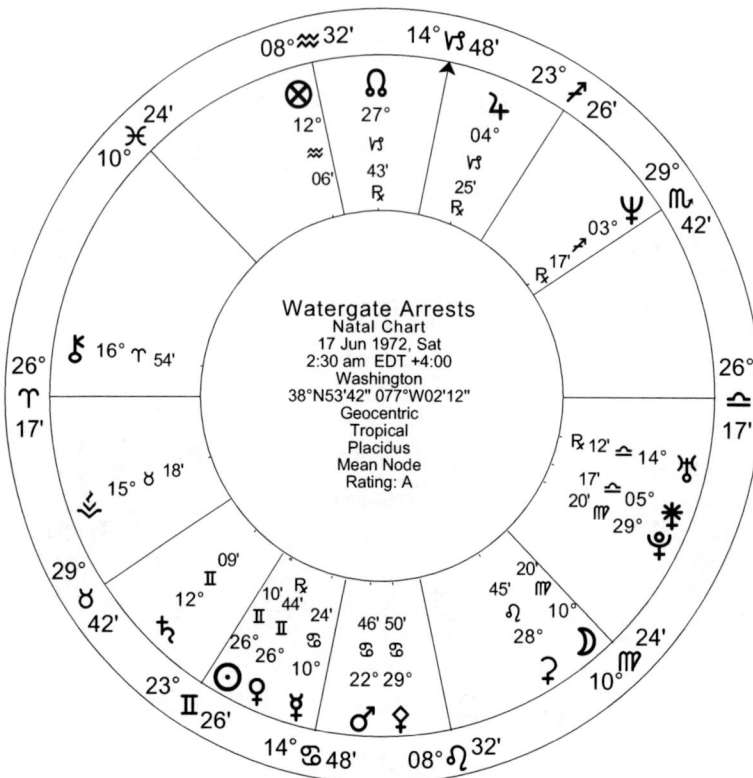

Data Source: www.watergate.info/chronology/brief.shtml

Notwithstanding a number of other significant transits to the US national chart at the time, including Uranus over Saturn and North Node over Pluto, this conjunction exposed a long era of political corruption within many tiers of government, culminating in the resignation of President Richard Nixon in 1974. Allegiances changed and political affiliations ended. Venus retreated from the unethical and illegal activities that had culminated in the Watergate burglary.

Richard Nixon's Degree of Passion sits at 18 Gemini 04, close to his Midheaven, revealing his intense desire for political power. 'Tricky Dicky' as he was nick-named, is an apt description for someone with a 'trickster' Gemini Degree of Passion. Indeed Nixon was the architect of his own downfall when recordings (Gemini) of his White House meetings were eventually made public (Midheaven).

Inner Wheel: USA Sibly Chart.
Outer Wheel: 16 May 1972. Degree of Separation, the final conjunction in series 13R/41R.

Nixon's televised resignation speech was broadcast at 9.05pm on 8 August 1974.[23] By this time the transiting South Node was crossing Nixon's Midheaven and his Degree of Passion. In the chart for the moment of his resignation the Part of Fortune is located at 2 Cancer 06 aligning with the 1972 Degree of Separation and Venus in the Sibly chart for the US, severing Nixon's relationship with the US and marking the end of an era.

Inner Wheel: Richard Nixon. 9 January 1913, 9.35pm, Yorba Linda, California. 33N53 117W48. Rating AA. Data Source: Astrotheme. Outer Wheel: 16 May 1972. Degree of Separation.

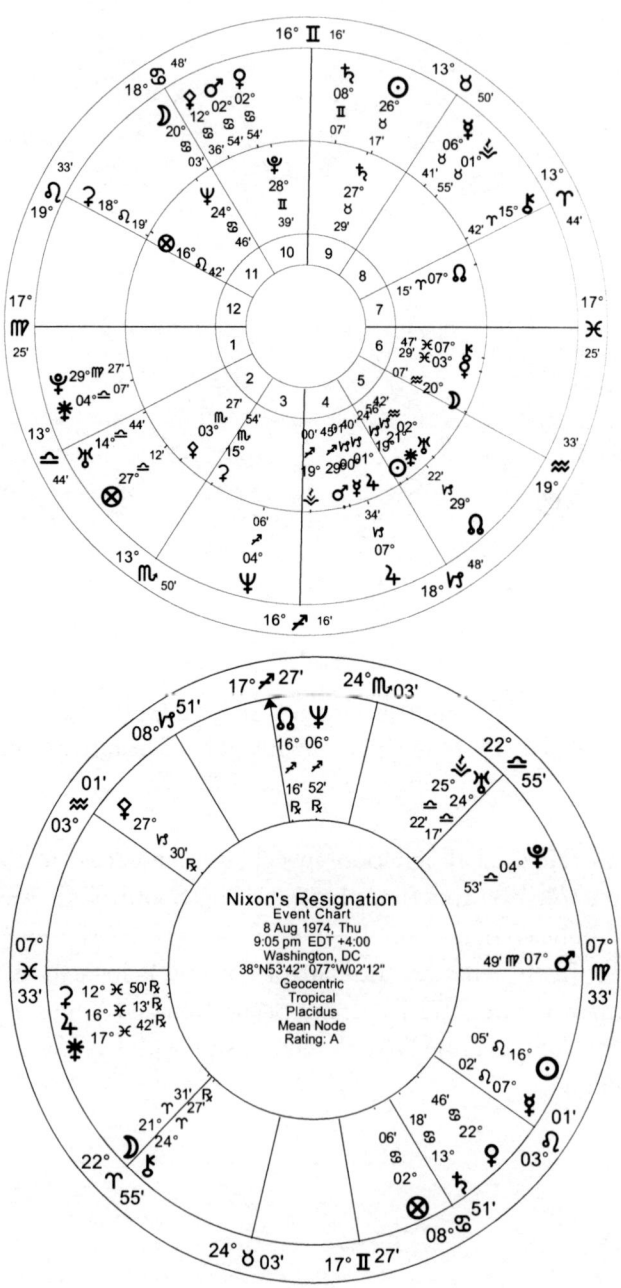

Final thoughts...

The Venus-Mars Saros is a new area of research. I feel it is important to point out that this kind of Saros-like cycle is not only seen in the Venus-Mars relationship, or in the Sun-Moon eclipse cycle, but is present in the way that all planets interact. Current ephemerides give us about 11,000 years of planetary data, but this is not long enough to examine the slower moving planets in terms of these much longer patterns.

My investigation of the Venus-Mars Saros is ongoing. I welcome comments and feedback. I can be contacted via my website:

www.celestialinsight.com.au

The Venus-Mars Saros Numbering System

I have numbered cycles 1-50 spanning the years 1000 CE through to circa 2500 CE. Because cycles overlap, I felt it was important to show that a cycle starts with one partner, but ends up with another, so all pairs which *start* and *end* within this time frame have a start number and an end number. For example cycle 14R/44R is a retrograde cycle (R) which began in 1723 and concluded in 2010.

Commencing with the first new retrograde cycle to begin after the year 1000 CE, which I have numbered 1R, the very next Venus Mars conjunction is a new direct and is numbered 1D.

The next new pair of cycles *in date sequence* I have numbered 2R and 2D. The first group of five cycles that commenced between the years 1048 and 1137 are numbered 1 through 5 in this manner.

The next group of five new cycles are numbered from 6R and 6D to 10R and 10D. These started during the years 1347 to 1436. I have numbered the five groups of five new cycles within the 1000-2500 period, up to 25R and 25D.

I then numbered all the cycles which *conclude* starting with 26D and 26R – through to 50D and 50R. Note that when cycles are concluding D comes before R because when cycles end, direct cycles end before retrograde ones.

If a cycle has only *one number*, and that number is 25 or less, it means the cycle commenced sometime *after* the year 1000 and it will conclude *after* 2500.

If a cycle has only *one number* and that number is 26 or higher, it means that the cycle started sometime *before* 1000 and finishes *before* 2500.

Cycles that have both a start number and an end number, begin and end within the 1000-2500 time period.

Footnotes

1. During periods when cycles are starting and stopping there are more than 25 conjunctions in 32 years. However, most of the time there will be 25 conjunctions of Venus and Mars in any given 32 year period.
2. Including Robert Blaschke, Alexander Ruperti, Nick Dagan Best and Adam Gainsburg.
3. *The Mountain Astrologer*, Issue 157, June/July 2011, p.50. See also http://www.earthwalkastrology.com/ [June 2011]
4. Alexander Ruperti, *Cycles of Becoming*, Second Edition, Earthwalk School of Astrology, Santa Monica CA, 2005.
5. Mark Littman, Ken Willcox and Fred Espenak, *Totality; Eclipses of the Sun*, University Press, Honolulu, 1st Ed, p.199. See also http://www.amazon.com/reader/019956552X?_encoding=UTF8&query=pliny#reader_019956552X
6. See Appendix for a full list of these groups.
7. It's so close to being exact and therefore an applying conjunction, that we can safely classify this as his 'pre-natal' conjunction.
8. Ibid
9. Ibid
10. Nick Campion, *The Book of World Horoscopes*, The Aquarian Press, 1988, p.140.
11. http://www.britainexpress.com/History/plague.htm [August 2011]
12. Benson Bobrick, *The Fated Sky*, Simon and Schuster, New York, 2005, p.217
13. Maurice McCann, http://www.skyscript.co.uk/fire.html [Sept. 2011]
14. Ibid
15. Hill and Hill P/L, *The Sabian Symbols as an Oracle*, Avalon, NSW, 1995.
16. http://en.wikipedia.org/wiki/Marlon_Brando [July 2011]
17. http://en.wikipedia.org/wiki/Keanu_Reeves [July 2011]
18. http://en.wikipedia.org/wiki/Jennifer_Syme [October 2011]
19. The idea that we 'evolve' as we travel through the signs of the zodiac, and can learn life lessons from the sign which follows our Sun sign was explored in the author's first book, *Secrets of the Zodiac*.
20. See case history for Amelia and Tom.
21. http://www.astro.com/astro-databank/Simpson,_Nicole_Brown [October 2011]
22. http://www.vanityfair.com/culture/features/2007/01/ojsimpson200701 [October 2011]
23. Robert Hand, *Planets in Transit*, Para Research Inc., Rockport Massachusetts, 1976, p.43.

Part Five
Case Histories

Case One: Alan and Bessie

Astrologer W. F. Allen, better known as Alan Leo, was born during a rare two week period when Venus and Mars were in opposition and both planets were retrograde. This celestial arrangement occurs only once in over 600 years.

A talented astrologer, Alan Leo, who changed his name from William Allen so that it would concur with his Sun sign, was also largely responsible for popularising modern day Sun sign astrology.[1] He and his wife Bessie were theosophists, vegetarians, teetotallers and apparently also celibate.[2]

Bessie was a phrenologist and a palmist. She was so impressed with Alan's written interpretation of her horoscope, she set up a meeting. At the time Bessie was engaged to be married, but it wasn't long before this marriage was annulled when her husband became frustrated with the platonic nature of their union.[3]

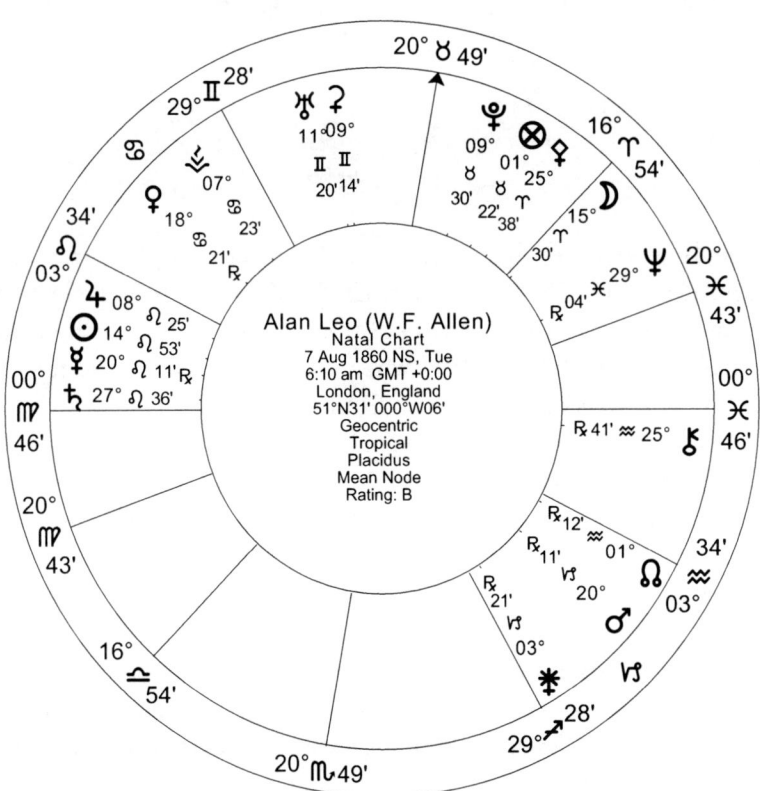

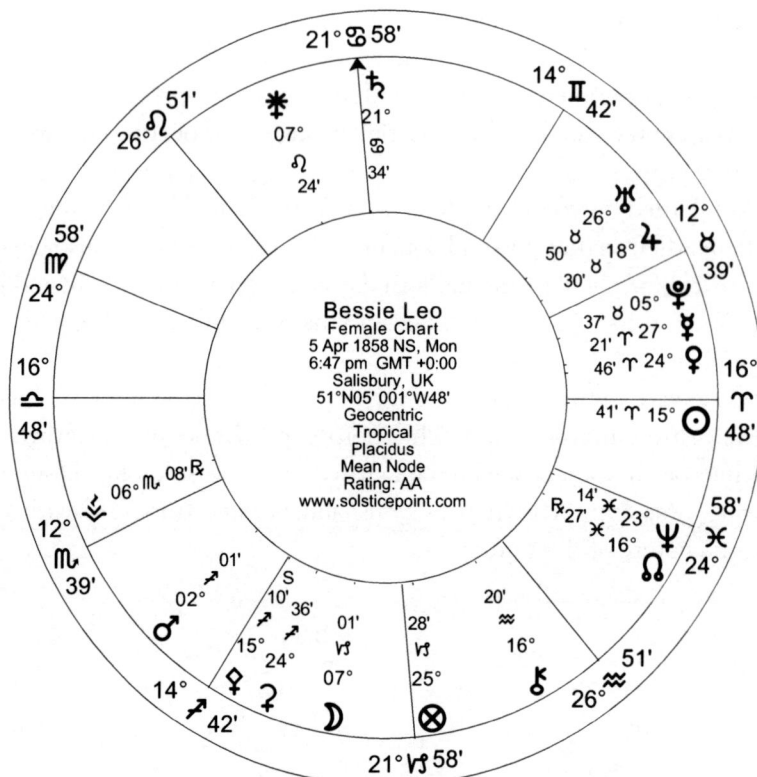

Leo, however, was apparently not at all concerned by her strict moral and ethical values, indeed his retrograde Mars and retrograde Venus were quite content with Bessie's position on such matters. The couple married on 23 September 1895 when Venus was retrograde, ten days after a Venus-Mars conjunction at 29 Virgo 50.

Alan Leo's dedication to strict guidelines is shown by the dispositors of his Venus (the Moon) and his Mars (Saturn). His strident Aries Moon sits close to his 9th house cusp implying a powerful conviction surrounding his beliefs. This Moon squares both Venus and Mars. Saturn in Leo close to his Ascendant confers a sense of personal pride in adhering to a set of strict rules and limitations.

Bessie was born shortly before Mars stationed retrograde. Venus is fast and emerging as the evening star. Heliocentrically, this places Venus and Mars on opposite sides of the Sun, suggesting a similar perspective to her husband, whose chart shows Venus and Mars opposing geocentrically.

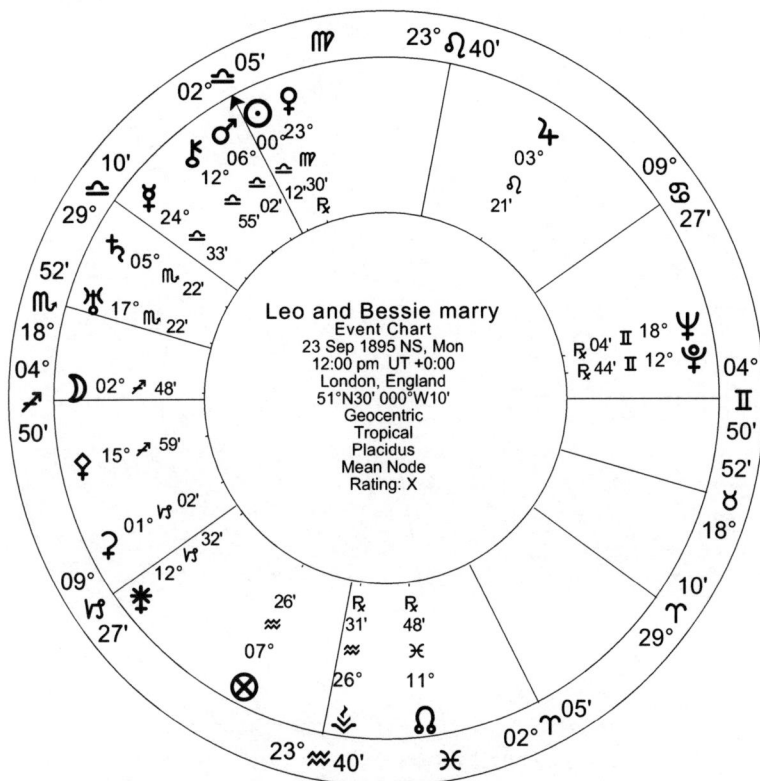

Alan Leo and Bessie marry.
23 September 1895, Time and place unknown.

Their synastry shows many areas of compatibility. Bessie's Sun at 15 Aries is within 11 minutes of Alan's Moon, an aspect often found in marriage partners.

Her slow Mars that turned retrograde by progression early in life, is the dispositor of her Aries Venus and Sun. Her Mars found a kindred spirit in his retrograde Mars. Her tough Saturn-Midheaven is conjunct his Venus and therefore opposes his Mars. Her Saturn-Midheaven which set down tough rules and strove to attain them has much in common with his responsible Saturn-Ascendant conjunction. Her Sun and Venus square off with his Venus-Mars opposition.

It is worth noting that Bessie's Juno, the asteroid goddess who represents the archetypal powerful wife, is making a conjunction to her

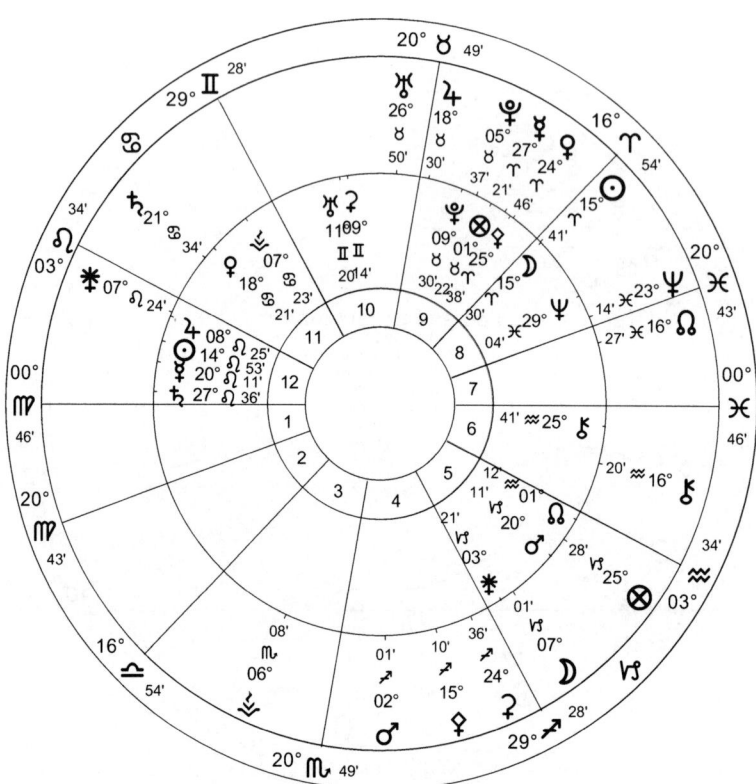

Inner Wheel: Alan Leo. Outer Wheel: Bessie Leo.

husband's Jupiter. I have often seen Jupiter-Juno links, especially the conjunction, in life-long marriage partners. The mythic Jupiter and Juno had a commitment to one another which endured. Despite constant squabbling, they really enjoyed each other's company. This combination does not necessarily indicate conflict between partners, but when present in synastry can be the glue that holds a union together through thick and thin.

Alan Leo's 'Degree of Passion' is located at 29 Taurus in his 10th house, squaring his natal Saturn/Ascendant, revealing his strong ambition, material wealth and high standards.

Bessie's 'Degree of Passion' at 29 Cancer is exactly sextile Alan's. It too falls in her 10th house very near her Midheaven conjunct her powerful Saturn.

Case Two: Diego and Frida

In the relationship of Frida Kahlo and Diego Rivera we see a completely different situation. This was a union of intense passion, infidelity, creativity and pain. Both were artists with temperaments to match. Their volatile relationship was depicted in the movie *Frida*.

Diego Rivera's chart shows Venus close to superior conjunction located in freedom loving Sagittarius. Diego, a notorious womaniser, met his match in Frida, who was openly bisexual. Yet his Mars, exalted in conservative Capricorn and adjacent to Juno shows that despite his infidelities he was the marrying kind – he married four times! Frida was his third wife. Mars in the 5th house found expression creatively as an artist and also fuelled his passionate and numerous love affairs.

Frida Kahlo has a fascinating chart. Like Diego, she too has Mars in Capricorn in the 5th house, giving rise to her passion for life and artistry. Her Mars is retrograde, conjunct Uranus and the South Node.

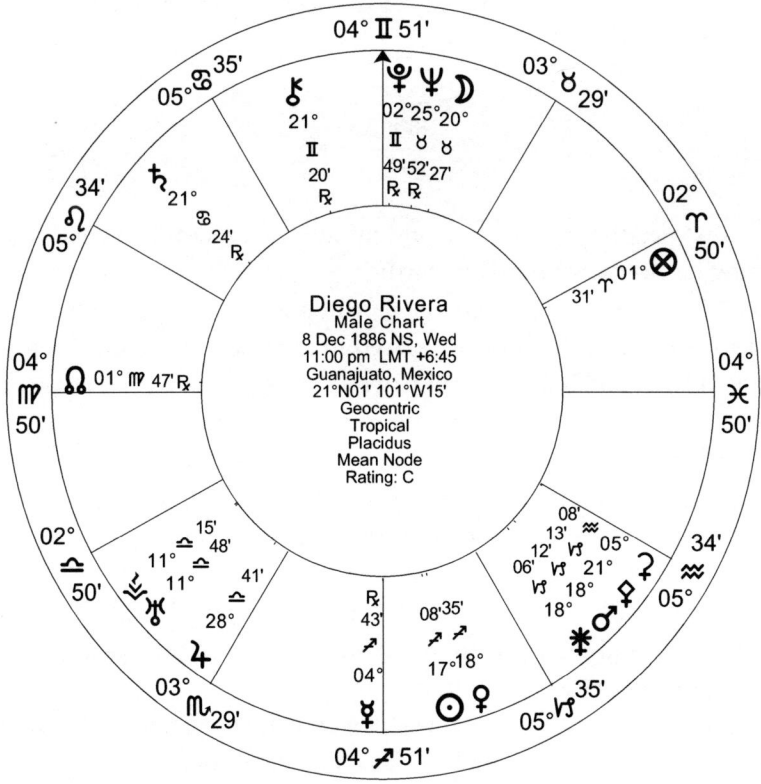

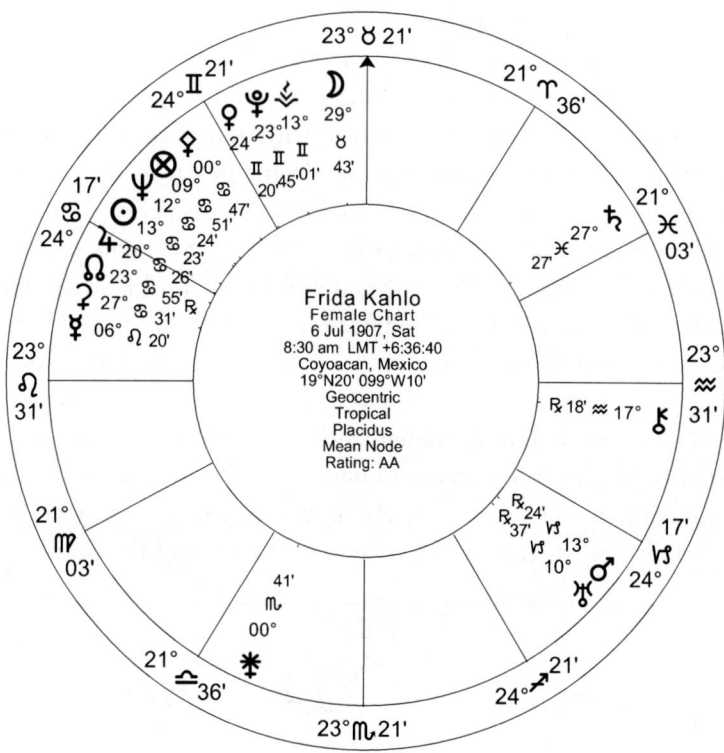

Mars opposes the Sun within one minute of exactness, hence it was making its closest approach to Earth.

Her Venus is equally intense; a morning star, it is highly animated in dualistic Gemini, which she expressed in her open bisexuality. Venus is also in a tight conjunction with powerful Pluto, fuelling her passionate emotions which she expressed in her life and her art.

Her Mars-Uranus conjunction in her 5th house played a pivotal role in her life. In her late teens she was involved in an horrific accident. It was during her convalescence that she began to paint. Her surrealistic self-portraits reveal her intense pain, both emotional and physical.

Diego was 21 years her senior. One would not describe him as a particularly handsome man, in many ways he was an unusual choice for a young passionate woman, but they were in love.

In their synastry we see some powerful links between Venus and Mars. They have Mars conjunct Mars and Venus opposite Venus. This

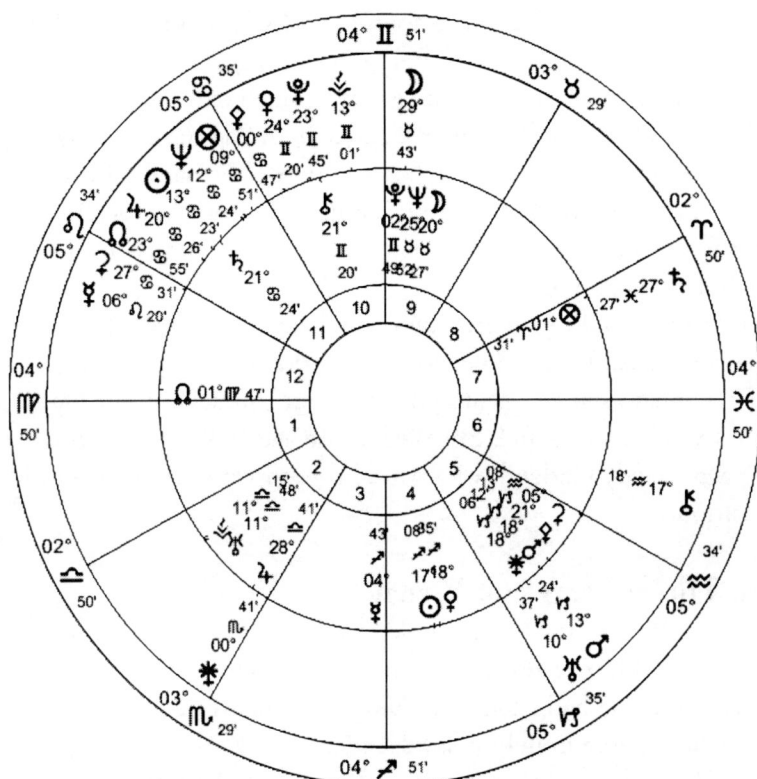

Inner Wheel: Diego Rivera. Outer Wheel: Frida Kahlo.

means Diego's Mars opposes Frida's Pluto adding more volatility to their relationship. Once again in this pairing we see her Juno conjunct his Jupiter.

On 21 August 1929,[4] Frida aged 22 and Diego 42 married on a Venus-Pluto conjunction. That day, transiting Venus and Pluto were located at 18 Cancer, opposing Diego's natal Mars and Juno exactly, therefore close to Frida's natal Jupiter.

Their roller-coaster relationship eventually led them to divorce in 1939, but they remarried the following year. The push-pull of their Venus-Mars was so intense that for much of their life together they lived in separate, but adjacent houses.

Their relationship was punctuated by sharp intense highs and deeply painful lows – compounded by their respective Degrees of Passion.

Frida's 'Degree of Passion' is found at 12 Capricorn 40 sandwiched between her Mars and Uranus. Being in Capricorn next to Mars might help to explain why she fell in love with a much older man.

Rivera's 'Degree of Passion' is located at 22 Sagittarius 10 right near his Sun-Venus which tightly opposes Chiron. His natal Chiron aligns closely with Frida's Venus-Pluto conjunction which describes her physical torment and also the emotional wounds which he seems to have inflicted upon her.

Frida once said, 'I suffered two grave accidents in my life. One in which a streetcar knocked me down... the other accident is Diego'.[5]

Though she suffered acute physical pain throughout her life, Frida Kahlo lived life to the full. She died at the age of 47 – interestingly the same age as Judy Garland, who was also born with an exact Sun-Mars opposition.

Case Three: Larry and Vivien

Laurence Oliver was born a couple of months before Frida Kahlo. His 'Degree of Passion' is also 12 Capricorn 40 and so conjunct his Uranus and Mars too. He had a long and tumultuous marriage to actress Vivien Leigh who suffered from bi-polar disorder.

His Venus is a morning star. It is placed at 29 Aries in its detriment, and his Mars, while exalted in Capricorn, is slow and about to station retrograde. Mars is the dispositor of Venus.

Vivien Leigh's beauty was legendary. Her Venus is a morning star and is located in Libra, the sign of its rulership. Venus also rules her physical appearance via her Taurus Ascendant. Her Mars, like Olivier's, is within weeks of stationing retrograde. In its fall, it sits next to Neptune and squares Venus, and is disposited by her highly visible, unpredictable and emotionally unstable Moon in Aquarius which is conjunct Uranus and her Midheaven.

Olivier's Venus and Mars combine with Vivien's Venus and Mars to form a grand cross that incorporates Olivier's nodal axis, Uranus and 'Degree of Passion', along with her Jupiter and Neptune.

This is a compelling and difficult soul connection with past life implications. It accurately describes the intense and unpredictable relationship he had with Vivien. With her Neptune-Mars and his Uranus-Mars involved, we see the confusion and instability which

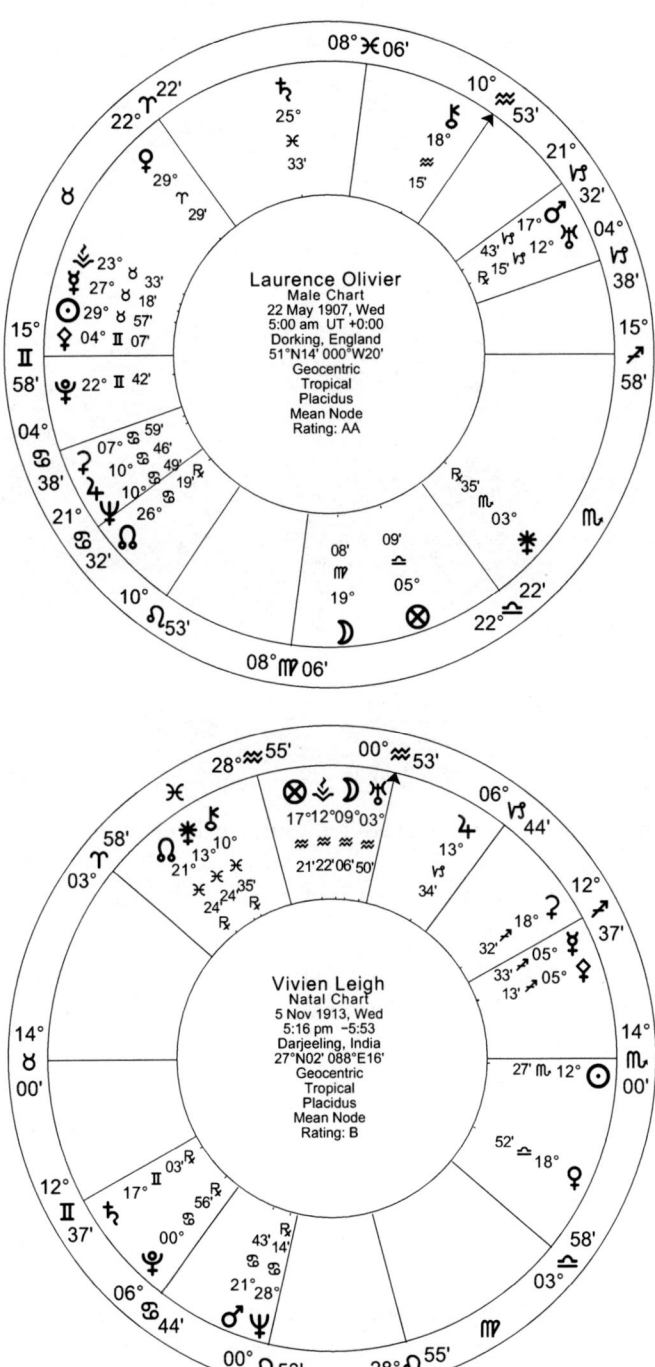

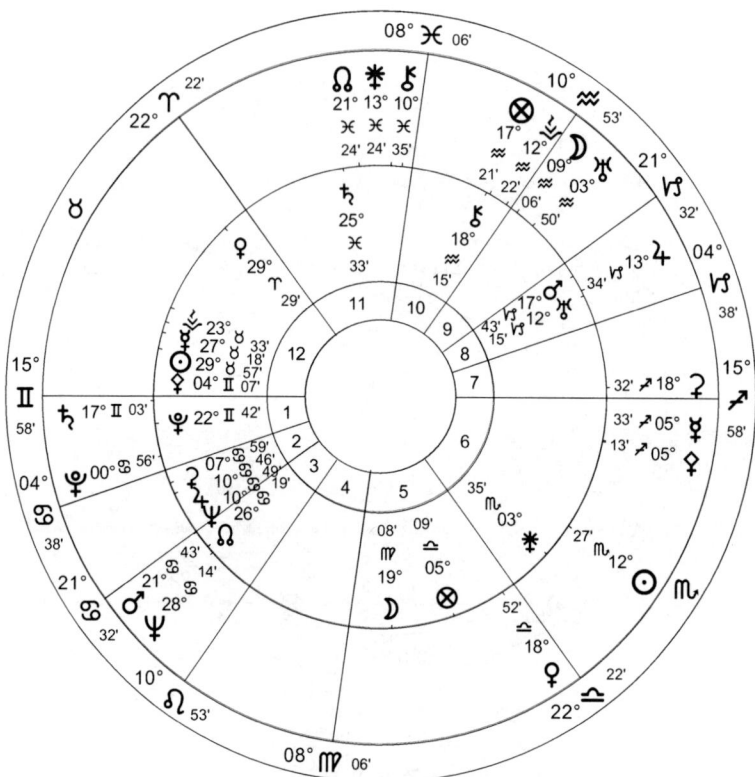

Inner Wheel: Laurence Olivier. Outer Wheel: Vivien Leigh.

plagued their relationship, mostly the result of Vivien's mental illness and emotional problems.

When their affair began they were both married to other people. They married on 31 August 1940 when Venus was at 21 Cancer, exactly conjunct Vivien's Mars and in close opposition to Olivier's Mars, near his North Node. Mars was conjunct the Sun at 7 Virgo.

Vivien's 'Degree of Passion' sits at 18 Gemini 04, very close to her 2nd house Saturn, showing her acute need for mental stimulation as well as a degree of stability and security in a partner. She found these qualities in Olivier, who had Mars in Capricorn and Gemini rising. Her 'Degree of Passion' is in close proximity to Olivier's Ascendant and natal Pluto.

After 20 years of marriage the couple divorced in 1960. Vivien Leigh died in 1967 at the age of 54 from tuberculosis, by which time she was apparently almost catatonic from repeated shock treatments.

The following year Olivier married actress Joan Plowright (28 October 1929) and they remained married until his death in 1989. Their synastry shows no Venus-Mars cross aspects. Since his death, a number of biographers have speculated that Olivier was bisexual.[6]

Case Four: Brad and Angelina

Brad Pitt has Mars exalted in Capricorn too. It is tightly conjunct his South Node and fast in motion, in the last phase of its heroic journey. Venus is in its evening phase too and also in Capricorn where it supports his Capricorn Moon. Pitt's 'Degree of Passion' is located at 19 Leo50 near his ninth house cusp showing his love of travel and foreign destinations. He and Jolie, (who has a prominent 9th house herself, with a dynamic conjunction involving Mars, the Moon and Jupiter in Aries) are keen to make a difference around the globe by drawing attention to humanitarian causes. They have adopted several children of different nationalities.

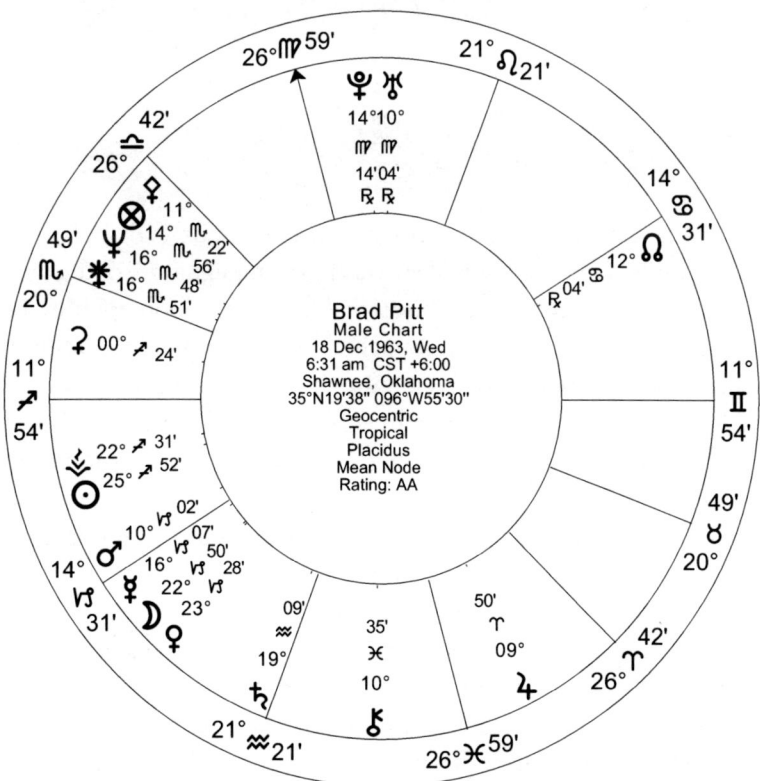

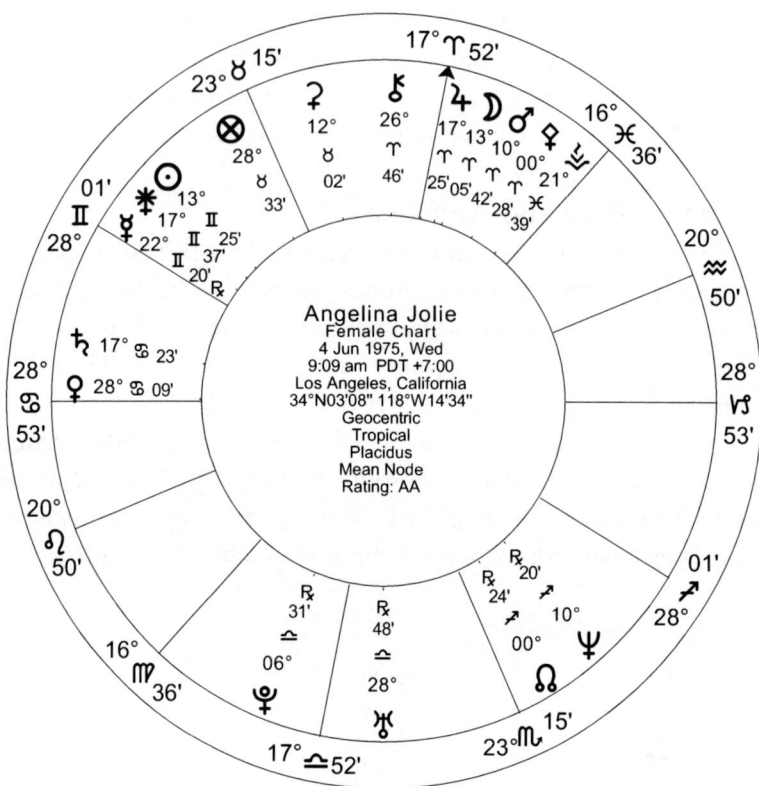

Angelina has Venus rising in Cancer, consistent with her physical beauty. This is an evening star Venus and a strong signature of the mother archetype. Her Venus square Chiron and her Mars/Moon opposite Pluto show that she has experienced some emotional scarring in relationships and has a propensity for involvement in dangerous liaisons.

Their synastry shows angular aspects between Venus and Mars. Her Cancerian Venus opposes Pitt's Capricorn Venus (and his Moon) while her Aries Mars (and Moon) square his Capricorn Mars and South Node. They are not married, but have been together since falling in love in 2005 while filming *Mr and Mrs Smith*.

Jolie's 'Degree of Passion' like Pitt's is in Leo, but at 10 Leo 23 and sits in her first house. In keeping with the sign of Leo in the first house, she is in the public limelight, and so too is her relationship with Pitt. They both seek a dynamic, creative, charismatic and outgoing partner and enjoy raising a large family. This is an adventurous love union as much as a creative one.

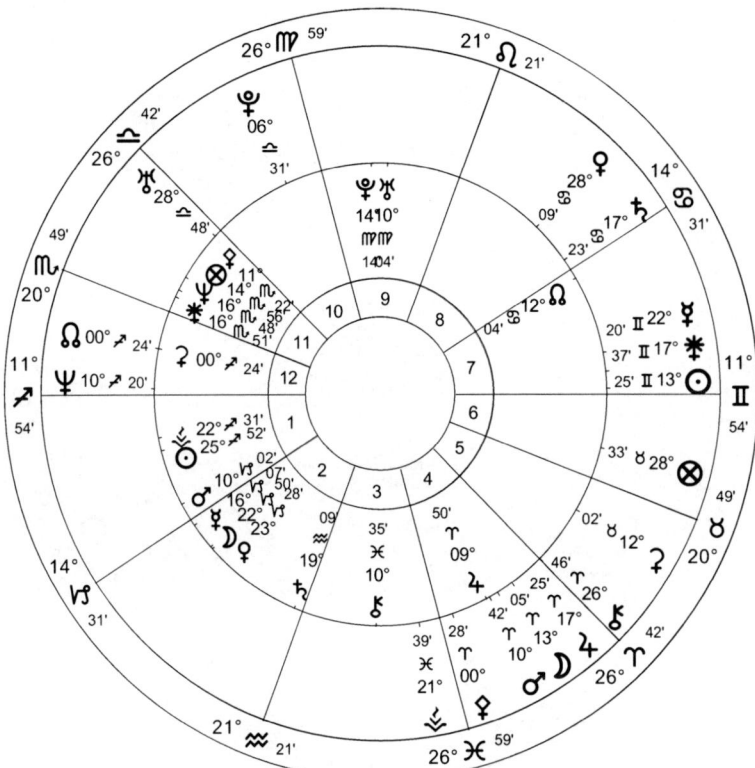

Inner Wheel: Brad Pitt. Outer Wheel: Angelina Jolie.

Case Five: Edward and Wallis

Though we only have a B rating for his birth, Edward VIII's chart has a strong Venus in Taurus as the morning star. His Mars is in its sign of rulership too, powerfully positioned at 0 Aries 23, conjunct his North Node, but forming a challenging waxing square to his Cancerian Sun.

This waxing square describes the external and internal pressures which surfaced when his father died and he ascended the throne. At that time, transiting Mars and Saturn were in close proximity to his Pisces Moon, compounding his fear and insecurity. Meanwhile transiting Pluto had just entered his 7th house of relationships. He was enraptured with Wallis Simpson and couldn't see any of her faults.

Although there is some uncertainty as to the exact birth time for Wallis Simpson too, the chart for 10.30pm works well. Her 'Degree of

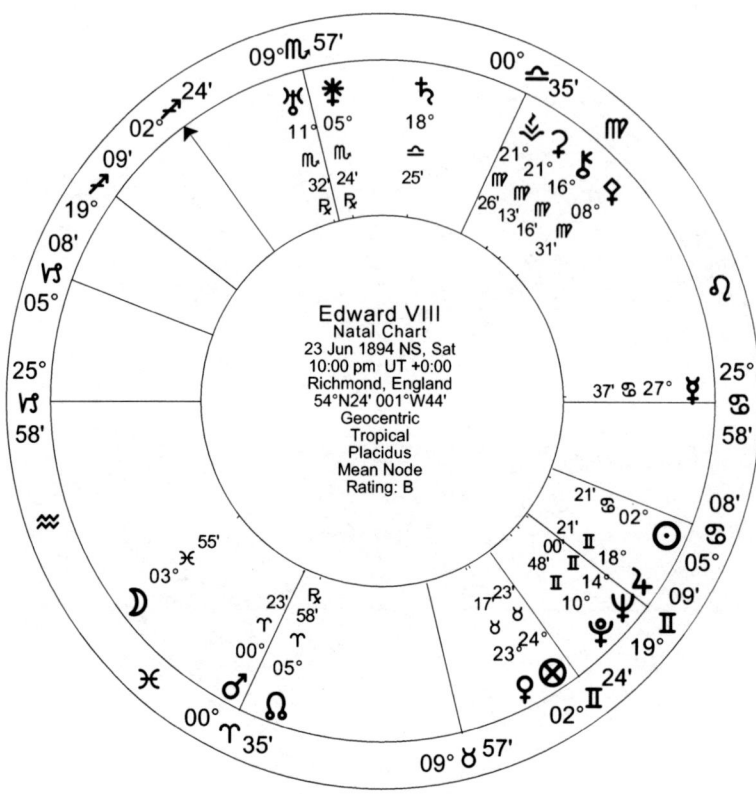

Edward VIII
Natal Chart
23 Jun 1894 NS, Sat
10:00 pm UT +0:00
Richmond, England
54°N24' 001°W44'
Geocentric
Tropical
Placidus
Mean Node
Rating: B

Passion' is 5 Sagittarius 45. Assuming her time of birth is accurate, this places it right on her Midheaven, which is very suggestive given her desire to marry a person of prominence.

By all accounts Wallis was determined to marry Edward and had serious ambitions to become queen.[7] While Sagittarius does not seem to depict Edward's persona in an obvious way, he was apparently quite a playboy and had numerous affairs before settling with Wallis. She is also rumoured to have had numerous liaisons. Wallis Simpson married three times, consistent with her Venus in Gemini approaching superior conjunction. With Venus in Gemini in her 5th house close to Neptune, she was an outgoing and highly social woman. She was still married to her second husband during her affair with Edward.[8]

Her strident Mars in Aries opposes Chiron and a wounded Libran Moon. When it looked as if she was not going to become queen, she

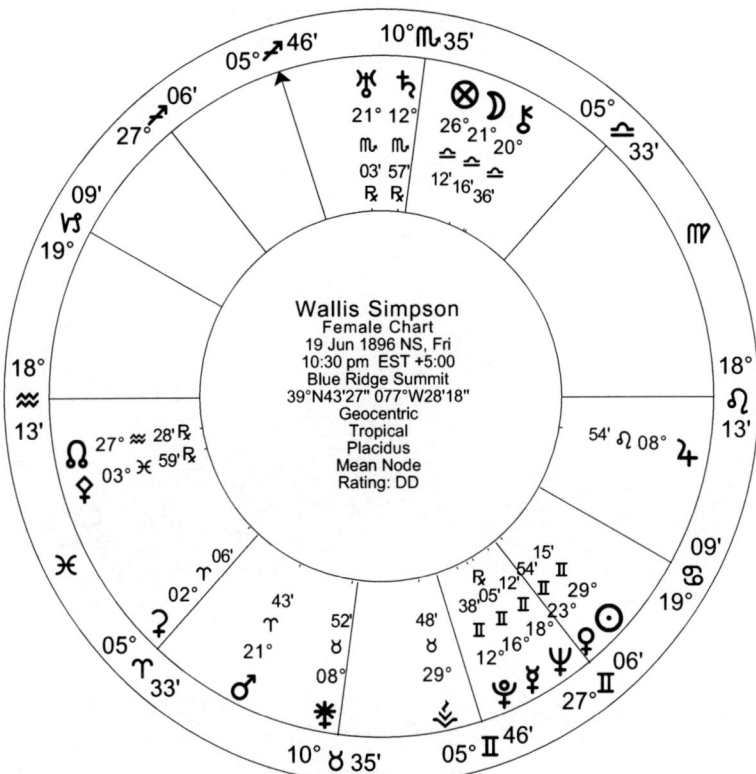

quickly made up her mind to walk away from Edward. She did not want him to abdicate. Accounts from insiders at the time suggest that she was bitterly disappointed not to have been made queen.[9]

Edward and Wallis were born almost exactly two years apart so they have a Sun-Sun conjunction, though it is out of sign. Save for a number of contacts between their respective planets in Gemini, there is not much else linking the two charts.

There are no major cross aspects between Venus and Mars, just one very tight semi-sextile between his Venus in Taurus and her Venus in Gemini. This may have had something to do with Edward's fascination for her. This semi-sextile has a very tight orb, perhaps enough to create a powerful magnetic attraction.

The semi-sextile aspect links two signs which have neither polarity, nor quality, nor element in common. From Edward's point of view this

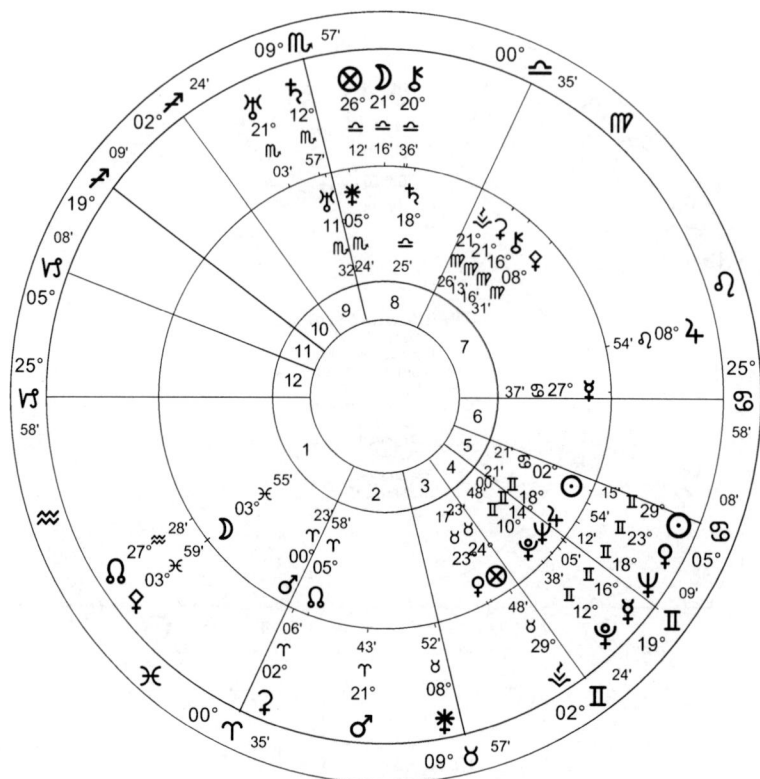

Inner Wheel: Edward VIII. Outer Wheel: Wallis Simpson.

added to her allure and mystery. Since Gemini follows Taurus, she represented his future. From her perspective, his Venus in Taurus offered material security and stability.

Edward's 'Degree of Passion' is found at 10 Aries 32 near his North Node and Mars showing his soul's desire for a tough, forthright and independent woman such as Wallis.

Case Six: Gough and Margaret

Former Australian Prime Minister Gough Whitlam has Venus retrograde in Cancer conjunct Pluto. Though there is no known time of birth available, this Venus shows him to be man of substance, passionate about his core values and eager to implement reform. Under Whitlam's leadership in the early 1970s Australia took great strides forward by

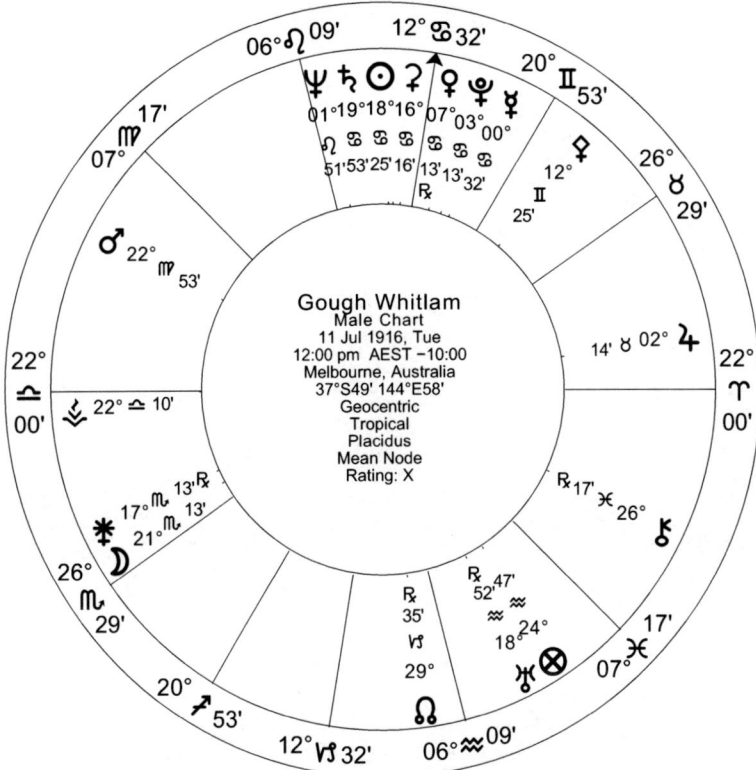

introducing new standards and policies, such as recognition of Aboriginal rights and the introduction of Medicare.

His retrograde Venus in Cancer with Pluto no doubt drew him towards a powerful woman such as Margaret, a Scorpio, who was a champion swimmer in her day. The couple towered over their contemporaries, not just in stature (both over 6 feet tall) but as an example of an enduring partnership that can survive the pressures of public life.

Their synastry shows Gough's Moon-Juno aligning powerfully with Margaret's Sun, North Node and Descendant.

They have Mars conjunct Mars and Venus square Venus. Gough's 'Degree of Passion' falls at 29 Aquarius 33 revealing his love of free-thinking types such as Margaret, who throughout her life spoke her mind and was engaged in the community. Gough's 'Degree of Passion' aligns with Margaret's 9th house Uranus which seems appropriate too. Both had vibrant personalities.

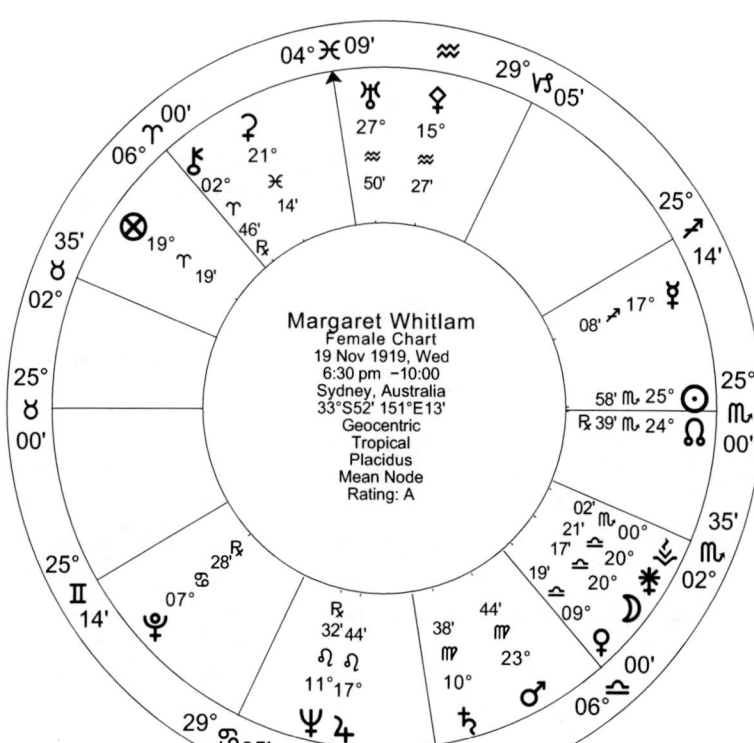

Margaret was born during the morning phase of Venus, just before greatest elongation, revealing her to be an independent woman of action. She had strong opinions and particular standards like Gough.

Her 'Degree of Passion' is located at 24 Libra 42, making a powerful conjunction to her Moon and Juno. Having her 'Degree of Passion' in Libra and in her 5th house describes her love for the arts, law, social justice, and politics, so it is not surprising that she fell in love with Gough, who was a solicitor when they met. Margaret's father was a Supreme Court Judge.

They married on 22 April 1942; nine days after Venus's greatest elongation as morning star.

Their union endured for 70 years; Margaret died in 2012, just as this book was being written.

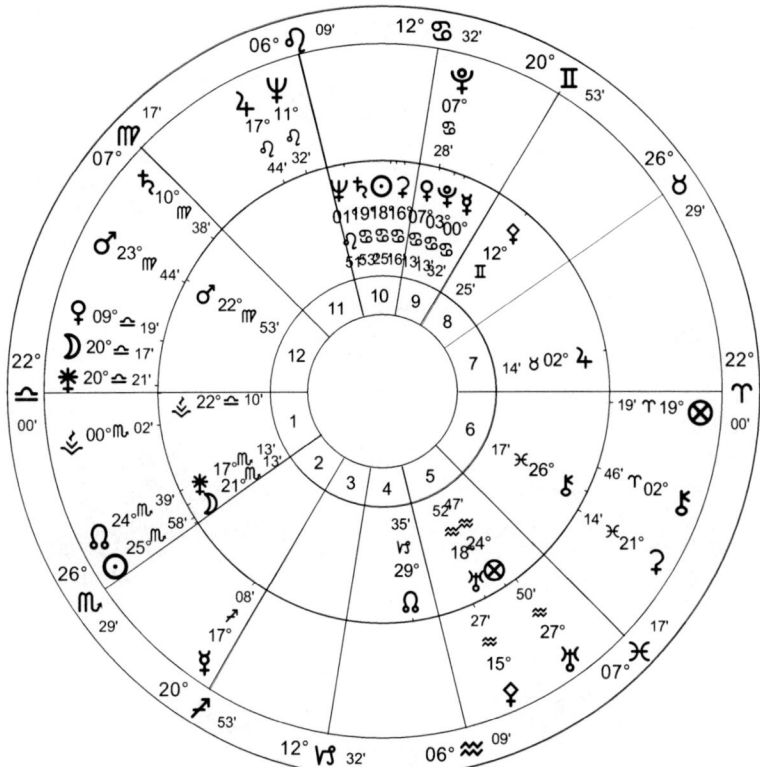

Inner Wheel: Gough Whitlam.
Outer Wheel: Margaret Whitlam.

Case Seven: Tom and Amelia

Friends of mine, 'Amelia' and 'Tom' first met on 15 August 1987 nine days before the central Venus-Mars conjunction of cycle 6D. With Venus-Mars and Sun all together this had a powerful sustaining influence on their relationship. This was a special moment.

Sun, Venus and Mars were located at 0 Virgo with the Moon and Mercury not far away. This stellium activated Amelia's Ascendant creating an atmosphere ripe for romance.

In Tom's chart, 0 Virgo 59 falls close to his second house cusp, Venus's natural house, where his natal Uranus and Ceres are found. Under the influence of this peak in Venus-Mars relations, Amelia and Tom suddenly fell in love.

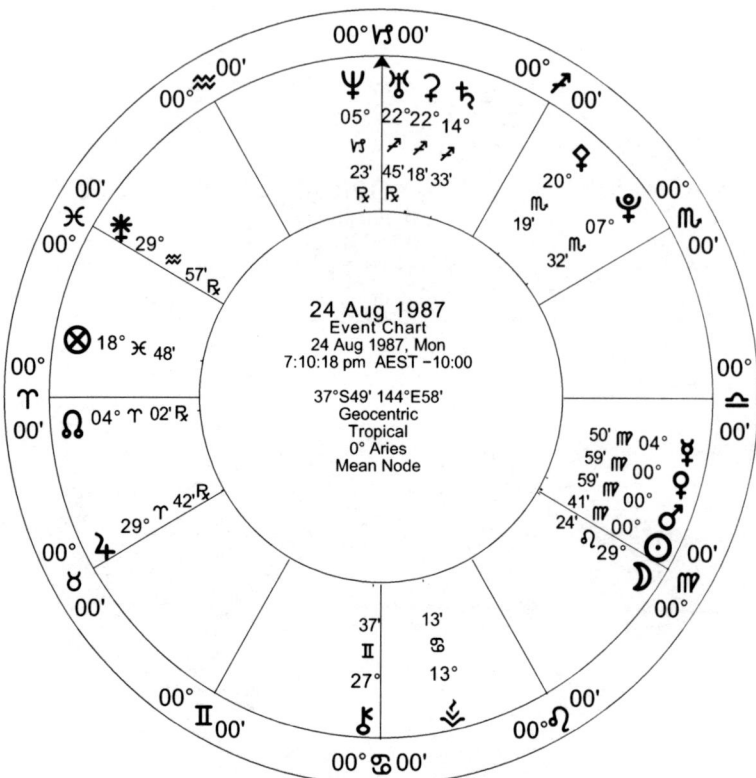

24 August 1987. Central conjunction of Cycle 6D.
Degree of Commitment.

Amelia's natal Venus is at 8 Capricorn 10, an evening star. Her 5th house Venus reached greatest elongation the day after she was born. Mars is at 29 Sagittarius 30, less than ten degrees away, with the Part of Fortune in between. Saturn in the 7th house sextiles Venus. These aspects suggest good fortune in love.

Tom was born with Venus at inferior conjunction with Venus at 19 Scorpio 31 retrograde. As we saw in Part One, we often find a special connection between one person who has Venus semi-square the Sun and another who has Venus conjunct the Sun. While no Venus aspects are in play in their synastry, this kind of connection between two Venus positions is often seen between charts of lovers and partners.

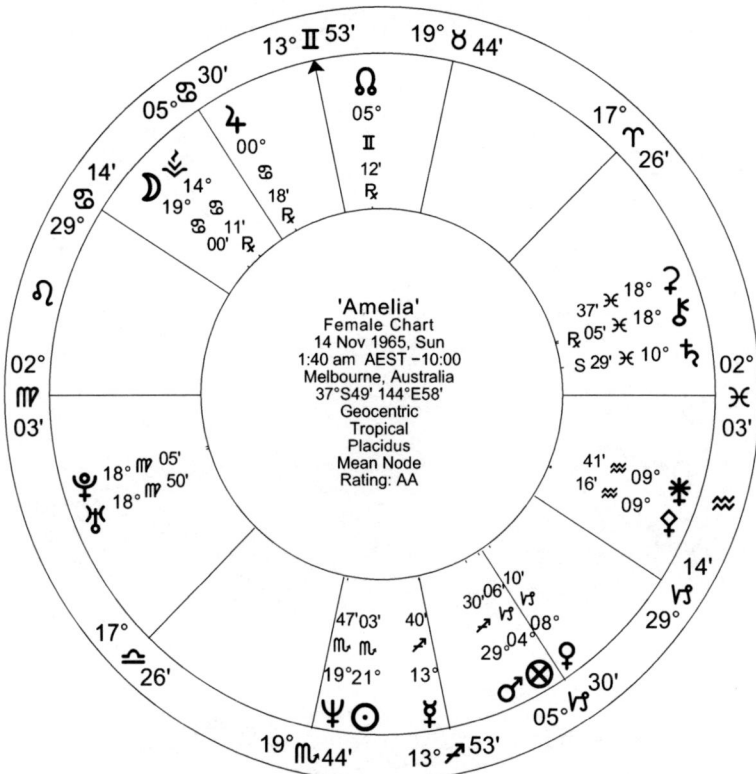

As Tom and Amelia were born almost exactly three years apart, his Venus and her Neptune are joined in a beautiful embrace that is illuminated and intensified by their dual Scorpio Suns.

Their synastry shows Amelia's Mars in late Sagittarius sesquiquadrate Tom's Leo Mars. Despite this tense Mars angle, the couple do not argue, or fight. When I discussed this aspect with Amelia, she said that the forcefulness of this energy allows them each the individual freedom to pursue their own interests. When we see powerful Mars cross aspects like this in synastry, it is vital that both parties acknowledge and allow free expression of Mars. In the case of Amelia and Tom who each have a fiery Mars, this freedom strengthens their union.

It is worth noting that Tom's pre-natal Venus-Mars conjunction took place in January 1962 at 8 Capricorn 04. This is exactly conjunct Amelia's natal Venus, within just six minutes of arc.

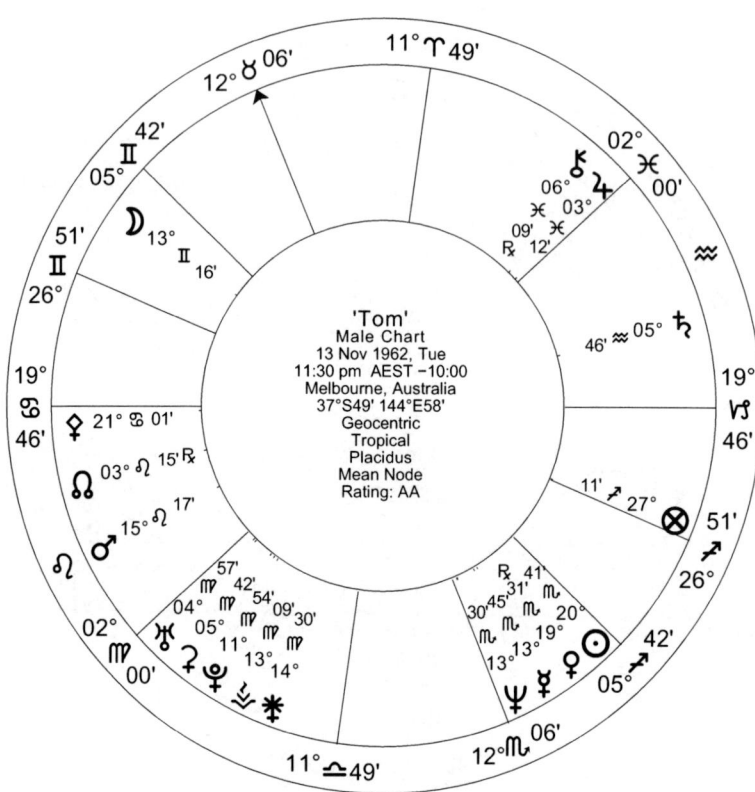

Amelia's 'Degree of Passion' is situated at 1 Cancer 48 conjunct her 10th house Jupiter, once again suggesting good fortune in matters of the heart. With her Moon in Cancer as well, it is important for her to exchange emotional support and nurturing with a partner. With Jupiter highlighted, she also needs a certain amount of freedom in relationships. These qualities have a similar feel to Tom's Cancerian Ascendant, and its dispositor, the Moon in Gemini.

Tom's 'Degree of Passion' is found at 1 Libra 19, in his second house. With its dispositor Venus at inferior conjunction, this shows a strong set of values. The security of a committed relationship is just as vital to him as it is to her. The pair married in 1990 when Venus was in her early morning star phase, after turning direct and before reaching greatest elongation; a perfect time to make a conscious choice to travel through life hand-in-hand. They have two children and are still wonderfully in love after 25 years.

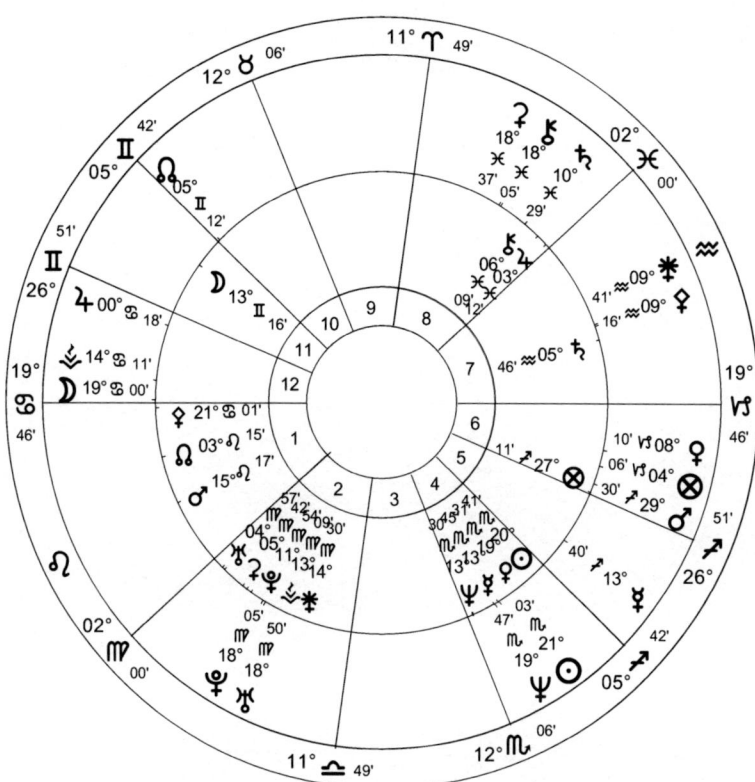

Inner Wheel: Tom. Outer Wheel: Amelia.

Footnotes

1. Benson Bobrick, *The Fated Sky*, Simon and Schuster Paperbacks, NY, 2005, p.266
2. Kim Farnell, *A Brief Biography of Alan Leo*, http://www.skyscript.co.uk/Alan_Leo.html [Oct 2009]
3. Ibid
4. http://www.lasmujeres.com/?m=kahlo_frida&s=articles&sc=art_frida-kahlo-and-diego-rivera [June 2010]
5. http://www.artchive.com/artchive/K/kahlo.html [June 2010]
6. http://en.wikipedia.org/wiki/Laurence_Olivier [April 2011]
7. Laurie Graham, *Gone with the Windsors*, Harper Perennial, London, 2006
8. Ibid
9. Ibid p.282 "David (Edward) has given up his throne so he can be with Wally, but Wally doesn't really want him without his throne."

Appendix 1
Venus Positions 1921-2020 UT

* Data courtesy of Astrodienst www.astro.com

inferior conj	1921 Apr 22	17:37	2 TA 2' 1"	5°58'43"
morning rise	1921 Apr 28	06:10	28 AR 39'47"	
direct	1921 May 14	00:27	23 AR 52' 8"	
greatest brilliancy	1921 May 26	03:52	26 AR 29'45"	-4.5m
morning max el	1921 Jul 1	18:31	23 TA 41'12"	45°44' 7"
morning set	1921 Dec 29	12:59	27 SA 17'55"	
superior conj	1922 Feb 9	07:16	19 AQ 46'32"	1°17'37"
evening rise	1922 Mar 21	16:43	10 AR 13'12"	
evening max el	1922 Sep 15	22:28	8 SC 36'18"	46°24'22"
greatest brilliancy	1922 Oct 24	22:35	7 SA 43'19"	-4.6m
retrograde	1922 Nov 4	15:21	9 SA 50'19"	
evening set	1922 Nov 19	09:05	5 SA 36'31"	
inferior conj	1922 Nov 25	05:57	2 SA 11'34"	2°11'53"
morning rise	1922 Dec 1	12:10	28 SC 32'53"	
direct	1922 Dec 15	17:08	24 SC 30'20"	
greatest brilliancy	1922 Dec 28	12:08	27 SC 32'22"	-4.7m
morning max el	1923 Feb 4	07:26	27 SA 39'44"	46°54'38"
morning set	1923 Aug 4	21:44	1 LE 29'15"	
superior conj	1923 Sep 10	11:01	16 VI 42'13"	1°24'51"
evening rise	1923 Oct 18	06:04	3 SC 48'39"	
evening max el	1924 Apr 22	02:58	17 GE 16'50"	45°40'30"
greatest brilliancy	1924 May 26	09:38	13 CN 50'48"	-4.5m
retrograde	1924 Jun 10	00:50	17 CN 35' 0"	
evening set	1924 Jun 25	04:36	13 CN 8'11"	
inferior conj	1924 Jul 1	12:20	9 CN 21' 6"	3°22'54"
morning rise	1924 Jul 7	06:09	5 CN 53' 8"	
direct	1924 Jul 23	03:34	1 CN 3'27"	
greatest brilliancy	1924 Aug 6	01:34	4 CN 25'49"	-4.5m
morning max el	1924 Sep 10	06:32	1 LE 19' 0"	45°59'30"
morning set	1925 Mar 16	07:05	15 PI 17'23"	
superior conj	1925 Apr 24	01:11	3 TA 20'43"	0°57'47"
evening rise	1925 May 31	14:40	19 GE 35'44"	
evening max el	1925 Nov 28	00:19	22 CP 28'58"	47°17'44"
greatest brilliancy	1926 Jan 5	05:55	23 AQ 4'17"	-4.7m
retrograde	1926 Jan 17	22:10	26 AQ 4'36"	
evening set	1926 Feb 3	10:59	20 AQ 39'16"	

inferior conj	1926 Feb 7	15:08	18 AQ 6'12"	7°57'31"
morning rise	1926 Feb 11	02:54	15 AQ 58'23"	
direct	1926 Feb 28	04:47	10 AQ 20' 1"	
greatest brilliancy	1926 Mar 10	18:27	12 AQ 25'32"	-4.6m
morning max el	1926 Apr 18	19:38	11 PI 44'30"	46°16' 2"
morning set	1926 Oct 13	10:37	9 LI 26'21"	
superior conj	1926 Nov 21	12:27	28 SC 26'31"	0°26' 3"
evening rise	1927 Jan 1	18:08	20 CP 17' 2"	
evening max el	1927 Jul 2	21:33	25 LE 25'18"	45°27' 2"
greatest brilliancy	1927 Aug 8	16:11	22 VI 31'57"	-4.5m
retrograde	1927 Aug 20	11:42	24 VI 59'46"	
evening set	1927 Sep 7	13:13	18 VI 58' 6"	
inferior conj	1927 Sep 10	17:51	17 VI 0'51"	8°43' 3"
morning rise	1927 Sep 13	22:19	15 VI 3'21"	
direct	1927 Oct 2	02:50	8 VI 51'24"	
greatest brilliancy	1927 Oct 16	12:24	12 VI 33'39"	-4.6m
morning max el	1927 Nov 21	11:45	11 LI 28'57"	46°42'23"
morning set	1928 May 25	23:20	24 TA 29'55"	
superior conj	1928 Jul 1	15:31	9 CN 30'42"	0°33'39"
evening rise	1928 Aug 6	11:00	23 LE 36'12"	
evening max el	1929 Feb 7	18:12	5 AR 17'47"	46°47'55"
greatest brilliancy	1929 Mar 16	00:04	4 TA 25' 9"	-4.6m
retrograde	1929 Mar 30	03:03	8 TA 2'37"	
evening set	1929 Apr 15	19:43	2 TA 37'58"	
inferior conj	1929 Apr 20	09:25	29 AR 48'24"	6°13'40"
morning rise	1929 Apr 25	19:08	26 AR 30' 8"	
direct	1929 May 11	15:01	21 AR 38'50"	
greatest brilliancy	1929 May 23	18:23	24 AR 16' 0"	-4.5m
morning max el	1929 Jun 29	09:45	21 TA 28'57"	45°44'39"
morning set	1929 Dec 26	22:52	24 SA 42'47"	
superior conj	1930 Feb 6	17:39	17 AQ 13'47"	1°15'48"
evening rise	1930 Mar 19	05:08	7 AR 48'14"	
evening max el	1930 Sep 13	11:50	6 SC 15' 7"	46°21'51"
greatest brilliancy	1930 Oct 22	10:24	5 SA 15'54"	-4.6m
retrograde	1930 Nov 2	03:50	7 SA 23'16"	
evening set	1930 Nov 16	23:23	3 SA 6'14"	

inferior conj	1930 Nov 22	18:16	29 SC 44' 2"	2°35'22"
morning rise	1930 Nov 29	00:08	26 SC 6' 9"	
direct	1930 Dec 13	06:23	22 SC 1'58"	
greatest brilliancy	1930 Dec 26	03:37	25 SC 7'15"	-4.7m
morning max el	1931 Feb 1	22:10	25 SA 17'24"	46°55'17"
morning set	1931 Aug 2	15:40	29 CN 23'39"	
superior conj	1931 Sep 8	04:11	14 VI 33' 2"	1°24'48"
evening rise	1931 Oct 15	20:13	1 SC 28'53"	
evening max el	1932 Apr 19	19:45	15 GE 7'40"	45°42'14"
greatest brilliancy	1932 May 24	01:40	11 CN 41'42"	-4.5m
retrograde	1932 Jun 7	17:35	15 CN 26'13"	
evening set	1932 Jun 22	20:07	11 CN 0'48"	
inferior conj	1932 Jun 29	04:39	7 CN 12'10"	3° 4'29"
morning rise	1932 Jul 5	00:27	3 CN 41'24"	
direct	1932 Jul 20	20:22	28 GE 54'48"	
greatest brilliancy	1932 Aug 3	15:46	2 CN 14'45"	-4.5m
morning max el	1932 Sep 7	22:35	29 CN 8'39"	45°58'20"
morning set	1933 Mar 13	19:34	12 PI 52'49"	
superior conj	1933 Apr 21	16:20	1 TA 5'56"	1° 0'18"
evening rise	1933 May 29	08:12	17 GE 29'13"	
evening max el	1933 Nov 25	15:04	20 CP 7'24"	47°16'58"
greatest brilliancy	1934 Jan 2	21:46	20 AQ 41'17"	-4.7m
retrograde	1934 Jan 15	11:45	23 AQ 38'34"	
evening set	1934 Jan 31	20:26	18 AQ 20' 6"	
inferior conj	1934 Feb 5	04:23	15 AQ 41'22"	7°46'55"
morning rise	1934 Feb 8	18:58	13 AQ 29'16"	
direct	1934 Feb 25	17:42	7 AQ 56'15"	
greatest brilliancy	1934 Mar 8	07:05	10 AQ 1'17"	-4.6m
morning max el	1934 Apr 16	08:33	9 PI 22'33"	46°17'29"
morning set	1934 Oct 11	01:29	7 LI 9' 8"	
superior conj	1934 Nov 19	00:19	25 SC 59' 8"	0°29'39"
evening rise	1934 Dec 30	04:30	17 CP 44'34"	
evening max el	1935 Jun 30	11:13	23 LE 9'22"	45°26'13"
greatest brilliancy	1935 Aug 6	04:12	20 VI 15'39"	-4.5m
retrograde	1935 Aug 18	01:41	22 VI 46' 9"	
evening set	1935 Sep 5	02:46	16 VI 45'38"	

inferior conj	1935 Sep 8	08:49	14 VI 46'25"	8°42' 8"
morning rise	1935 Sep 11	12:58	12 VI 49'21"	
direct	1935 Sep 29	17:46	6 VI 35'59"	
greatest brilliancy	1935 Oct 14	05:01	10 VI 19'22"	-4.6m
morning max el	1935 Nov 19	01:41	9 LI 7'24"	46°41'17"
morning set	1936 May 23	16:42	22 TA 23' 9"	
superior conj	1936 Jun 29	09:43	7 CN 26'42"	0°30'44"
evening rise	1936 Aug 4	05:23	21 LE 32' 7"	
evening max el	1937 Feb 5	08:15	2 AR 57'50"	46°50'14"
greatest brilliancy	1937 Mar 13	15:53	2 TA 11'32"	-4.6m
retrograde	1937 Mar 27	19:06	5 TA 50' 1"	
evening set	1937 Apr 13	14:23	0 TA 20'46"	
inferior conj	1937 Apr 18	01:13	27 AR 35'45"	6°27'56"
morning rise	1937 Apr 23	08:01	24 AR 21'50"	
direct	1937 May 9	05:56	19 AR 26'22"	
greatest brilliancy	1937 May 21	09:06	22 AR 3'28"	-4.5m
morning max el	1937 Jun 27	01:52	19 TA 19'29"	45°45' 1"
morning set	1937 Dec 24	08:52	22 SA 8'44"	
superior conj	1938 Feb 4	04:04	14 AQ 41'48"	1°13'51"
evening rise	1938 Mar 16	17:43	5 AR 24'41"	
evening max el	1938 Sep 11	01:53	3 SC 56' 3"	46°19'25"
greatest brilliancy	1938 Oct 19	22:01	2 SA 48'54"	-4.6m
retrograde	1938 Oct 30	16:22	4 SA 56'24"	
evening set	1938 Nov 14	13:52	0 SA 36'13"	
inferior conj	1938 Nov 20	06:30	27 SC 16'46"	2°58'24"
morning rise	1938 Nov 26	11:46	23 SC 39'51"	
direct	1938 Dec 10	19:52	19 SC 34' 4"	
greatest brilliancy	1938 Dec 23	18:06	22 SC 41'11"	-4.7m
morning max el	1939 Jan 30	12:43	22 SA 54'55"	46°55'51"
morning set	1939 Jul 31	09:31	27 CN 18' 7"	
superior conj	1939 Sep 5	21:14	12 VI 23'34"	1°24'36"
evening rise	1939 Oct 13	10:09	29 LI 8'26"	
evening max el	1940 Apr 17	12:21	12 GE 58'14"	45°44' 5"
greatest brilliancy	1940 May 21	18:40	9 CN 34'25"	-4.5m
retrograde	1940 Jun 5	10:05	13 CN 18'16"	
evening set	1940 Jun 20	12:03	8 CN 54' 7"	

inferior conj	1940 Jun 26	21:13	5 CN	4'11"	2°46' 2"
morning rise	1940 Jul 2	18:51	1 CN	30'34"	
direct	1940 Jul 18	13:13	26 GE	47' 7"	
greatest brilliancy	1940 Aug 1	05:38	0 CN	3'42"	-4.5m
morning max el	1940 Sep 5	13:53	26 CN	56'29"	45°56'55"
morning set	1941 Mar 11	07:57	10 PI	27'28"	
superior conj	1941 Apr 19	07:34	28 AR	50'59"	1° 2'44"
evening rise	1941 May 27	01:50	15 GE	22'42"	
evening max el	1941 Nov 23	04:55	17 CP	42'23"	47°16' 5"
greatest brilliancy	1941 Dec 31	13:55	18 AQ	17'14"	-4.7m
retrograde	1942 Jan 13	00:41	21 AQ	11'14"	
evening set	1942 Jan 29	05:46	15 AQ	59'33"	
inferior conj	1942 Feb 2	17:32	13 AQ	15'23"	7°35'30"
morning rise	1942 Feb 6	10:59	10 AQ	58'57"	
direct	1942 Feb 23	06:02	5 AQ	31' 9"	
greatest brilliancy	1942 Mar 5	20:36	7 AQ	36'53"	-4.6m
morning max el	1942 Apr 13	20:54	6 PI	58'17"	46°19' 5"
morning set	1942 Oct 8	16:31	4 LI	51'49"	
superior conj	1942 Nov 16	12:09	23 SC	30'36"	0°33'12"
evening rise	1942 Dec 27	14:31	15 CP	9'53"	
evening max el	1943 Jun 28	01:24	20 LE	54' 9"	45°25'41"
greatest brilliancy	1943 Aug 3	15:26	17 VI	58'36"	-4.5m
retrograde	1943 Aug 15	16:37	20 VI	33' 9"	
evening set	1943 Sep 2	16:22	14 VI	33'56"	
inferior conj	1943 Sep 6	00:05	12 VI	32'22"	8°40'19"
morning rise	1943 Sep 9	04:15	10 VI	35'26"	
direct	1943 Sep 27	09:15	4 VI	21' 4"	
greatest brilliancy	1943 Oct 11	22:20	8 VI	6'20"	-4.6m
morning max el	1943 Nov 16	16:36	6 LI	47'53"	46°39'52"
morning set	1944 May 21	09:54	20 TA	14'44"	
superior conj	1944 Jun 27	03:57	5 CN	21'46"	0°27'47"
evening rise	1944 Aug 2	00:07	19 LE	28' 8"	
evening max el	1945 Feb 2	23:14	0 AR	38'23"	46°52'25"
greatest brilliancy	1945 Mar 11	07:39	29 AR	55'39"	-4.6m
retrograde	1945 Mar 25	11:24	3 TA	34'51"	
evening set	1945 Apr 11	08:50	28 AR	1' 4"	

inferior conj	1945 Apr 15	16:44	25 AR 20'32"	6°41'48"
morning rise	1945 Apr 20	20:28	22 AR 11'25"	
direct	1945 May 6	21:03	17 AR 11'36"	
greatest brilliancy	1945 May 18	22:53	19 AR 48' 2"	-4.5m
morning max el	1945 Jun 24	18:16	17 TA 9'29"	45°45'30"
morning set	1945 Dec 21	19:25	19 SA 35'39"	
superior conj	1946 Feb 1	14:19	12 AQ 8'10"	1°11'44"
evening rise	1946 Mar 14	05:47	2 AR 58'11"	
evening max el	1946 Sep 8	16:25	1 SC 37'36"	46°17' 1"
greatest brilliancy	1946 Oct 17	10:39	0 SA 23'11"	-4.6m
retrograde	1946 Oct 28	04:52	2 SA 29'49"	
evening set	1946 Nov 12	04:47	28 SC 6'42"	
inferior conj	1946 Nov 17	19:02	24 SC 50' 4"	3°20'49"
morning rise	1946 Nov 23	23:22	21 SC 14'15"	
direct	1946 Dec 8	09:32	17 SC 6'56"	
greatest brilliancy	1946 Dec 21	08:11	20 SC 14'46"	-4.7m
morning max el	1947 Jan 28	02:23	20 SA 29'52"	46°56'11"
morning set	1947 Jul 29	03:13	25 CN 11'30"	
superior conj	1947 Sep 3	14:23	10 VI 14' 1"	1°24'18"
evening rise	1947 Oct 11	00:25	26 LI 48'34"	
evening max el	1948 Apr 15	04:01	10 GE 45'37"	45°45'42"
greatest brilliancy	1948 May 19	11:45	7 CN 25'56"	-4.5m
retrograde	1948 Jun 3	02:01	11 CN 9' 1"	
evening set	1948 Jun 18	03:55	6 CN 45'53"	
inferior conj	1948 Jun 24	13:37	2 CN 55' 4"	2°27'13"
morning rise	1948 Jun 30	12:58	29 GE 18'41"	
direct	1948 Jul 16	05:25	24 GE 38'14"	
greatest brilliancy	1948 Jul 29	19:58	27 GE 52'13"	-4.5m
morning max el	1948 Sep 3	04:10	24 CN 41'24"	45°55'44"
morning set	1949 Mar 8	20:26	8 PI 2'31"	
superior conj	1949 Apr 16	22:48	26 AR 36'10"	1° 5' 3"
evening rise	1949 May 24	19:12	13 GE 15'17"	
evening max el	1949 Nov 20	17:48	15 CP 15'18"	47°15'11"
greatest brilliancy	1949 Dec 29	05:43	15 AQ 52'57"	-4.7m
retrograde	1950 Jan 10	13:35	18 AQ 44'25"	
evening set	1950 Jan 26	15:06	13 AQ 39' 3"	

inferior conj	1950 Jan 31	06:40	10 AQ 49'48"	7°23' 7"
morning rise	1950 Feb 4	03:05	8 AQ 29' 5"	
direct	1950 Feb 20	18:04	3 AQ 6'14"	
greatest brilliancy	1950 Mar 3	10:51	5 AQ 13'47"	-4.6m
morning max el	1950 Apr 11	09:29	4 PI 35' 6"	46°20'47"
morning set	1950 Oct 6	07:30	2 LI 34'50"	
superior conj	1950 Nov 13	23:59	21 SC 2'44"	0°36'40"
evening rise	1950 Dec 25	00:41	12 CP 36'21"	
evening max el	1951 Jun 25	16:08	18 LE 40'58"	45°25' 2"
greatest brilliancy	1951 Aug 1	02:07	15 VI 41'14"	-4.5m
retrograde	1951 Aug 13	07:51	18 VI 20' 5"	
evening set	1951 Aug 31	05:22	12 VI 22'52"	
inferior conj	1951 Sep 3	15:08	10 VI 18'16"	8°37'46"
morning rise	1951 Sep 6	19:46	8 VI 20'48"	
direct	1951 Sep 25	00:58	2 VI 6'14"	
greatest brilliancy	1951 Oct 9	15:12	5 VI 53' 8"	-4.6m
morning max el	1951 Nov 14	08:07	4 LI 30'42"	46°38'33"
morning set	1952 May 19	03:17	18 TA 7'52"	
superior conj	1952 Jun 24	22:17	3 CN 18'11"	0°24'47"
evening rise	1952 Jul 30	18:58	17 LE 25'26"	
evening max el	1953 Jan 31	14:55	28 PI 21'49"	46°54'35"
greatest brilliancy	1953 Mar 9	00:17	27 AR 42' 1"	-4.6m
retrograde	1953 Mar 23	03:53	1 TA 20'36"	
evening set	1953 Apr 9	03:19	25 AR 42'29"	
inferior conj	1953 Apr 13	08:15	23 AR 6'18"	6°55' 9"
morning rise	1953 Apr 18	08:48	20 AR 2' 4"	
direct	1953 May 4	12:33	14 AR 58' 3"	
greatest brilliancy	1953 May 16	11:41	17 AR 32'33"	-4.5m
morning max el	1953 Jun 22	10:39	15 TA 0'37"	45°46' 1"
morning set	1953 Dec 19	05:45	17 SA 2'45"	
superior conj	1954 Jan 30	00:17	9 AQ 34'37"	1° 9'27"
evening rise	1954 Mar 11	17:43	0 AR 32'14"	
evening max el	1954 Sep 6	06:12	29 LI 18'23"	46°14'22"
greatest brilliancy	1954 Oct 14	23:53	27 SC 58'53"	-4.6m
retrograde	1954 Oct 25	16:36	0 SA 3'39"	
evening set	1954 Nov 9	19:42	25 SC 37'24"	

inferior conj	1954 Nov 15	07:26	22 SC 23'51"	3°42'57"	
morning rise	1954 Nov 21	10:33	18 SC 49'11"		
direct	1954 Dec 5	22:39	14 SC 40' 2"		
greatest brilliancy	1954 Dec 18	22:43	17 SC 49' 0"	-4.7m	
morning max el	1955 Jan 25	15:06	18 SA 2'37"	46°56'36"	
morning set	1955 Jul 26	21:11	23 CN 6'39"		
superior conj	1955 Sep 1	07:57	8 VI 6'46"	1°23'52"	
evening rise	1955 Oct 8	15:05	24 LI 31' 0"		
evening max el	1956 Apr 12	18:45	8 GE 31'25"	45°47'35"	
greatest brilliancy	1956 May 17	04:02	5 CN 17'21"	-4.5m	
retrograde	1956 May 31	18:04	9 CN 1' 6"		
evening set	1956 Jun 15	20:04	4 CN 38'21"		

inferior conj	1956 Jun 22	06:09	0 CN 47' 5"	2° 8' 9"	
morning rise	1956 Jun 28	07:05	27 GE 8'10"		
direct	1956 Jul 13	21:20	22 GE 30'16"		
greatest brilliancy	1956 Jul 27	11:28	25 GE 43' 5"	-4.5m	
morning max el	1956 Aug 31	18:43	22 CN 27'48"	45°54'44"	
morning set	1957 Mar 6	08:16	5 PI 35'36"		
superior conj	1957 Apr 14	13:39	24 AR 20'18"	1° 7'18"	
evening rise	1957 May 22	12:22	11 GE 7'37"		
evening max el	1957 Nov 18	06:36	12 CP 48'44"	47°14'14"	
greatest brilliancy	1957 Dec 26	20:24	13 AQ 27'35"	-4.7m	
retrograde	1958 Jan 8	02:47	16 AQ 17'59"		
evening set	1958 Jan 24	00:21	11 AQ 18'27"		

inferior conj	1958 Jan 28	19:47	8 AQ 24'11"	7° 9'41"	
morning rise	1958 Feb 1	19:24	5 AQ 59' 4"		
direct	1958 Feb 18	06:17	0 AQ 41' 2"		
greatest brilliancy	1958 Mar 1	01:18	2 AQ 50'47"	-4.6m	
morning max el	1958 Apr 8	23:02	2 PI 13'51"	46°22'26"	
morning set	1958 Oct 3	22:52	0 LI 19' 8"		
superior conj	1958 Nov 11	12:20	18 SC 36'29"	0°40' 2"	
evening rise	1958 Dec 22	11:19	10 CP 4'24"		
evening max el	1959 Jun 23	07:50	16 LE 29'55"	45°24'39"	
greatest brilliancy	1959 Jul 29	13:23	13 VI 24'44"	-4.5m	
retrograde	1959 Aug 10	23:16	16 VI 7'16"		
evening set	1959 Aug 28	18:23	10 VI 12'32"		

inferior conj	1959 Sep 1	06:23	8 VI 4'30"	8°34'29"
morning rise	1959 Sep 4	11:46	6 VI 5'54"	
direct	1959 Sep 22	17:15	29 LE 51'55"	
greatest brilliancy	1959 Oct 7	07:10	3 VI 38'55"	-4.6m
morning max el	1959 Nov 12	00:02	2 LI 14'26"	46°37' 9"
morning set	1960 May 16	20:33	15 TA 59'58"	
superior conj	1960 Jun 22	16:25	1 CN 13'15"	0°21'44"
evening rise	1960 Jul 28	13:39	15 LE 21'45"	
evening max el	1961 Jan 29	06:53	26 PI 5'17"	46°56'42"
greatest brilliancy	1961 Mar 6	17:52	25 AR 29'12"	-4.6m
retrograde	1961 Mar 20	20:13	29 AR 5'45"	
evening set	1961 Apr 6	21:54	23 AR 23'39"	

inferior conj	1961 Apr 10	23:51	20 AR 51'40"	7° 7'47"
morning rise	1961 Apr 15	21:03	17 AR 52'18"	
direct	1961 May 2	04:15	12 AR 44'15"	
greatest brilliancy	1961 May 13	23:50	15 AR 15'40"	-4.5m
morning max el	1961 Jun 20	02:27	12 TA 49'31"	45°46'26"
morning set	1961 Dec 16	16:10	14 SA 29'15"	
superior conj	1962 Jan 27	10:19	7 AQ 0'18"	1° 7' 0"
evening rise	1962 Mar 9	05:39	28 PI 5'21"	
evening max el	1962 Sep 3	19:14	26 LI 56'35"	46°11'51"
greatest brilliancy	1962 Oct 12	13:55	25 SC 35' 4"	-4.6m
retrograde	1962 Oct 23	04:14	27 SC 37'36"	
evening set	1962 Nov 7	10:56	23 SC 7'47"	

inferior conj	1962 Nov 12	20:07	19 SC 57'42"	4° 4'20"
morning rise	1962 Nov 18	21:44	16 SC 24'29"	
direct	1962 Dec 3	11:26	12 SC 12'56"	
greatest brilliancy	1962 Dec 16	14:10	15 SC 24' 3"	-4.7m
morning max el	1963 Jan 23	03:34	15 SA 33'46"	46°56'54"
morning set	1963 Jul 24	15:10	21 CN 0'54"	
superior conj	1963 Aug 30	01:30	5 VI 58'28"	1°23'19"
evening rise	1963 Oct 6	05:47	22 LI 12'33"	
evening max el	1964 Apr 10	09:11	6 GE 15'21"	45°49'38"
greatest brilliancy	1964 May 14	19:19	3 CN 6'28"	-4.5m
retrograde	1964 May 29	10:29	6 CN 52'25"	
evening set	1964 Jun 13	12:20	2 CN 29'34"	

inferior conj	1964 Jun 19	22:40	28 GE 38'15"	1°48'57"
morning rise	1964 Jun 26	01:06	24 GE 57'12"	
direct	1964 Jul 11	13:00	20 GE 21'23"	
greatest brilliancy	1964 Jul 25	03:36	23 GE 34' 4"	-4.5m
morning max el	1964 Aug 29	10:04	20 CN 15'21"	45°53'42"
morning set	1965 Mar 3	19:49	3 PI 6'54"	
superior conj	1965 Apr 12	04:21	22 AR 3' 4"	1° 9'26"
evening rise	1965 May 20	05:28	8 GE 58'55"	
evening max el	1965 Nov 15	20:12	10 CP 23'16"	47°13'13"
greatest brilliancy	1965 Dec 24	10:14	10 AQ 59'49"	-4.7m
retrograde	1966 Jan 5	16:21	13 AQ 49'56"	
evening set	1966 Jan 21	09:32	8 AQ 55'52"	

inferior conj	1966 Jan 26	08:38	5 AQ 56'51"	6°55'17"
morning rise	1966 Jan 30	11:31	3 AQ 27'26"	
direct	1966 Feb 15	18:41	28 CP 14'17"	
greatest brilliancy	1966 Feb 26	14:39	0 AQ 25'24"	-4.6m
morning max el	1966 Apr 6	13:18	29 AQ 53'38"	46°24' 2"
morning set	1966 Oct 1	14:24	28 VI 3'39"	
superior conj	1966 Nov 9	00:40	16 SC 9'39"	0°43'19"
evening rise	1966 Dec 19	21:33	7 CP 30'29"	
evening max el	1967 Jun 21	00:05	14 LE 19'54"	45°24'17"
greatest brilliancy	1967 Jul 27	01:49	11 VI 9'35"	-4.5m
retrograde	1967 Aug 8	14:29	13 VI 54'24"	
evening set	1967 Aug 26	07:12	8 VI 3' 2"	

inferior conj	1967 Aug 29	21:40	5 VI 50'59"	8°30'23"
morning rise	1967 Sep 2	04:02	3 VI 50'48"	
direct	1967 Sep 20	09:34	27 LE 38' 9"	
greatest brilliancy	1967 Oct 4	21:36	1 VI 23' 6"	-4.6m
morning max el	1967 Nov 9	15:17	29 VI 56'50"	46°35'34"
morning set	1968 May 14	13:30	13 TA 51' 8"	
superior conj	1968 Jun 20	10:22	29 GE 7'51"	0°18'39"
evening rise	1968 Jul 26	08:20	13 LE 18' 3"	
evening max el	1969 Jan 26	22:18	23 PI 47' 1"	46°58'31"
greatest brilliancy	1969 Mar 4	12:08	23 AR 16'24"	-4.6m
retrograde	1969 Mar 18	11:49	26 AR 49'42"	
evening set	1969 Apr 4	16:14	21 AR 3'52"	

inferior conj	1969 Apr 8	15:11	18 AR 36' 8"	7°19'50"
morning rise	1969 Apr 13	08:52	15 AR 41'39"	
direct	1969 Apr 29	19:20	10 AR 29'39"	
greatest brilliancy	1969 May 11	11:47	12 AR 57'57"	-4.5m
morning max el	1969 Jun 17	17:06	10 TA 35'38"	45°46'57"
morning set	1969 Dec 14	03:00	11 SA 57'53"	
superior conj	1970 Jan 24	20:27	4 AQ 27' 4"	1° 4'26"
evening rise	1970 Mar 6	17:15	25 PI 37'49"	
evening max el	1970 Sep 1	07:37	24 LI 33'59"	46° 9'25"
greatest brilliancy	1970 Oct 10	03:41	23 SC 11'53"	-4.6m
retrograde	1970 Oct 20	15:57	25 SC 12'53"	
evening set	1970 Nov 5	02:15	20 SC 39' 0"	
inferior conj	1970 Nov 10	08:49	17 SC 32'47"	4°25' 5"
morning rise	1970 Nov 16	08:45	14 SC 1'30"	
direct	1970 Dec 1	00:03	9 SC 46'50"	
greatest brilliancy	1970 Dec 14	06:19	13 SC 1'20"	-4.7m
morning max el	1971 Jan 20	16:24	13 SA 7' 3"	46°57'19"
morning set	1971 Jul 22	08:54	18 CN 55'19"	
superior conj	1971 Aug 27	18:54	3 VI 50'42"	1°22'38"
evening rise	1971 Oct 3	20:36	19 LI 55'32"	
evening max el	1972 Apr 8	00:08	4 GE 1'48"	45°51'37"
greatest brilliancy	1972 May 12	09:53	0 CN 55'40"	-4.5m
retrograde	1972 May 27	03:14	4 CN 44'38"	
evening set	1972 Jun 11	04:43	0 CN 21'18"	
inferior conj	1972 Jun 17	15:09	26 GE 30' 9"	1°29'34"
morning rise	1972 Jun 23	19:01	22 GE 47'18"	
direct	1972 Jul 9	04:55	18 GE 13'11"	
greatest brilliancy	1972 Jul 22	20:03	21 GE 26'26"	-4.5m
morning max el	1972 Aug 27	02:16	18 CN 6' 9"	45°52'41"
morning set	1973 Mar 1	07:37	0 PI 40'11"	
superior conj	1973 Apr 9	19:13	19 AR 47'38"	1°11'27"
evening rise	1973 May 17	22:41	6 GE 51'49"	
evening max el	1973 Nov 13	10:43	8 CP 1'15"	47°12' 4"
greatest brilliancy	1973 Dec 21	23:54	8 AQ 32'43"	-4.7m
retrograde	1974 Jan 3	06:07	11 AQ 22'25"	
evening set	1974 Jan 18	18:42	6 AQ 33'52"	

inferior conj	1974 Jan 23	21:20	3 AQ 30' 5"	6°40' 3"
morning rise	1974 Jan 28	03:28	0 AQ 56'23"	
direct	1974 Feb 13	07:28	25 CP 48'16"	
greatest brilliancy	1974 Feb 24	03:08	27 CP 59'49"	-4.6m
morning max el	1974 Apr 4	03:49	27 AQ 35'13"	46°25'46"
morning set	1974 Sep 29	05:57	25 VI 49'16"	
superior conj	1974 Nov 6	13:09	13 SC 44'21"	0°46'29"
evening rise	1974 Dec 17	07:49	4 CP 57'32"	
evening max el	1975 Jun 18	16:07	12 LE 10'22"	45°23'52"
greatest brilliancy	1975 Jul 24	15:12	8 VI 56'38"	-4.5m
retrograde	1975 Aug 6	05:21	11 VI 42'47"	
evening set	1975 Aug 23	19:58	5 VI 55'16"	
inferior conj	1975 Aug 27	13:11	3 VI 38'52"	8°25'34"
morning rise	1975 Aug 30	20:49	1 VI 36'29"	
direct	1975 Sep 18	01:46	25 LE 25'42"	
greatest brilliancy	1975 Oct 2	11:52	29 LE 7'52"	-4.6m
morning max el	1975 Nov 7	05:46	27 VI 37'55"	46°33'57"
morning set	1976 May 12	06:38	11 TA 43'16"	
superior conj	1976 Jun 18	04:36	27 GE 3'55"	0°15'34"
evening rise	1976 Jul 24	03:18	11 LE 15'50"	
evening max el	1977 Jan 24	12:43	21 PI 26' 3"	47° 0'17"
greatest brilliancy	1977 Mar 2	06:20	21 AR 3'14"	-4.6m
retrograde	1977 Mar 16	03:01	24 AR 33'28"	
evening set	1977 Apr 2	10:28	18 AR 43'57"	
inferior conj	1977 Apr 6	06:29	16 AR 20'29"	7°31'22"
morning rise	1977 Apr 10	20:32	13 AR 31' 3"	
direct	1977 Apr 27	09:49	8 AR 14'45"	
greatest brilliancy	1977 May 9	00:34	10 AR 40'53"	-4.5m
morning max el	1977 Jun 15	07:23	8 TA 20'44"	45°47'45"
morning set	1977 Dec 11	13:40	9 SA 25'28"	
superior conj	1978 Jan 22	06:15	1 AQ 52'23"	1° 1'42"
evening rise	1978 Mar 4	04:33	23 PI 8'57"	
evening max el	1978 Aug 29	19:54	22 LI 11'17"	46° 7' 2"
greatest brilliancy	1978 Oct 7	16:05	20 SC 47'19"	-4.6m
retrograde	1978 Oct 18	03:58	22 SC 48'20"	
evening set	1978 Nov 2	17:43	18 SC 9'43"	

inferior conj	1978 Nov 7	21:34	15 SC 7'32"	4°45'13"
morning rise	1978 Nov 13	19:39	11 SC 38'44"	
direct	1978 Nov 28	13:09	7 SC 20' 9"	
greatest brilliancy	1978 Dec 11	23:07	10 SC 38'52"	-4.7m
morning max el	1979 Jan 18	06:20	10 SA 42' 5"	46°57'34"
morning set	1979 Jul 20	02:50	16 CN 49'32"	
superior conj	1979 Aug 25	12:38	1 VI 43'21"	1°21'51"
evening rise	1979 Oct 1	11:57	17 LI 39'40"	
evening max el	1980 Apr 5	15:45	1 GE 48'31"	45°53'47"
greatest brilliancy	1980 May 10	00:50	28 GE 43'58"	-4.5m
retrograde	1980 May 24	20:10	2 CN 35' 9"	
evening set	1980 Jun 8	21:11	28 GE 11'17"	
inferior conj	1980 Jun 15	07:27	24 GE 20'17"	1° 9'54"
morning rise	1980 Jun 21	12:40	20 GE 35'55"	
direct	1980 Jul 6	21:15	16 GE 3'21"	
greatest brilliancy	1980 Jul 20	11:48	19 GE 16'34"	-4.5m
morning max el	1980 Aug 24	19:05	15 CN 57'26"	45°51'50"
morning set	1981 Feb 26	18:52	28 AQ 10'12"	
superior conj	1981 Apr 7	09:22	17 AR 28'20"	1°13'23"
evening rise	1981 May 15	15:18	4 GE 41'28"	
evening max el	1981 Nov 11	01:55	5 CP 40'20"	47°10'52"
greatest brilliancy	1981 Dec 19	13:49	6 AQ 5'29"	-4.7m
retrograde	1981 Dec 31	19:45	8 AQ 54' 5"	
evening set	1982 Jan 16	04:10	4 AQ 11' 5"	
inferior conj	1982 Jan 21	10:06	1 AQ 2'33"	6°23'58"
morning rise	1982 Jan 25	19:34	28 CP 24'20"	
direct	1982 Feb 10	20:38	23 CP 21'39"	
greatest brilliancy	1982 Feb 21	15:31	25 CP 32'56"	-4.6m
morning max el	1982 Apr 1	17:50	25 AQ 14' 3"	46°27'10"
morning set	1982 Sep 26	21:31	23 VI 33'46"	
superior conj	1982 Nov 4	02:02	11 SC 19'20"	0°49'33"
evening rise	1982 Dec 14	18:29	2 CP 24'56"	
evening max el	1983 Jun 16	07:15	9 LE 57' 8"	45°23'33"
greatest brilliancy	1983 Jul 22	04:46	6 VI 42'21"	-4.5m
retrograde	1983 Aug 3	19:44	9 VI 29'46"	
evening set	1983 Aug 21	08:28	3 VI 46'18"	

inferior conj	1983 Aug 25	04:35	1 VI 25'26"	8°20' 3"	
morning rise	1983 Aug 28	13:46	29 LE 20'26"		
direct	1983 Sep 15	17:22	23 LE 11'49"		
greatest brilliancy	1983 Sep 30	02:41	26 LE 52' 6"	-4.6m	
morning max el	1983 Nov 4	19:22	25 VI 15'47"	46°32'29"	
morning set	1984 May 9	23:33	9 TA 33'55"		
superior conj	1984 Jun 15	22:32	24 GE 58'12"	0°12'25"	
evening rise	1984 Jul 21	21:56	9 LE 11'46"		
evening max el	1985 Jan 22	02:29	19 PI 3'11"	47° 2'12"	
greatest brilliancy	1985 Feb 27	23:44	18 AR 49' 5"	-4.6m	
retrograde	1985 Mar 13	18:17	22 AR 17'46"		
evening set	1985 Mar 31	04:43	16 AR 24'29"		

inferior conj	1985 Apr 3	22:00	14 AR 5'18"	7°42' 2"	
morning rise	1985 Apr 8	08:27	11 AR 20'58"		
direct	1985 Apr 25	00:09	6 AR 0' 6"		
greatest brilliancy	1985 May 6	14:30	8 AR 25'20"	-4.5m	
morning max el	1985 Jun 12	21:56	6 TA 6'10"	45°48'24"	
morning set	1985 Dec 9	00:23	6 SA 53' 2"		
superior conj	1986 Jan 19	16:05	29 CP 17'32"	0°58'50"	
evening rise	1986 Mar 1	16:02	20 PI 40'36"		
evening max el	1986 Aug 27	08:52	19 LI 50'15"	46° 4'43"	
greatest brilliancy	1986 Oct 5	03:33	18 SC 21'48"	-4.6m	
retrograde	1986 Oct 15	16:33	20 SC 23'49"		
evening set	1986 Oct 31	09:15	15 SC 40'20"		

inferior conj	1986 Nov 5	10:17	12 SC 42'11"	5° 4'46"	
morning rise	1986 Nov 11	06:19	9 SC 16'25"		
direct	1986 Nov 26	02:46	4 SC 53'38"		
greatest brilliancy	1986 Dec 9	15:23	8 SC 16' 2"	-4.7m	
morning max el	1987 Jan 15	20:58	8 SA 19'13"	46°57'45"	
morning set	1987 Jul 17	20:59	14 CN 45' 5"		
superior conj	1987 Aug 23	06:25	29 LE 36'30"	1°20'57"	
evening rise	1987 Sep 29	03:13	15 LI 23'47"		
evening max el	1988 Apr 3	08:18	29 TA 38'22"	45°56' 4"	
greatest brilliancy	1988 May 7	17:17	26 GE 35'35"	-4.5m	
retrograde	1988 May 22	13:26	0 CN 27'14"		
evening set	1988 Jun 6	14:07	26 GE 2'58"		

inferior conj	1988 Jun 13	00:00	22 GE 12'10"	0°50'15"	
morning rise	1988 Jun 19	06:23	18 GE 26'26"		
direct	1988 Jul 4	14:09	13 GE 55'32"		
greatest brilliancy	1988 Jul 18	02:30	17 GE 7' 4"	-4.5m	
morning max el	1988 Aug 22	11:46	13 CN 49'43"	45°50'44"	
morning set	1989 Feb 24	05:58	25 AQ 40'45"		
superior conj	1989 Apr 4	23:29	15 AR 9'50"	1°15'12"	
evening rise	1989 May 13	08:02	2 GE 32'25"		
evening max el	1989 Nov 8	16:49	3 CP 19'13"	47° 9'19"	
greatest brilliancy	1989 Dec 17	04:43	3 AQ 39'34"	-4.7m	
retrograde	1989 Dec 29	08:50	6 AQ 25'30"		
evening set	1990 Jan 13	13:39	1 AQ 48'11"		
inferior conj	1990 Jan 18	22:42	28 CP 35'10"	6° 6'56"	
morning rise	1990 Jan 23	11:24	25 CP 52'18"		
direct	1990 Feb 8	09:16	20 CP 55'16"		
greatest brilliancy	1990 Feb 19	04:07	23 CP 6'30"	-4.6m	
morning max el	1990 Mar 30	06:41	22 AQ 50'46"	46°28'40"	
morning set	1990 Sep 24	13:32	21 VI 21' 1"		
superior conj	1990 Nov 1	15:15	8 SC 56'30"	0°52'29"	
evening rise	1990 Dec 12	04:57	29 SA 52'35"		
evening max el	1991 Jun 13	21:50	7 LE 43'55"	45°23'25"	
greatest brilliancy	1991 Jul 19	18:11	4 VI 29'46"	-4.5m	
retrograde	1991 Aug 1	10:35	7 VI 19'26"		
evening set	1991 Aug 18	21:05	1 VI 40' 0"		
inferior conj	1991 Aug 22	20:21	29 LE 14'34"	8°13'43"	
morning rise	1991 Aug 26	07:17	27 LE 6'49"		
direct	1991 Sep 13	08:56	21 LE 0'25"		
greatest brilliancy	1991 Sep 27	18:39	24 LE 40' 7"	-4.6m	
morning max el	1991 Nov 2	09:08	22 VI 55'46"	46°30'56"	
morning set	1992 May 7	16:10	7 TA 24'28"		
superior conj	1992 Jun 13	16:30	22 GE 53'33"	0° 9'16"	
evening rise	1992 Jul 19	16:53	7 LE 9'43"		
evening max el	1993 Jan 19	16:06	16 PI 40'12"	47° 3'49"	
greatest brilliancy	1993 Feb 25	16:07	16 AR 33' 6"	-4.6m	
retrograde	1993 Mar 11	09:28	20 AR 1'23"		
evening set	1993 Mar 28	22:32	14 AR 4'10"		

inferior conj	1993 Apr 1	13:12	11 AR 49'15"	7°51'58"
morning rise	1993 Apr 5	20:02	9 AR 10'23"	
direct	1993 Apr 22	14:13	3 AR 44'27"	
greatest brilliancy	1993 May 4	04:46	6 AR 9'51"	-4.5m
morning max el	1993 Jun 10	12:54	3 TA 52'53"	45°49'19"
morning set	1993 Dec 6	11:47	4 SA 23'44"	
superior conj	1994 Jan 17	02:04	26 CP 43'52"	0°55'50"
evening rise	1994 Feb 27	03:22	18 PI 12'11"	
evening max el	1994 Aug 24	22:52	17 LI 32'30"	46° 2'32"
greatest brilliancy	1994 Oct 2	14:50	15 SC 57'28"	-4.6m
retrograde	1994 Oct 13	05:41	18 SC 0'39"	
evening set	1994 Oct 29	01:08	13 SC 12'27"	
inferior conj	1994 Nov 2	23:12	10 SC 18'11"	5°23'31"
morning rise	1994 Nov 8	17:01	6 SC 55'42"	
direct	1994 Nov 23	16:57	2 SC 28'47"	
greatest brilliancy	1994 Dec 7	06:47	5 SC 53'21"	-4.7m
morning max el	1995 Jan 13	11:55	5 SA 58' 5"	46°57'49"
morning set	1995 Jul 15	14:55	12 CN 39'56"	
superior conj	1995 Aug 21	00:04	27 LE 29'25"	1°19'55"
evening rise	1995 Sep 26	18:35	13 LI 8'21"	
evening max el	1996 Apr 1	00:47	27 TA 27'41"	45°58' 3"
greatest brilliancy	1996 May 5	10:35	24 GE 27'24"	-4.5m
retrograde	1996 May 20	06:08	28 GE 17'53"	
evening set	1996 Jun 4	07:00	23 GE 53'18"	
inferior conj	1996 Jun 10	16:19	20 GE 2'46"	0°30'24"
morning rise	1996 Jun 16	23:40	16 GE 15'39"	
direct	1996 Jul 2	06:51	11 GE 46'33"	
greatest brilliancy	1996 Jul 15	16:24	14 GE 55'26"	-4.5m
morning max el	1996 Aug 20	03:28	11 CN 38'57"	45°49'48"
morning set	1997 Feb 21	17:16	23 AQ 11'32"	
superior conj	1997 Apr 2	13:45	12 AR 51'24"	1°16'52"
evening rise	1997 May 11	00:42	0 GE 22'38"	
evening max el	1997 Nov 6	06:37	0 CP 54'45"	47° 7'46"
greatest brilliancy	1997 Dec 14	20:18	1 AQ 13'50"	-4.7m
retrograde	1997 Dec 26	21:21	3 AQ 56'17"	
evening set	1998 Jan 10	23:14	29 CP 24'24"	

inferior conj	1998 Jan 16	11:18	26 CP	7'13"	5°49'11"
morning rise	1998 Jan 21	03:09	23 CP	19'45"	
direct	1998 Feb 5	21:26	18 CP	28' 3"	
greatest brilliancy	1998 Feb 16	17:48	20 CP	40'22"	-4.6m
morning max el	1998 Mar 27	18:39	20 AQ	24'27"	46°30'18"
morning set	1998 Sep 22	05:18	19 VI	6'29"	
superior conj	1998 Oct 30	04:22	6 SC	32'32"	0°55'20"
evening rise	1998 Dec 9	15:26	27 SA	19'34"	
evening max el	1999 Jun 11	11:54	5 LE	28'36"	45°23'18"
greatest brilliancy	1999 Jul 17	06:15	2 VI	14'22"	-4.5m
retrograde	1999 Jul 30	01:42	5 VI	7'48"	
evening set	1999 Aug 16	09:25	29 LE	32'13"	
inferior conj	1999 Aug 20	11:58	27 LE	2' 7"	8° 6'36"
morning rise	1999 Aug 24	00:52	24 LE	51'29"	
direct	1999 Sep 11	00:23	18 LE	47'17"	
greatest brilliancy	1999 Sep 25	11:43	22 LE	28' 8"	-4.6m
morning max el	1999 Oct 30	23:35	20 VI	36'12"	46°29'30"
morning set	2000 May 5	08:46	5 TA	13'45"	
superior conj	2000 Jun 11	10:31	20 GE	48' 3"	0° 6' 7"
evening rise	2000 Jul 17	11:57	5 LE	7' 5"	
evening max el	2001 Jan 17	06:09	14 PI	17'16"	47° 5'36"
greatest brilliancy	2001 Feb 23	07:43	14 AR	14'59"	-4.6m
retrograde	2001 Mar 9	01:07	17 AR	43'46"	
evening set	2001 Mar 26	16:14	11 AR	42'25"	
inferior conj	2001 Mar 30	04:17	9 AR	31'42"	8° 1'17"
morning rise	2001 Apr 3	07:32	6 AR	58'29"	
direct	2001 Apr 20	04:34	1 AR	27'23"	
greatest brilliancy	2001 May 1	18:30	3 AR	52'36"	-4.5m
morning max el	2001 Jun 8	04:41	1 TA	40'35"	45°50'18"
morning set	2001 Dec 3	22:56	1 SA	52'22"	
superior conj	2002 Jan 14	11:32	24 CP	7'22"	0°52'42"
evening rise	2002 Feb 24	14:23	15 PI	41'48"	
evening max el	2002 Aug 22	13:18	15 LI	15'19"	46° 0'16"
greatest brilliancy	2002 Sep 30	02:22	13 SC	32'58"	-4.6m
retrograde	2002 Oct 10	18:35	15 SC	36'35"	
evening set	2002 Oct 26	17:05	10 SC	43'51"	

inferior conj	2002 Oct 31	12:06	7 SC 53'26"	5°41'32"		
morning rise	2002 Nov 6	03:22	4 SC 34'18"			
direct	2002 Nov 21	07:13	0 SC 3'13"			
greatest brilliancy	2002 Dec 4	21:21	3 SC 28'29"	-4.7m		
morning max el	2003 Jan 11	02:27	3 SA 34'33"	46°57'41"		
morning set	2003 Jul 13	09:02	10 CN 34'52"			
superior conj	2003 Aug 18	18:05	25 LE 23' 2"	1°18'47"		
evening rise	2003 Sep 24	10:22	10 LI 53'51"			
evening max el	2004 Mar 29	16:40	25 TA 14'45"	46° 0'16"		
greatest brilliancy	2004 May 3	04:32	22 GE 19'38"	-4.5m		
retrograde	2004 May 17	22:28	26 GE 8'18"			
evening set	2004 Jun 2	00:07	21 GE 43'16"			
inferior conj	2004 Jun 8	08:43	17 GE 53'20"	0°10'35"		
transit begin	2004 Jun 8	05:14	17 GE 58'50"			
transit end	2004 Jun 8	11:26	17 GE 49' 5"			
morning rise	2004 Jun 14	16:52	14 GE 4'49"			
direct	2004 Jun 29	23:15	9 GE 37'32"			
greatest brilliancy	2004 Jul 13	06:12	12 GE 43'26"	-4.5m		
morning max el	2004 Aug 17	18:31	9 CN 26'32"	45°48'58"		
morning set	2005 Feb 19	04:05	20 AQ 40'30"			
superior conj	2005 Mar 31	03:30	10 AR 31' 4"	1°18'27"		
evening rise	2005 May 8	16:49	28 TA 11' 2"			
evening max el	2005 Nov 3	19:34	28 SA 28'48"	47° 6'10"		
greatest brilliancy	2005 Dec 12	11:44	28 CP 48'35"	-4.7m		
retrograde	2005 Dec 24	09:36	1 AQ 28' 1"			
evening set	2006 Jan 8	09:07	27 CP 0'47"			
inferior conj	2006 Jan 13	23:59	23 CP 40' 6"	5°30'44"		
morning rise	2006 Jan 18	19:00	20 CP 48' 3"			
direct	2006 Feb 3	09:19	16 CP 1'19"			
greatest brilliancy	2006 Feb 14	08:27	18 CP 15'53"	-4.6m		
morning max el	2006 Mar 25	06:45	17 AQ 58'28"	46°31'49"		
morning set	2006 Sep 19	21:10	16 VI 53' 1"			
superior conj	2006 Oct 27	17:50	4 SC 10'16"	0°58' 3"		
evening rise	2006 Dec 7	02:24	24 SA 48'50"			
evening max el	2007 Jun 9	02:45	3 LE 15'54"	45°23'27"		
greatest brilliancy	2007 Jul 14	17:41	29 LE 59'15"	-4.5m		
retrograde	2007 Jul 27	17:28	2 VI 57'23"			
evening set	2007 Aug 13	21:46	27 LE 25'45"			

inferior conj	2007 Aug 18	03:41	24 LE 50'52"	7°58'54"
morning rise	2007 Aug 21	18:51	22 LE 37' 1"	
direct	2007 Sep 8	16:14	16 LE 35'27"	
greatest brilliancy	2007 Sep 23	04:52	20 LE 17'45"	-4.6m
morning max el	2007 Oct 28	15:05	18 VI 20'38"	46°27'59"
morning set	2008 May 3	01:17	3 TA 3'50"	
superior conj	2008 Jun 9	04:20	18 GE 42'52"	0° 2'56"
evening rise	2008 Jul 15	06:49	3 LE 4'56"	
evening max el	2009 Jan 14	21:24	11 PI 58'34"	47° 7'21"
greatest brilliancy	2009 Feb 20	23:28	11 AR 58'26"	-4.6m
retrograde	2009 Mar 6	17:17	15 AR 27'27"	
evening set	2009 Mar 24	09:49	9 AR 22'25"	
inferior conj	2009 Mar 27	19:24	7 AR 15'32"	8° 9'51"
morning rise	2009 Mar 31	19:08	4 AR 47'52"	
direct	2009 Apr 17	19:24	29 PI 11'57"	
greatest brilliancy	2009 Apr 29	07:08	1 AR 35'42"	-4.5m
morning max el	2009 Jun 5	20:51	29 AR 30'33"	45°51' 7"
morning set	2009 Dec 1	10:19	29 SC 23' 7"	
superior conj	2010 Jan 11	21:06	21 CP 32'15"	0°49'27"
evening rise	2010 Feb 22	01:26	13 PI 12'28"	
evening max el	2010 Aug 20	03:48	12 LI 59'17"	45°57'59"
greatest brilliancy	2010 Sep 27	15:05	11 SC 11' 8"	-4.6m
retrograde	2010 Oct 8	07:05	13 SC 13'58"	
evening set	2010 Oct 24	09:14	8 SC 16'56"	
inferior conj	2010 Oct 29	01:10	5 SC 30'25"	5°58'48"
morning rise	2010 Nov 3	13:41	2 SC 14'37"	
direct	2010 Nov 18	21:18	27 LI 39'26"	
greatest brilliancy	2010 Dec 2	11:36	1 SC 4'37"	-4.7m
morning max el	2011 Jan 8	16:02	1 SA 9'49"	46°57'24"
morning set	2011 Jul 11	03:13	8 CN 31' 5"	
superior conj	2011 Aug 16	12:08	23 LE 17'47"	1°17'33"
evening rise	2011 Sep 22	02:08	8 LI 40'10"	
evening max el	2012 Mar 27	07:44	23 TA 0'19"	46° 2'27"
greatest brilliancy	2012 Apr 30	22:07	20 GE 11'55"	-4.5m
retrograde	2012 May 15	14:33	23 GE 59'32"	
evening set	2012 May 30	17:21	19 GE 33'39"	

inferior conj	2012 Jun 6	01:09	15 GE 44'46"	0° 9'21"	
transit begin	2012 Jun 5	22:10	15 GE 49'29"		
transit end	2012 Jun 6	04:49	15 GE 38'59"		
morning rise	2012 Jun 12	09:53	11 GE 55' 1"		
direct	2012 Jun 27	15:07	7 GE 29'16"		
greatest brilliancy	2012 Jul 10	20:26	10 GE 32'46"	-4.5m	
morning max el	2012 Aug 15	09:07	7 CN 13'45"	45°48'10"	
morning set	2013 Feb 16	14:36	18 AQ 8'55"		
superior conj	2013 Mar 28	17:05	8 AR 10'36"	1°19'53"	
evening rise	2013 May 6	08:47	25 TA 59'11"		
evening max el	2013 Nov 1	07:59	26 SA 1'29"	47° 4'26"	
greatest brilliancy	2013 Dec 10	02:30	26 CP 21'40"	-4.7m	
retrograde	2013 Dec 21	21:53	28 CP 58'57"		
evening set	2014 Jan 5	18:51	24 CP 35'44"		
inferior conj	2014 Jan 11	12:25	21 CP 11'59"	5°11'17"	
morning rise	2014 Jan 16	10:35	18 CP 15'40"		
direct	2014 Jan 31	20:49	13 CP 33'23"		
greatest brilliancy	2014 Feb 11	23:13	15 CP 50'55"	-4.6m	
morning max el	2014 Mar 22	19:31	15 AQ 33'55"	46°33'26"	
morning set	2014 Sep 17	13:24	14 VI 40'36"		
superior conj	2014 Oct 25	07:31	1 SC 48'31"	1° 0'39"	
evening rise	2014 Dec 4	13:19	22 SA 17'36"		
evening max el	2015 Jun 6	18:29	1 LE 4'50"	45°23'40"	
greatest brilliancy	2015 Jul 12	05:23	27 LE 43'58"	-4.5m	
retrograde	2015 Jul 25	09:29	0 VI 46'23"		
evening set	2015 Aug 11	10:09	25 LE 18'48"		
inferior conj	2015 Aug 15	19:22	22 LE 39' 6"	7°50'26"	
morning rise	2015 Aug 19	12:55	20 LE 21'50"		
direct	2015 Sep 6	08:29	14 LE 23'18"		
greatest brilliancy	2015 Sep 20	20:59	18 LE 5'49"	-4.5m	
morning max el	2015 Oct 26	07:11	16 VI 6'25"	46°26'29"	
morning set	2016 Apr 30	17:26	0 TA 51'51"		
superior conj	2016 Jun 6	21:48	16 GE 35'42"	0° 0'21"	
evening rise	2016 Jul 13	01:40	1 LE 1'47"		
evening max el	2017 Jan 12	13:18	9 PI 40'27"	47° 8'46"	
greatest brilliancy	2017 Feb 18	15:51	9 AR 41' 1"	-4.6m	
retrograde	2017 Mar 4	09:09	13 AR 8'50"		
evening set	2017 Mar 22	03:00	7 AR 0'42"		

inferior conj	2017 Mar 25	10:17	4 AR 57'13"	8°17'38"
morning rise	2017 Mar 29	06:32	2 AR 34'54"	
direct	2017 Apr 15	10:18	26 PI 54'34"	
greatest brilliancy	2017 Apr 26	18:44	29 PI 15'42"	-4.5m
morning max el	2017 Jun 3	12:30	27 AR 17'53"	45°51'59"
morning set	2017 Nov 28	22:13	26 SC 54'32"	
superior conj	2018 Jan 9	07:02	18 CP 57'28"	0°46' 6"
evening rise	2018 Feb 19	12:30	10 PI 42' 4"	
evening max el	2018 Aug 17	17:31	10 LI 40' 9"	45°55'40"
greatest brilliancy	2018 Sep 25	04:25	8 SC 48'50"	-4.6m
retrograde	2018 Oct 5	19:04	10 SC 50'22"	
evening set	2018 Oct 22	01:22	5 SC 48'55"	
inferior conj	2018 Oct 26	14:16	3 SC 6'29"	6°15'22"
morning rise	2018 Oct 31	23:44	29 LI 54'23"	
direct	2018 Nov 16	10:51	25 LI 14'32"	
greatest brilliancy	2018 Nov 30	02:31	28 LI 40'30"	-4.7m
morning max el	2019 Jan 6	04:53	28 SC 42'12"	46°57'22"
morning set	2019 Jul 8	21:14	6 CN 25'38"	
superior conj	2019 Aug 14	06:07	21 LE 11'22"	1°16'12"
evening rise	2019 Sep 19	18:02	6 LI 25'58"	
evening max el	2020 Mar 24	22:13	20 TA 43'48"	46° 4'39"
greatest brilliancy	2020 Apr 28	14:35	18 GE 2' 6"	-4.5m
retrograde	2020 May 13	06:45	21 GE 50'25"	
evening set	2020 May 28	10:50	17 GE 23' 5"	

Appendix 2
Sun-Mars Positions
1921-2020 UT

Date	Sun	Mars
01/01/1921	10°Cp03'	26°Aq39'
01/02/1921	11°Aq36'	20°Pi38'
01/03/1921	09°Pi52'	11°Ar57'
01/04/1921	10°Ar43'	04°Ta55'
01/05/1921	10°Ta04'	26°Ta26'
01/06/1921	09°Ge57'	17°Ge56'
01/07/1921	08°Cn36'	08°Cn06'
01/08/1921	08°Le11'	28°Cn24'
01/09/1921	08°Vi00'	18°Le18'
01/10/1921	07°Li16'	07°Vi14'
01/11/1921	08°Sc02'	26°Vi30'
01/12/1921	08°Sg16'	14°Li49'
01/01/1922	09°Cp48'	03°Sc13'
01/02/1922	11°Aq22'	20°Sc42'
01/03/1922	09°Pi38'	05°Sg06'
01/04/1922	10°Ar29'	18°Sg07'
01/05/1922	09°Ta50'	24°Sg58'
01/06/1922	09°Ge43'	21°Sg49' R
01/07/1922	08°Cn22'	12°Sg53'
01/08/1922	07°Le57'	12°Sg37' D
01/09/1922	07°Vi46'	23°Sg32'
01/10/1922	07°Li02'	10°Cp16'
01/11/1922	07°Sc47'	00°Aq51'
01/12/1922	08°Sg01'	22°Aq18'
01/01/1923	09°Cp33'	15°Pi02'
01/02/1923	11°Aq07'	07°Ar42'
01/03/1923	09°Pi23'	27°Ar51'
01/04/1923	10°Ar15'	19°Ta36'
01/05/1923	09°Ta36'	10°Ge06'
01/06/1923	09°Ge29'	00°Cn44'
01/07/1923	08°Cn08'	20°Cn18'
01/08/1923	07°Le43'	10°Le13'
01/09/1923	07°Vi32'	29°Le58'
01/10/1923	06°Li47'	19°Vi03'
01/11/1923	07°Sc32'	08°Li49'
01/12/1923	07°Sg46'	28°Li01'
01/01/1924	09°Cp18'	17°Sc55'
01/02/1924	10°Aq52'	07°Sg50'
01/03/1924	10°Pi09'	26°Sg20'
01/04/1924	11°Ar00'	15°Cp45'
01/05/1924	10°Ta20'	03°Aq41'
01/06/1924	10°Ge13'	20°Aq14'
01/07/1924	08°Cn52'	01°Pi55'
01/08/1924	08°Le27'	04°Pi56' R
01/09/1924	08°Vi16'	28°Aq07'
01/10/1924	07°Li32'	25°Aq49' D
01/11/1924	08°Sc18'	04°Pi30'
01/12/1924	08°Sg32'	19°Pi19'

Date	Sun	Mars
01/01/1925	10°Cp05'	07°Ar37'
01/02/1925	11°Aq38'	27°Ar10'
01/03/1925	09°Pi54'	15°Ta10'
01/04/1925	10°Ar45'	05°Ge07'
01/05/1925	10°Ta06'	24°Ge19'
01/06/1925	09°Ge59'	13°Cn59'
01/07/1925	08°Cn38'	02°Le55'
01/08/1925	08°Le13'	22°Le29'
01/09/1925	08°Vi02'	12°Vi09'
01/10/1925	07°Li17'	01°Li26'
01/11/1925	08°Sc03'	21°Li40'
01/12/1925	08°Sg17'	11°Sc39'
01/01/1926	09°Cp49'	02°Sg44'
01/02/1926	11°Aq23'	24°Sg16'
01/03/1926	09°Pi39'	14°Cp05'
01/04/1926	10°Ar31'	06°Aq21'
01/05/1926	09°Ta52'	28°Aq03'
01/06/1926	09°Ge45'	20°Pi13'
01/07/1926	08°Cn24'	10°Ar46'
01/08/1926	07°Le59'	29°Ar47'
01/09/1926	07°Vi48'	14°Ta11'
01/10/1926	07°Li03'	19°Ta26' R
01/11/1926	07°Sc49'	12°Ta24'
01/12/1926	08°Sg02'	04°Ta47'
01/01/1927	09°Cp34'	08°Ta11' D
01/02/1927	11°Aq08'	19°Ta47'
01/03/1927	09°Pi24'	03°Ge38'
01/04/1927	10°Ar16'	20°Ge44'
01/05/1927	09°Ta38'	08°Cn10'
01/06/1927	09°Ge31'	26°Cn41'
01/07/1927	08°Cn10'	14°Le57'
01/08/1927	07°Le45'	04°Vi10'
01/09/1927	07°Vi34'	23°Vi49'
01/10/1927	06°Li49'	13°Li19'
01/11/1927	07°Sc34'	04°Sc03'
01/12/1927	07°Sg48'	24°Sc45'
01/01/1928	09°Cp20'	16°Sg49'
01/02/1928	10°Aq53'	09°Cp33'
01/03/1928	10°Pi10'	01°Aq19'
01/04/1928	11°Ar01'	24°Aq57'
01/05/1928	10°Ta22'	17°Pi55'
01/06/1928	10°Ge15'	11°Ar21'
01/07/1928	08°Cn54'	03°Ta19'
01/08/1928	08°Le29'	24°Ta41'
01/09/1928	08°Vi18'	13°Ge54'
01/10/1928	07°Li34'	29°Ge06'
01/11/1928	08°Sc19'	08°Cn27'
01/12/1928	08°Sg34'	06°Cn46' R

Date	Sun	Mars
01/01/1929	10°Cp06'	25°Ge36'
01/02/1929	11°Aq39'	21°Ge07' D
01/03/1929	09°Pi55'	26°Ge36'
01/04/1929	10°Ar47'	08°Cn44'
01/05/1929	10°Ta08'	23°Cn32'
01/06/1929	10°Ge00'	10°Le30'
01/07/1929	08°Cn40'	27°Le58'
01/08/1929	08°Le15'	16°Vi50'
01/09/1929	08°Vi04'	06°Li29'
01/10/1929	07°Li20'	26°Li16'
01/11/1929	08°Sc05'	17°Sc33'
01/12/1929	08°Sg19'	08°Sg59'
01/01/1930	09°Cp51'	01°Cp55'
01/02/1930	11°Aq25'	25°Cp33'
01/03/1930	09°Pi41'	17°Aq18'
01/04/1930	10°Ar32'	11°Pi32'
01/05/1930	09°Ta54'	04°Ar51'
01/06/1930	09°Ge46'	28°Ar24'
01/07/1930	08°Cn26'	20°Ta24'
01/08/1930	08°Le01'	12°Ge02'
01/09/1930	07°Vi50'	02°Cn12'
01/10/1930	07°Li06'	19°Cn52'
01/11/1930	07°Sc51'	05°Le10'
01/12/1930	08°Sg04'	14°Le56'
01/01/1931	09°Cp37'	15°Le35' R
01/02/1931	11°Aq10'	05°Le14'
01/03/1931	09°Pi27'	27°Cn47'
01/04/1931	10°Ar18'	00°Le26' D
01/05/1931	09°Ta40'	10°Le30'
01/06/1931	09°Ge33'	24°Le59'
01/07/1931	08°Cn12'	11°Vi14'
01/08/1931	07°Le47'	29°Vi35'
01/09/1931	07°Vi36'	19°Li11'
01/10/1931	06°Li51'	09°Sc15'
01/11/1931	07°Sc36'	01°Sg03'
01/12/1931	07°Sg50'	23°Sg07'
01/01/1932	09°Cp22'	16°Cp45'
01/02/1932	10°Aq55'	10°Aq58'
01/03/1932	10°Pi12'	03°Pi52'
01/04/1932	11°Ar03'	28°Pi13'
01/05/1932	10°Ta24'	21°Ar20'
01/06/1932	10°Ge16'	14°Ta31'
01/07/1932	08°Cn56'	06°Ge06'
01/08/1932	08°Le31'	27°Ge26'
01/09/1932	08°Vi20'	17°Cn42'
01/10/1932	07°Li36'	06°Le06'
01/11/1932	08°Sc22'	23°Le28'
01/12/1932	08°Sg36'	07°Vi48'

Date	Sun	Mars
01/01/1933	10°Cp08'	18°Vi00'
01/02/1933	11°Aq42'	19°Vi30' R
01/03/1933	09°Pi58'	11°Vi10'
01/04/1933	10°Ar49'	01°Vi39'
01/05/1933	10°Ta10'	02°Vi52' D
01/06/1933	10°Ge03'	12°Vi43'
01/07/1933	08°Cn42'	26°Vi51'
01/08/1933	08°Le17'	14°Li17'
01/09/1933	08°Vi06'	03°Sc43'
01/10/1933	07°Li22'	24°Sc01'
01/11/1933	08°Sc07'	16°Sg19'
01/12/1933	08°Sg21'	08°Cp55'
01/01/1934	09°Cp54'	03°Aq01'
01/02/1934	11°Aq27'	27°Aq29'
01/03/1934	09°Pi43'	19°Pi33'
01/04/1934	10°Ar35'	13°Ar36'
01/05/1934	09°Ta56'	06°Ta13'
01/06/1934	09°Ge49'	28°Ta48'
01/07/1934	08°Cn28'	19°Ge50'
01/08/1934	08°Le03'	10°Cn46'
01/09/1934	07°Vi52'	00°Le55'
01/10/1934	07°Li07'	19°Le38'
01/11/1934	07°Sc53'	08°Vi04'
01/12/1934	08°Sg07'	24°Vi39'
01/01/1935	09°Cp39'	09°Li42'
01/02/1935	11°Aq12'	20°Li51'
01/03/1935	09°Pi29'	24°Li36' R
01/04/1935	10°Ar20'	18°Li09'
01/05/1935	09°Ta42'	07°Li56'
01/06/1935	09°Ge35'	07°Li15' D
01/07/1935	08°Cn15'	16°Li12'
01/08/1935	07°Le50'	01°Sc14'
01/09/1935	07°Vi38'	19°Sc47'
01/10/1935	06°Li53'	09°Sg57'
01/11/1935	07°Sc38'	02°Cp24'
01/12/1935	07°Sg52'	25°Cp13'
01/01/1936	09°Cp24'	19°Aq22'
01/02/1936	10°Aq58'	13°Pi37'
01/03/1936	10°Pi15'	06°Ar00'
01/04/1936	11°Ar06'	29°Ar20'
01/05/1936	10°Ta26'	21°Ta12'
01/06/1936	10°Ge19'	13°Ge00'
01/07/1936	08°Cn58'	03°Cn25'
01/08/1936	08°Le33'	23°Cn54'
01/09/1936	08°Vi22'	13°Le51'
01/10/1936	07°Li38'	02°Vi44'
01/11/1936	08°Sc23'	21°Vi48'
01/12/1936	08°Sg38'	09°Li42'

Date	Sun	Mars
01/01/1937	10°Cp10'	27°Li21'
01/02/1937	11°Aq44'	13°Sc31'
01/03/1937	10°Pi00'	25°Sc48'
01/04/1937	10°Ar51'	04°Sg27'
01/05/1937	10°Ta12'	03°Sg51' R
01/06/1937	10°Ge05'	24°Sc08'
01/07/1937	08°Cn44'	19°Sc37' D
01/08/1937	08°Le19'	26°Sc44'
01/09/1937	08°Vi08'	11°Sg44'
01/10/1937	07°Li24'	00°Cp25'
01/11/1937	08°Sc09'	22°Cp07'
01/12/1937	08°Sg23'	14°Aq20'
01/01/1938	09°Cp55'	07°Pi46'
01/02/1938	11°Aq29'	01°Ar06'
01/03/1938	09°Pi45'	21°Ar47'
01/04/1938	10°Ar37'	14°Ta04'
01/05/1938	09°Ta58'	04°Ge59'
01/06/1938	09°Ge51'	25°Ge58'
01/07/1938	08°Cn30'	15°Cn46'
01/08/1938	08°Le05'	05°Le50'
01/09/1938	07°Vi54'	25°Le39'
01/10/1938	07°Li09'	14°Vi40'
01/11/1938	07°Sc55'	04°Li15'
01/12/1938	08°Sg08'	23°Li07'
01/01/1939	09°Cp40'	12°Sc30'
01/02/1939	11°Aq14'	01°Sg35'
01/03/1939	09°Pi31'	18°Sg20'
01/04/1939	10°Ar23'	05°Cp53'
01/05/1939	09°Ta44'	20°Cp50'
01/06/1939	09°Ge37'	01°Aq55'
01/07/1939	08°Cn17'	04°Aq17' R
01/08/1939	07°Le51'	27°Cp14'
01/09/1939	07°Vi40'	24°Cp21' D
01/10/1939	06°Li55'	02°Aq44'
01/11/1939	07°Sc40'	18°Aq37'
01/12/1939	07°Sg53'	07°Pi17'
01/01/1940	09°Cp25'	27°Pi58'
01/02/1940	10°Aq59'	19°Ar04'
01/03/1940	10°Pi16'	08°Ta44'
01/04/1940	11°Ar07'	29°Ta29'
01/05/1940	10°Ta28'	19°Ge13'
01/06/1940	10°Ge20'	09°Cn16'
01/07/1940	09°Cn00'	28°Cn27'
01/08/1940	08°Le35'	18°Le09'
01/09/1940	08°Vi24'	07°Vi51'
01/10/1940	07°Li39'	27°Vi02'
01/11/1940	08°Sc25'	17°Li06'
01/12/1940	08°Sg39'	06°Sc47'

Date	Sun	Mars
01/01/1941	10°Cp12'	27°Sc26'
01/02/1941	11°Aq45'	18°Sg24'
01/03/1941	10°Pi01'	07°Cp34'
01/04/1941	10°Ar53'	28°Cp58'
01/05/1941	10°Ta14'	19°Aq39'
01/06/1941	10°Ge06'	10°Pi31'
01/07/1941	08°Cn46'	29°Pi17'
01/08/1941	08°Le21'	15°Ar11'
01/09/1941	08°Vi10'	23°Ar29'
01/10/1941	07°Li25'	19°Ar46' R
01/11/1941	08°Sc11'	11°Ar39'
01/12/1941	08°Sg25'	13°Ar42' D
01/01/1942	09°Cp57'	24°Ar50'
01/02/1942	11°Aq30'	10°Ta27'
01/03/1942	09°Pi46'	26°Ta18'
01/04/1942	10°Ar38'	14°Ge42'
01/05/1942	09°Ta59'	02°Cn53'
01/06/1942	09°Ge52'	21°Cn53'
01/07/1942	08°Cn32'	10°Le25'
01/08/1942	08°Le07'	29°Le47'
01/09/1942	07°Vi56'	19°Vi26'
01/10/1942	07°Li11'	08°Li50'
01/11/1942	07°Sc56'	29°Li22'
01/12/1942	08°Sg10'	19°Sc47'
01/01/1943	09°Cp42'	11°Sg29'
01/02/1943	11°Aq15'	03°Cp47'
01/03/1943	09°Pi32'	24°Cp24'
01/04/1943	10°Ar23'	17°Aq36'
01/05/1943	09°Ta45'	10°Pi14'
01/06/1943	09°Ge38'	03°Ar25'
01/07/1943	08°Cn18'	25°Ar08'
01/08/1943	07°Le53'	16°Ta05'
01/09/1943	07°Vi42'	04°Ge22'
01/10/1943	06°Li57'	17°Ge28'
01/11/1943	07°Sc42'	22°Ge08' R
01/12/1943	07°Sg55'	14°Ge36'
01/01/1944	09°Cp27'	05°Ge25'
01/02/1944	11°Aq01'	07°Ge36' D
01/03/1944	10°Pi18'	17°Ge20'
01/04/1944	11°Ar09'	01°Cn49'
01/05/1944	10°Ta29'	17°Cn48'
01/06/1944	10°Ge22'	05°Le27'
01/07/1944	09°Cn01'	23°Le15'
01/08/1944	08°Le36'	12°Vi16'
01/09/1944	08°Vi25'	01°Li55'
01/10/1944	07°Li41'	21°Li36'
01/11/1944	08°Sc27'	12°Sc40'
01/12/1944	08°Sg41'	03°Sg48'

Date	Sun	Mars
01/01/1945	10°Cp13'	26°Sg25'
01/02/1945	11°Aq46'	19°Cp44'
01/03/1945	10°Pi03'	11°Aq15'
01/04/1945	10°Ar54'	05°Pi19'
01/05/1945	10°Ta15'	28°Pi34'
01/06/1945	10°Ge08'	22°Ar10'
01/07/1945	08°Cn47'	14°Ta15'
01/08/1945	08°Le22'	05°Ge53'
01/09/1945	08°Vi11'	25°Ge52'
01/10/1945	07°Li27'	12°Cn54'
01/11/1945	08°Sc12'	26°Cn39'
01/12/1945	08°Sg26'	03°Le08'
01/01/1946	09°Cp59'	28°Cn17' R
01/02/1946	11°Aq32'	16°Cn56'
01/03/1946	09°Pi48'	14°Cn25' D
01/04/1946	10°Ar40'	21°Cn25'
01/05/1946	10°Ta01'	03°Le42'
01/06/1946	09°Ge54'	19°Le19'
01/07/1946	08°Cn33'	06°Vi06'
01/08/1946	08°Le09'	24°Vi41'
01/09/1946	07°Vi57'	14°Li19'
01/10/1946	07°Li13'	04°Sc17'
01/11/1946	07°Sc58'	25°Sc53'
01/12/1946	08°Sg12'	17°Sg41'
01/01/1947	09°Cp44'	11°Cp04'
01/02/1947	11°Aq17'	05°Aq05'
01/03/1947	09°Pi34'	27°Aq05'
01/04/1947	10°Ar26'	21°Pi27'
01/05/1947	09°Ta47'	14°Ar42'
01/06/1947	09°Ge40'	08°Ta06'
01/07/1947	08°Cn20'	29°Ta54'
01/08/1947	07°Le55'	21°Ge24'
01/09/1947	07°Vi43'	11°Cn42'
01/10/1947	06°Li58'	29°Cn56'
01/11/1947	07°Sc43'	16°Le45'
01/12/1947	07°Sg57'	29°Le49'
01/01/1948	09°Cp29'	07°Vi15'
01/02/1948	11°Aq02'	04°Vi01' R
01/03/1948	10°Pi19'	23°Le15'
01/04/1948	11°Ar10'	18°Le08' D
01/05/1948	10°Ta31'	23°Le35'
01/06/1948	10°Ge24'	05°Vi42'
01/07/1948	09°Cn03'	20°Vi52'
01/08/1948	08°Le38'	08°Li45'
01/09/1948	08°Vi27'	28°Li18'
01/10/1948	07°Li43'	18°Sc33'
01/11/1948	08°Sc29'	10°Sg41'
01/12/1948	08°Sg43'	03°Cp06'

Date	Sun	Mars
01/01/1949	10°Cp15'	27°Cp04'
01/02/1949	11°Aq49'	21°Aq30'
01/03/1949	10°Pi05'	13°Pi37'
01/04/1949	10°Ar56'	07°Ar49'
01/05/1949	10°Ta17'	00°Ta40'
01/06/1949	10°Ge10'	23°Ta30'
01/07/1949	08°Cn49'	14°Ge46'
01/08/1949	08°Le24'	05°Cn52'
01/09/1949	08°Vi13'	26°Cn04'
01/10/1949	07°Li29'	14°Le42'
01/11/1949	08°Sc14'	02°Vi48'
01/12/1949	08°Sg28'	18°Vi40'
01/01/1950	10°Cp00'	02°Li13'
01/02/1950	11°Aq34'	10°Li18'
01/03/1950	09°Pi50'	09°Li14' R
01/04/1950	10°Ar42'	28°Vi40'
01/05/1950	10°Ta03'	22°Vi03'
01/06/1950	09°Ge56'	26°Vi26' D
01/07/1950	08°Cn36'	08°Li02'
01/08/1950	08°Le11'	24°Li18'
01/09/1950	07°Vi59'	13°Sc19'
01/10/1950	07°Li15'	03°Sg37'
01/11/1950	08°Sc00'	26°Sg03'
01/12/1950	08°Sg13'	18°Cp50'
01/01/1951	09°Cp45'	13°Aq02'
01/02/1951	11°Aq19'	07°Pi26'
01/03/1951	09°Pi35'	29°Pi17'
01/04/1951	10°Ar28'	22°Ar58'
01/05/1951	09°Ta49'	15°Ta10'
01/06/1951	09°Ge43'	07°Ge18'
01/07/1951	08°Cn22'	27°Ge59'
01/08/1951	07°Le57'	18°Cn39'
01/09/1951	07°Vi45'	08°Le41'
01/10/1951	07°Li00'	27°Le31'
01/11/1951	07°Sc45'	16°Vi22'
01/12/1951	07°Sg59'	03°Li51'
01/01/1952	09°Cp31'	20°Li40'
01/02/1952	11°Aq04'	05°Sc16'
01/03/1952	10°Pi22'	15°Sc13'
01/04/1952	11°Ar13'	18°Sc12' R
01/05/1952	10°Ta34'	10°Sc39'
01/06/1952	10°Ge26'	01°Sc44'
01/07/1952	09°Cn06'	03°Sc52' D
01/08/1952	08°Le41'	15°Sc28'
01/09/1952	08°Vi29'	02°Sg33'
01/10/1952	07°Li45'	22°Sg09'
01/11/1952	08°Sc31'	14°Cp23'
01/12/1952	08°Sg45'	07°Aq00'

Date	Sun	Mars
01/01/1953	10°Cp17'	00°Pi51'
01/02/1953	11°Aq50'	24°Pi39'
01/03/1953	10°Pi07'	15°Ar46'
01/04/1953	10°Ar58'	08°Ta31'
01/05/1953	10°Ta19'	29°Ta49'
01/06/1953	10°Ge12'	21°Ge09'
01/07/1953	08°Cn52'	11°Cn11'
01/08/1953	08°Le27'	01°Le25'
01/09/1953	08°Vi15'	21°Le17'
01/10/1953	07°Li31'	10°Vi15'
01/11/1953	08°Sc16'	29°Vi38'
01/12/1953	08°Sg30'	18°Li09'
01/01/1954	10°Cp02'	06°Sc55'
01/02/1954	11°Aq36'	25°Sc02'
01/03/1954	09°Pi52'	10°Sg24'
01/04/1954	10°Ar44'	25°Sg20'
01/05/1954	10°Ta05'	05°Cp40'
01/06/1954	09°Ge58'	08°Cp05' R
01/07/1954	08°Cn38'	00°Cp42'
01/08/1954	08°Le13'	25°Sg38' D
01/09/1954	08°Vi02'	02°Cp39'
01/10/1954	07°Li17'	17°Cp26'
01/11/1954	08°Sc02'	06°Aq54'
01/12/1954	08°Sg16'	27°Aq39'
01/01/1955	09°Cp48'	19°Pi49'
01/02/1955	11°Aq21'	12°Ar01'
01/03/1955	09°Pi38'	01°Ta48'
01/04/1955	10°Ar30'	23°Ta14'
01/05/1955	09°Ta52'	13°Ge28'
01/06/1955	09°Ge45'	03°Cn54'
01/07/1955	08°Cn24'	23°Cn20'
01/08/1955	07°Le59'	13°Le10'
01/09/1955	07°Vi48'	02°Vi55'
01/10/1955	07°Li03'	22°Vi02'
01/11/1955	07°Sc47'	11°Li53'
01/12/1955	08°Sg01'	01°Sc15'
01/01/1956	09°Cp33'	21°Sc26'
01/02/1956	11°Aq06'	11°Sg44'
01/03/1956	10°Pi23'	00°Cp46'
01/04/1956	11°Ar15'	21°Cp00'
01/05/1956	10°Ta35'	10°Aq08'
01/06/1956	10°Ge28'	28°Aq42'
01/07/1956	09°Cn07'	13°Pi51'
01/08/1956	08°Le42'	23°Pi01'
01/09/1956	08°Vi31'	20°Pi48' R
01/10/1956	07°Li47'	13°Pi45'
01/11/1956	08°Sc33'	16°Pi04' D
01/12/1956	08°Sg47'	27°Pi22'

Date	Sun	Mars
01/01/1957	10°Cp19'	13°Ar41'
01/02/1957	11°Aq53'	02°Ta04'
01/03/1957	10°Pi09'	19°Ta24'
01/04/1957	11°Ar00'	08°Ge52'
01/05/1957	10°Ta21'	27°Ge43'
01/06/1957	10°Ge14'	17°Cn09'
01/07/1957	08°Cn53'	05°Le57'
01/08/1957	08°Le29'	25°Le26'
01/09/1957	08°Vi17'	15°Vi06'
01/10/1957	07°Li33'	04°Li25'
01/11/1957	08°Sc18'	24°Li46'
01/12/1957	08°Sg32'	14°Sc53'
01/01/1958	10°Cp04'	06°Sg12'
01/02/1958	11°Aq38'	28°Sg01'
01/03/1958	09°Pi54'	18°Cp08'
01/04/1958	10°Ar46'	10°Aq47'
01/05/1958	10°Ta07'	02°Pi52'
01/06/1958	10°Ge00'	25°Pi30'
01/07/1958	08°Cn40'	16°Ar37'
01/08/1958	08°Le15'	06°Ta36'
01/09/1958	08°Vi03'	22°Ta55'
01/10/1958	07°Li19'	01°Ge54'
01/11/1958	08°Sc04'	29°Ta10' R
01/12/1958	08°Sg17'	19°Ta06'
01/01/1959	09°Cp49'	17°Ta26' D
01/02/1959	11°Aq23'	26°Ta05'
01/03/1959	09°Pi39'	08°Ge33'
01/04/1959	10°Ar31'	24°Ge47'
01/05/1959	09°Ta53'	11°Cn44'
01/06/1959	09°Ge46'	29°Cn56'
01/07/1959	08°Cn26'	18°Le02'
01/08/1959	08°Le01'	07°Vi11'
01/09/1959	07°Vi49'	26°Vi49'
01/10/1959	07°Li04'	16°Li22'
01/11/1959	07°Sc49'	07°Sc12'
01/12/1959	08°Sg02'	28°Sc03'
01/01/1960	09°Cp34'	20°Sg18'
01/02/1960	11°Aq08'	13°Cp15'
01/03/1960	10°Pi25'	05°Aq12'
01/04/1960	11°Ar16'	29°Aq01'
01/05/1960	10°Ta37'	22°Pi07'
01/06/1960	10°Ge30'	15°Ar39'
01/07/1960	09°Cn09'	07°Ta42'
01/08/1960	08°Le44'	29°Ta13'
01/09/1960	08°Vi33'	18°Ge48'
01/10/1960	07°Li49'	04°Cn51'
01/11/1960	08°Sc34'	16°Cn11'
01/12/1960	08°Sg48'	17°Cn54' R

Date	Sun	Mars
01/01/1961	10°Cp20'	08°Cn07'
01/02/1961	11°Aq54'	00°Cn10'
01/03/1961	10°Pi10'	02°Cn55' D
01/04/1961	11°Ar02'	13°Cn26'
01/05/1961	10°Ta23'	27°Cn25'
01/06/1961	10°Ge16'	13°Le57'
01/07/1961	08°Cn55'	01°Vi11'
01/08/1961	08°Le30'	19°Vi57'
01/09/1961	08°Vi19'	09°Li36'
01/10/1961	07°Li34'	29°Li26'
01/11/1961	08°Sc20'	20°Sc49'
01/12/1961	08°Sg33'	12°Sg23'
01/01/1962	10°Cp05'	05°Cp28'
01/02/1962	11°Aq39'	29°Cp15'
01/03/1962	09°Pi55'	21°Aq06'
01/04/1962	10°Ar47'	15°Pi25'
01/05/1962	10°Ta09'	08°Ar44'
01/06/1962	10°Ge02'	02°Ta15'
01/07/1962	08°Cn41'	24°Ta12'
01/08/1962	08°Le16'	15°Ge48'
01/09/1962	08°Vi05'	06°Cn03'
01/10/1962	07°Li20'	23°Cn59'
01/11/1962	08°Sc05'	09°Le56'
01/12/1962	08°Sg19'	21°Le08'
01/01/1963	09°Cp51'	24°Le35' R
01/02/1963	11°Aq24'	16°Le21'
01/03/1963	09°Pi41'	06°Le55'
01/04/1963	10°Ar33'	06°Le40' D
01/05/1963	09°Ta55'	15°Le11'
01/06/1963	09°Ge48'	28°Le52'
01/07/1963	08°Cn28'	14°Vi45'
01/08/1963	08°Le03'	02°Li56'
01/09/1963	07°Vi51'	22°Li30'
01/10/1963	07°Li06'	12°Sc37'
01/11/1963	07°Sc50'	04°Sg31'
01/12/1963	08°Sg04'	26°Sg42'
01/01/1964	09°Cp36'	20°Cp26'
01/02/1964	11°Aq09'	14°Aq44'
01/03/1964	10°Pi26'	07°Pi39'
01/04/1964	11°Ar18'	01°Ar58'
01/05/1964	10°Ta39'	25°Ar01'
01/06/1964	10°Ge31'	18°Ta05'
01/07/1964	09°Cn11'	09°Ge34'
01/08/1964	08°Le46'	00°Cn50'
01/09/1964	08°Vi35'	21°Cn05'
01/10/1964	07°Li50'	09°Le35'
01/11/1964	08°Sc36'	27°Le15'
01/12/1964	08°Sg50'	12°Vi13'

Date	Sun	Mars
01/01/1965	10°Cp22'	23°Vi49'
01/02/1965	11°Aq55'	27°Vi59' R
01/03/1965	10°Pi12'	22°Vi00'
01/04/1965	11°Ar03'	11°Vi01'
01/05/1965	10°Ta24'	09°Vi27' D
01/06/1965	10°Ge17'	17°Vi37'
01/07/1965	08°Cn57'	00°Li59'
01/08/1965	08°Le32'	18°Li04'
01/09/1965	08°Vi21'	07°Sc23'
01/10/1965	07°Li36'	27°Sc42'
01/11/1965	08°Sc21'	20°Sg03'
01/12/1965	08°Sg35'	12°Cp44'
01/01/1966	10°Cp07'	06°Aq53'
01/02/1966	11°Aq41'	01°Pi21'
01/03/1966	09°Pi57'	23°Pi21'
01/04/1966	10°Ar49'	17°Ar17'
01/05/1966	10°Ta10'	09°Ta46'
01/06/1966	10°Ge04'	02°Ge11'
01/07/1966	08°Cn43'	23°Ge06'
01/08/1966	08°Le18'	13°Cn57'
01/09/1966	08°Vi07'	04°Le03'
01/10/1966	07°Li22'	22°Le50'
01/11/1966	08°Sc07'	11°Vi25'
01/12/1966	08°Sg20'	28°Vi22'
01/01/1967	09°Cp52'	14°Li07'
01/02/1967	11°Aq26'	26°Li41'
01/03/1967	09°Pi42'	02°Sc50'
01/04/1967	10°Ar34'	29°Li47' R
01/05/1967	09°Ta56'	19°Li12'
01/06/1967	09°Ge50'	15°Li11' D
01/07/1967	08°Cn29'	22°Li02'
01/08/1967	08°Le04'	06°Sc03'
01/09/1967	07°Vi53'	24°Sc10'
01/10/1967	07°Li08'	14°Sg10'
01/11/1967	07°Sc52'	06°Cp35'
01/12/1967	08°Sg06'	29°Cp21'
01/01/1968	09°Cp38'	23°Aq26'
01/02/1968	11°Aq11'	17°Pi34'
01/03/1968	10°Pi29'	09°Ar48'
01/04/1968	11°Ar20'	02°Ta57'
01/05/1968	10°Ta41'	24°Ta38'
01/06/1968	10°Ge34'	16°Ge16'
01/07/1968	09°Cn13'	06°Cn33'
01/08/1968	08°Le48'	26°Cn57'
01/09/1968	08°Vi37'	16°Le52'
01/10/1968	07°Li52'	05°Vi47'
01/11/1968	08°Sc38'	24°Vi58'
01/12/1968	08°Sg52'	13°Li06'

Date	Sun	Mars
01/01/1969	10°Cp24'	01°Sc11'
01/02/1969	11°Aq58'	18°Sc07'
01/03/1969	10°Pi14'	01°Sg40'
01/04/1969	11°Ar05'	12°Sg56'
01/05/1969	10°Ta27'	16°Sg41' R
01/06/1969	10°Ge20'	09°Sg53'
01/07/1969	08°Cn59'	02°Sg04'
01/08/1969	08°Le34'	05°Sg21' D
01/09/1969	08°Vi23'	18°Sg23'
01/10/1969	07°Li38'	06°Cp08'
01/11/1969	08°Sc24'	27°Cp18'
01/12/1969	08°Sg37'	19°Aq09'
01/01/1970	10°Cp09'	12°Pi14'
01/02/1970	11°Aq43'	05°Ar14'
01/03/1970	09°Pi59'	25°Ar39'
01/04/1970	10°Ar51'	17°Ta39'
01/05/1970	10°Ta13'	08°Ge21'
01/06/1970	10°Ge06'	29°Ge09'
01/07/1970	08°Cn45'	18°Cn49'
01/08/1970	08°Le20'	08°Le49'
01/09/1970	08°Vi09'	28°Le36'
01/10/1970	07°Li24'	17°Vi39'
01/11/1970	08°Sc09'	07°Li20'
01/12/1970	08°Sg23'	26°Li23'
01/01/1971	09°Cp55'	16°Sc04'
01/02/1971	11°Aq28'	05°Sg37'
01/03/1971	09°Pi45'	23°Sg01'
01/04/1971	10°Ar37'	11°Cp41'
01/05/1971	09°Ta59'	28°Cp30'
01/06/1971	09°Ge52'	13°Aq03'
01/07/1971	08°Cn32'	21°Aq18'
01/08/1971	08°Le07'	19°Aq21' R
01/09/1971	07°Vi55'	12°Aq22'
01/10/1971	07°Li10'	14°Aq51' D
01/11/1971	07°Sc54'	27°Aq10'
01/12/1971	08°Sg08'	13°Pi55'
01/01/1972	09°Cp40'	03°Ar23'
01/02/1972	11°Aq13'	23°Ar40'
01/03/1972	10°Pi31'	12°Ta49'
01/04/1972	11°Ar22'	03°Ge08'
01/05/1972	10°Ta43'	22°Ge35'
01/06/1972	10°Ge36'	12°Cn26'
01/07/1972	09°Cn15'	01°Le28'
01/08/1972	08°Le50'	21°Le06'
01/09/1972	08°Vi39'	10°Vi47'
01/10/1972	07°Li54'	00°Li01'
01/11/1972	08°Sc40'	20°Li10'
01/12/1972	08°Sg54'	10°Sc01'

Date	Sun	Mars
01/01/1973	10°Cp26'	00°Sg54'
01/02/1973	12°Aq00'	22°Sg11'
01/03/1973	10°Pi16'	11°Cp44'
01/04/1973	11°Ar08'	03°Aq38'
01/05/1973	10°Ta29'	24°Aq56'
01/06/1973	10°Ge22'	16°Pi37'
01/07/1973	09°Cn01'	06°Ar32'
01/08/1973	08°Le36'	24°Ar30'
01/09/1973	08°Vi25'	06°Ta47'
01/10/1973	07°Li40'	08°Ta22' R
01/11/1973	08°Sc26'	29°Ar22'
01/12/1973	08°Sg39'	25°Ar28' D
01/01/1974	10°Cp11'	02°Ta33'
01/02/1974	11°Aq45'	16°Ta04'
01/03/1974	10°Pi01'	00°Ge52'
01/04/1974	10°Ar53'	18°Ge35'
01/05/1974	10°Ta15'	06°Cn22'
01/06/1974	10°Ge08'	25°Cn06'
01/07/1974	08°Cn48'	13°Le29'
01/08/1974	08°Le23'	02°Vi46'
01/09/1974	08°Vi11'	22°Vi25'
01/10/1974	07°Li26'	11°Li51'
01/11/1974	08°Sc11'	02°Sc30'
01/12/1974	08°Sg24'	23°Sc04'
01/01/1975	09°Cp56'	14°Sg58'
01/02/1975	11°Aq30'	07°Cp29'
01/03/1975	09°Pi46'	28°Cp19'
01/04/1975	10°Ar39'	21°Aq47'
01/05/1975	10°Ta01'	14°Pi37'
01/06/1975	09°Ge54'	07°Ar59'
01/07/1975	08°Cn34'	29°Ar53'
01/08/1975	08°Le09'	21°Ta10'
01/09/1975	07°Vi57'	10°Ge07'
01/10/1975	07°Li12'	24°Ge40'
01/11/1975	07°Sc56'	02°Cn27'
01/12/1975	08°Sg10'	28°Ge25' R
01/01/1976	09°Cp41'	17°Ge22'
01/02/1976	11°Aq15'	15°Ge29' D
01/03/1976	10°Pi32'	22°Ge57'
01/04/1976	11°Ar24'	06°Cn10'
01/05/1976	10°Ta45'	21°Cn31'
01/06/1976	10°Ge38'	08°Le48'
01/07/1976	09°Cn17'	26°Le24'
01/08/1976	08°Le52'	15°Vi20'
01/09/1976	08°Vi41'	04°Li59'
01/10/1976	07°Li56'	24°Li43'
01/11/1976	08°Sc42'	15°Sc54'
01/12/1976	08°Sg56'	07°Sg11'

Date	Sun	Mars
01/01/1977	10°Cp28'	29°Sg59'
01/02/1977	12°Aq01'	23°Cp28'
01/03/1977	10°Pi18'	15°Aq07'
01/04/1977	11°Ar09'	09°Pi17'
01/05/1977	10°Ta30'	02°Ar35'
01/06/1977	10°Ge23'	26°Ar10'
01/07/1977	09°Cn03'	18°Ta13'
01/08/1977	08°Le38'	09°Ge52'
01/09/1977	08°Vi27'	29°Ge59'
01/10/1977	07°Li42'	17°Cn26'
01/11/1977	08°Sc27'	02°Le09'
01/12/1977	08°Sg41'	10°Le41'
01/01/1978	10°Cp13'	09°Le03' R
01/02/1978	11°Aq46'	27°Cn47'
01/03/1978	10°Pi03'	22°Cn17'
01/04/1978	10°Ar54'	26°Cn54' D
01/05/1978	10°Ta16'	07°Le59'
01/06/1978	10°Ge09'	22°Le59'
01/07/1978	08°Cn49'	09°Vi28'
01/08/1978	08°Le24'	27°Vi55'
01/09/1978	08°Vi13'	17°Li32'
01/10/1978	07°Li28'	07°Sc32'
01/11/1978	08°Sc13'	29°Sc15'
01/12/1978	08°Sg26'	21°Sg11'
01/01/1979	09°Cp58'	14°Cp42'
01/02/1979	11°Aq31'	08°Aq51'
01/03/1979	09°Pi48'	00°Pi54'
01/04/1979	10°Ar40'	25°Pi17'
01/05/1979	10°Ta02'	18°Ar29'
01/06/1979	09°Ge56'	11°Ta47'
01/07/1979	08°Cn35'	03°Ge30'
01/08/1979	08°Le10'	24°Ge56'
01/09/1979	07°Vi59'	15°Cn15'
01/10/1979	07°Li13'	03°Le37'
01/11/1979	07°Sc58'	20°Le49'
01/12/1979	08°Sg11'	04°Vi44'
01/01/1980	09°Cp43'	13°Vi58'
01/02/1980	11°Aq16'	13°Vi44' R
01/03/1980	10°Pi34'	03°Vi54'
01/04/1980	11°Ar25'	26°Le03'
01/05/1980	10°Ta46'	29°Le11' D
01/06/1980	10°Ge39'	10°Vi05'
01/07/1980	09°Cn18'	24°Vi41'
01/08/1980	08°Le53'	12°Li19'
01/09/1980	08°Vi42'	01°Sc48'
01/10/1980	07°Li58'	22°Sc04'
01/11/1980	08°Sc43'	14°Sg16'
01/12/1980	08°Sg57'	06°Cp47'

Date	Sun	Mars
01/01/1981	10°Cp29'	00°Aq50'
01/02/1981	12°Aq03'	25°Aq18'
01/03/1981	10°Pi19'	17°Pi24'
01/04/1981	11°Ar11'	11°Ar31'
01/05/1981	10°Ta32'	04°Ta16'
01/06/1981	10°Ge25'	26°Ta58'
01/07/1981	09°Cn04'	18°Ge07'
01/08/1981	08°Le39'	09°Cn08'
01/09/1981	08°Vi28'	29°Cn19'
01/10/1981	07°Li44'	18°Le01'
01/11/1981	08°Sc29'	06°Vi18'
01/12/1981	08°Sg42'	22°Vi37'
01/01/1982	10°Cp15'	07°Li03'
01/02/1982	11°Aq48'	16°Li59'
01/03/1982	10°Pi04'	18°Li45' R
01/04/1982	10°Ar56'	10°Li09'
01/05/1982	10°Ta18'	01°Li08'
01/06/1982	10°Ge11'	02°Li46' D
01/07/1982	08°Cn51'	12°Li58'
01/08/1982	08°Le26'	28°Li35'
01/09/1982	08°Vi14'	17°Sc21'
01/10/1982	07°Li29'	07°Sg34'
01/11/1982	08°Sc14'	00°Cp02'
01/12/1982	08°Sg27'	22°Cp49'
01/01/1983	09°Cp59'	17°Aq00'
01/02/1983	11°Aq33'	11°Pi20'
01/03/1983	09°Pi50'	03°Ar04'
01/04/1983	10°Ar42'	26°Ar35'
01/05/1983	10°Ta04'	18°Ta37'
01/06/1983	09°Ge57'	10°Ge36'
01/07/1983	08°Cn37'	01°Cn09'
01/08/1983	08°Le12'	21°Cn44'
01/09/1983	08°Vi00'	11°Le45'
01/10/1983	07°Li15'	00°Vi37'
01/11/1983	07°Sc59'	19°Vi36'
01/12/1983	08°Sg13'	07°Li20'
01/01/1984	09°Cp45'	24°Li40'
01/02/1984	11°Aq18'	10°Sc14'
01/03/1984	10°Pi36'	21°Sc52'
01/04/1984	11°Ar27'	28°Sc13'
01/05/1984	10°Ta48'	24°Sc20' R
01/06/1984	10°Ge41'	14°Sc05'
01/07/1984	09°Cn20'	12°Sc32' D
01/08/1984	08°Le55'	21°Sc53'
01/09/1984	08°Vi44'	07°Sg56'
01/10/1984	08°Li00'	27°Sg05'
01/11/1984	08°Sc45'	19°Cp04'
01/12/1984	08°Sg59'	11°Aq30'

Date	Sun	Mars
01/01/1985	10°Cp31'	05°Pi08'
01/02/1985	12°Aq05'	28°Pi42'
01/03/1985	10°Pi21'	19°Ar36'
01/04/1985	11°Ar13'	12°Ta06'
01/05/1985	10°Ta34'	03°Ge12'
01/06/1985	10°Ge27'	24°Ge21'
01/07/1985	09°Cn07'	14°Cn16'
01/08/1985	08°Le42'	04°Le24'
01/09/1985	08°Vi30'	24°Le15'
01/10/1985	07°Li46'	13°Vi15'
01/11/1985	08°Sc30'	02°Li44'
01/12/1985	08°Sg44'	21°Li27'
01/01/1986	10°Cp16'	10°Sc34'
01/02/1986	11°Aq49'	29°Sc15'
01/03/1986	10°Pi06'	15°Sg26'
01/04/1986	10°Ar58'	01°Cp56'
01/05/1986	10°Ta20'	15°Cp05'
01/06/1986	10°Ge13'	22°Cp43'
01/07/1986	08°Cn53'	20°Cp13' R
01/08/1986	08°Le28'	12°Cp18'
01/09/1986	08°Vi16'	14°Cp00' D
01/10/1986	07°Li31'	25°Cp46'
01/11/1986	08°Sc16'	13°Aq34'
01/12/1986	08°Sg29'	03°Pi19'
01/01/1987	10°Cp01'	24°Pi45'
01/02/1987	11°Aq35'	16°Ar24'
01/03/1987	09°Pi52'	05°Ta46'
01/04/1987	10°Ar44'	26°Ta51'
01/05/1987	10°Ta06'	16°Ge49'
01/06/1987	10°Ge00'	07°Cn04'
01/07/1987	08°Cn40'	26°Cn21'
01/08/1987	08°Le14'	16°Le07'
01/09/1987	08°Vi02'	05°Vi50'
01/10/1987	07°Li17'	24°Vi59'
01/11/1987	08°Sc02'	14°Li57'
01/12/1987	08°Sg15'	04°Sc29'
01/01/1988	09°Cp47'	24°Sc56'
01/02/1988	11°Aq20'	15°Sg36'
01/03/1988	10°Pi37'	05°Cp06'
01/04/1988	11°Ar29'	26°Cp01'
01/05/1988	10°Ta50'	16°Aq06'
01/06/1988	10°Ge43'	06°Pi07'
01/07/1988	09°Cn23'	23°Pi36'
01/08/1988	08°Le58'	07°Ar10'
01/09/1988	08°Vi46'	11°Ar16' R
01/10/1988	08°Li02'	04°Ar24'
01/11/1988	08°Sc47'	29°Pi58' D
01/12/1988	09°Sg01'	06°Ar30'

Date	Sun	Mars
01/01/1989	10°Cp33'	20°Ar12'
01/02/1989	12°Aq06'	07°Ta10'
01/03/1989	10°Pi23'	23°Ta43'
01/04/1989	11°Ar14'	12°Ge37'
01/05/1989	10°Ta36'	01°Cn07'
01/06/1989	10°Ge29'	20°Cn19'
01/07/1989	09°Cn09'	08°Le58'
01/08/1989	08°Le44'	28°Le23'
01/09/1989	08°Vi32'	18°Vi02'
01/10/1989	07°Li48'	07°Li24'
01/11/1989	08°Sc33'	27°Li50'
01/12/1989	08°Sg46'	18°Sc08'
01/01/1990	10°Cp18'	09°Sg39'
01/02/1990	11°Aq52'	01°Cp44'
01/03/1990	10°Pi08'	22°Cp08'
01/04/1990	11°Ar00'	15°Aq07'
01/05/1990	10°Ta22'	07°Pi32'
01/06/1990	10°Ge16'	00°Ar31'
01/07/1990	08°Cn55'	22°Ar01'
01/08/1990	08°Le31'	12°Ta39'
01/09/1990	08°Vi19'	00°Ge15'
01/10/1990	07°Li34'	11°Ge54'
01/11/1990	08°Sc18'	13°Ge38' R
01/12/1990	08°Sg32'	04°Ge11'
01/01/1991	10°Cp03'	27°Ta45'
01/02/1991	11°Aq37'	02°Ge54' D
01/03/1991	09°Pi54'	13°Ge41'
01/04/1991	10°Ar46'	28°Ge56'
01/05/1991	10°Ta08'	15°Cn20'
01/06/1991	10°Ge02'	03°Le13'
01/07/1991	08°Cn41'	21°Le08'
01/08/1991	08°Le16'	10°Vi12'
01/09/1991	08°Vi05'	29°Vi49'
01/10/1991	07°Li19'	19°Li25'
01/11/1991	08°Sc04'	10°Sc22'
01/12/1991	08°Sg17'	01°Sg21'
01/01/1992	09°Cp49'	23°Sg47'
01/02/1992	11°Aq22'	16°Cp55'
01/03/1992	10°Pi40'	09°Aq04'
01/04/1992	11°Ar31'	03°Pi02'
01/05/1992	10°Ta52'	26°Pi14'
01/06/1992	10°Ge45'	19°Ar50'
01/07/1992	09°Cn25'	11°Ta55'
01/08/1992	09°Le00'	03°Ge32'
01/09/1992	08°Vi49'	23°Ge23'
01/10/1992	08°Li04'	10°Cn05'
01/11/1992	08°Sc49'	22°Cn56'
01/12/1992	09°Sg03'	27°Cn36' R

Date	Sun	Mars
01/01/1993	10°Cp35'	20°Cn25'
01/02/1993	12°Aq09'	10°Cn00'
01/03/1993	10°Pi25'	09°Cn46' D
01/04/1993	11°Ar17'	18°Cn23'
01/05/1993	10°Ta38'	01°Le27'
01/06/1993	10°Ge31'	17°Le28'
01/07/1993	09°Cn11'	04°Vi28'
01/08/1993	08°Le46'	23°Vi07'
01/09/1993	08°Vi35'	12°Li45'
01/10/1993	07°Li50'	02°Sc38'
01/11/1993	08°Sc35'	24°Sc08'
01/12/1993	08°Sg48'	15°Sg50'
01/01/1994	10°Cp20'	09°Cp04'
01/02/1994	11°Aq54'	02°Aq59'
01/03/1994	10°Pi10'	24°Aq55'
01/04/1994	11°Ar02'	19°Pi16'
01/05/1994	10°Ta24'	12°Ar34'
01/06/1994	10°Ge17'	06°Ta01'
01/07/1994	08°Cn57'	27°Ta54'
01/08/1994	08°Le32'	19°Ge29'
01/09/1994	08°Vi20'	09°Cn47'
01/10/1994	07°Li35'	27°Cn55'
01/11/1994	08°Sc20'	14°Le25'
01/12/1994	08°Sg33'	26°Le46'
01/01/1995	10°Cp05'	02°Vi39'
01/02/1995	11°Aq39'	27°Le11' R
01/03/1995	09°Pi56'	16°Le45'
01/04/1995	10°Ar48'	13°Le29' D
01/05/1995	10°Ta10'	20°Le11'
01/06/1995	10°Ge04'	02°Vi55'
01/07/1995	08°Cn43'	18°Vi22'
01/08/1995	08°Le18'	06°Li21'
01/09/1995	08°Vi06'	25°Li52'
01/10/1995	07°Li21'	16°Sc01'
01/11/1995	08°Sc05'	08°Sg02'
01/12/1995	08°Sg18'	00°Cp19'
01/01/1996	09°Cp50'	24°Cp10'
01/02/1996	11°Aq24'	18°Aq32'
01/03/1996	10°Pi42'	11°Pi28'
01/04/1996	11°Ar33'	05°Ar44'
01/05/1996	10°Ta54'	28°Ar40'
01/06/1996	10°Ge47'	21°Ta38'
01/07/1996	09°Cn26'	13°Ge00'
01/08/1996	09°Le01'	04°Cn11'
01/09/1996	08°Vi50'	24°Cn25'
01/10/1996	08°Li05'	13°Le01'
01/11/1996	08°Sc51'	00°Vi56'
01/12/1996	09°Sg04'	16°Vi28'

Date	Sun	Mars
01/01/1997	10°Cp36'	29°Vi14'
01/02/1997	12°Aq10'	05°Li46'
01/03/1997	10°Pi27'	02°Li33' R
01/04/1997	11°Ar18'	21°Vi19'
01/05/1997	10°Ta40'	16°Vi48' D
01/06/1997	10°Ge33'	22°Vi56'
01/07/1997	09°Cn12'	05°Li22'
01/08/1997	08°Le47'	22°Li00'
01/09/1997	08°Vi36'	11°Sc09'
01/10/1997	07°Li51'	01°Sg27'
01/11/1997	08°Sc36'	23°Sg51'
01/12/1997	08°Sg49'	16°Cp35'
01/01/1998	10°Cp21'	10°Aq46'
01/02/1998	11°Aq55'	05°Pi13'
01/03/1998	10°Pi12'	27°Pi09'
01/04/1998	11°Ar04'	20°Ar57'
01/05/1998	10°Ta26'	13°Ta17'
01/06/1998	10°Ge19'	05°Ge34'
01/07/1998	08°Cn59'	26°Ge21'
01/08/1998	08°Le34'	17°Cn06'
01/09/1998	08°Vi22'	07°Le11'
01/10/1998	07°Li37'	26°Le00'
01/11/1998	08°Sc22'	14°Vi45'
01/12/1998	08°Sg35'	02°Li00'
01/01/1999	10°Cp06'	18°Li23'
01/02/1999	11°Aq40'	02°Sc11'
01/03/1999	09°Pi57'	10°Sc27'
01/04/1999	10°Ar49'	11°Sc04' R
01/05/1999	10°Ta11'	01°Sc46'
01/06/1999	10°Ge05'	24°Li31'
01/07/1999	08°Cn45'	28°Li42' D
01/08/1999	08°Le20'	11°Sc21'
01/09/1999	08°Vi08'	28°Sc52'
01/10/1999	07°Li22'	18°Sg38'
01/11/1999	08°Sc07'	10°Cp56'
01/12/1999	08°Sg20'	03°Aq37'
01/01/2000	09°Cp52'	27°Aq35'
01/02/2000	11°Aq25'	21°Pi33'
01/03/2000	10°Pi42'	13°Ar36'
01/04/2000	11°Ar34'	06°Ta32'
01/05/2000	10°Ta55'	28°Ta02'
01/06/2000	10°Ge49'	19°Ge30'
01/07/2000	09°Cn28'	09°Cn40'
01/08/2000	09°Le03'	29°Cn58'
01/09/2000	08°Vi52'	19°Le51'
01/10/2000	08°Li07'	08°Vi48'
01/11/2000	08°Sc52'	28°Vi06'
01/12/2000	09°Sg06'	16°Li27'

Date	Sun	Mars
01/01/2001	10°Cp38'	04°Sc56'
01/02/2001	12°Aq11'	22°Sc34'
01/03/2001	10°Pi28'	07°Sg12'
01/04/2001	11°Ar20'	20°Sg40'
01/05/2001	10°Ta41'	28°Sg23'
01/06/2001	10°Ge35'	26°Sg29' R
01/07/2001	09°Cn14'	17°Sg33'
01/08/2001	08°Le49'	16°Sg07' D
01/09/2001	08°Vi38'	26°Sg14'
01/10/2001	07°Li53'	12°Cp35'
01/11/2001	08°Sc38'	02°Aq56'
01/12/2001	08°Sg51'	24°Aq15'
01/01/2002	10°Cp23'	16°Pi53'
01/02/2002	11°Aq56'	09°Ar29'
01/03/2002	10°Pi13'	29°Ar33'
01/04/2002	11°Ar05'	21°Ta15'
01/05/2002	10°Ta27'	11°Ge42'
01/06/2002	10°Ge20'	02°Cn19'
01/07/2002	09°Cn00'	21°Cn51'
01/08/2002	08°Le35'	11°Le46'
01/09/2002	08°Vi24'	01°Vi31'
01/10/2002	07°Li39'	20°Vi37'
01/11/2002	08°Sc23'	10°Li23'
01/12/2002	08°Sg36'	29°Li37'
01/01/2003	10°Cp08'	19°Sc34'
01/02/2003	11°Aq42'	09°Sg33'
01/03/2003	09°Pi59'	27°Sg31'
01/04/2003	10°Ar51'	17°Cp07'
01/05/2003	10°Ta13'	05°Aq22'
01/06/2003	10°Ge07'	22°Aq29'
01/07/2003	08°Cn47'	05°Pi14'
01/08/2003	08°Le22'	10°Pi05' R
01/09/2003	08°Vi10'	04°Pi09'
01/10/2003	07°Li24'	00°Pi13' D
01/11/2003	08°Sc09'	07°Pi18'
01/12/2003	08°Sg22'	21°Pi19'
01/01/2004	09°Cp53'	09°Ar10'
01/02/2004	11°Aq27'	28°Ar28'
01/03/2004	10°Pi45'	16°Ta59'
01/04/2004	11°Ar36'	06°Ge50'
01/05/2004	10°Ta58'	25°Ge58'
01/06/2004	10°Ge51'	15°Cn35'
01/07/2004	09°Cn30'	04°Le29'
01/08/2004	09°Le05'	24°Le02'
01/09/2004	08°Vi54'	13°Vi43'
01/10/2004	08°Li09'	02°Li59'
01/11/2004	08°Sc54'	23°Li14'
01/12/2004	09°Sg08'	13°Sc14'

Date	Sun	Mars
01/01/2005	10°Cp40'	04°Sg21'
01/02/2005	12°Aq13'	25°Sg56'
01/03/2005	10°Pi30'	15°Cp48'
01/04/2005	11°Ar22'	08°Aq08'
01/05/2005	10°Ta43'	29°Aq55'
01/06/2005	10°Ge36'	22°Pi12'
01/07/2005	09°Cn16'	12°Ar53'
01/08/2005	08°Le51'	02°Ta11'
01/09/2005	08°Vi40'	17°Ta07'
01/10/2005	07°Li55'	23°Ta22'
01/11/2005	08°Sc40'	17°Ta15' R
01/12/2005	08°Sg53'	08°Ta49'
01/01/2006	10°Cp25'	11°Ta05' D
01/02/2006	11°Aq59'	22°Ta03'
01/03/2006	10°Pi15'	05°Ge37'
01/04/2006	11°Ar08'	22°Ge33'
01/05/2006	10°Ta30'	09°Cn53'
01/06/2006	10°Ge23'	28°Cn20'
01/07/2006	09°Cn03'	16°Le33'
01/08/2006	08°Le38'	05°Vi45'
01/09/2006	08°Vi26'	25°Vi23'
01/10/2006	07°Li41'	14°Li53'
01/11/2006	08°Sc25'	05°Sc37'
01/12/2006	08°Sg39'	26°Sc20'
01/01/2007	10°Cp10'	18°Sg26'
01/02/2007	11°Aq44'	11°Cp11'
01/03/2007	10°Pi01'	02°Aq13'
01/04/2007	10°Ar53'	25°Aq53'
01/05/2007	10°Ta16'	18°Pi53'
01/06/2007	10°Ge09'	12°Ar22'
01/07/2007	08°Cn49'	04°Ta24'
01/08/2007	08°Le24'	25°Ta53'
01/09/2007	08°Vi12'	15°Ge19'
01/10/2007	07°Li26'	00°Cn54'
01/11/2007	08°Sc11'	11°Cn05'
01/12/2007	08°Sg24'	10°Cn42' R
01/01/2008	09°Cp56'	29°Ge53'
01/02/2008	11°Aq29'	24°Ge05' D
01/03/2008	10°Pi47'	28°Ge57'
01/04/2008	11°Ar38'	10°Cn43'
01/05/2008	11°Ta00'	25°Cn20'
01/06/2008	10°Ge53'	12°Le12'
01/07/2008	09°Cn32'	29°Le36'
01/08/2008	09°Le07'	18°Vi26'
01/09/2008	08°Vi56'	08°Li04'
01/10/2008	08°Li11'	27°Li51'
01/11/2008	08°Sc56'	19°Sc08'
01/12/2008	09°Sg10'	10°Sg34'

Date	Sun	Mars
01/01/2009	10°Cp42'	03°Cp31'
01/02/2009	12°Aq16'	27°Cp10'
01/03/2009	10°Pi32'	18°Aq56'
01/04/2009	11°Ar24'	13°Pi12'
01/05/2009	10°Ta46'	06°Ar31'
01/06/2009	10°Ge39'	00°Ta05'
01/07/2009	09°Cn19'	22°Ta06'
01/08/2009	08°Le54'	13°Ge44'
01/09/2009	08°Vi42'	03°Cn58'
01/10/2009	07°Li57'	21°Cn43'
01/11/2009	08°Sc42'	07°Le13'
01/12/2009	08°Sg55'	17°Le24'
01/01/2010	10°Cp27'	18°Le49' R
01/02/2010	12°Aq00'	08°Le56'
01/03/2010	10°Pi17'	00°Le54'
01/04/2010	11°Ar10'	02°Le48' D
01/05/2010	10°Ta32'	12°Le30'
01/06/2010	10°Ge25'	26°Le47'
01/07/2010	09°Cn05'	12°Vi56'
01/08/2010	08°Le40'	01°Li14'
01/09/2010	08°Vi28'	20°Li49'
01/10/2010	07°Li43'	10°Sc52'
01/11/2010	08°Sc27'	02°Sg40'
01/12/2010	08°Sg40'	24°Sg44'
01/01/2011	10°Cp12'	18°Cp22'
01/02/2011	11°Aq46'	12°Aq36'
01/03/2011	10°Pi03'	04°Pi42'
01/04/2011	10°Ar55'	29°Pi04'
01/05/2011	10°Ta18'	22°Ar12'
01/06/2011	10°Ge11'	15°Ta25'
01/07/2011	08°Cn51'	07°Ge01'
01/08/2011	08°Le26'	28°Ge24'
01/09/2011	08°Vi14'	18°Cn42'
01/10/2011	07°Li29'	07°Le12'
01/11/2011	08°Sc13'	24°Le43'
01/12/2011	08°Sg26'	09°Vi20'
01/01/2012	09°Cp57'	20°Vi07'
01/02/2012	11°Aq31'	22°Vi41' R
01/03/2012	10°Pi48'	14°Vi47'
01/04/2012	11°Ar40'	04°Vi47'
01/05/2012	11°Ta02'	05°Vi18' D
01/06/2012	10°Ge55'	14°Vi44'
01/07/2012	09°Cn34'	28°Vi41'
01/08/2012	09°Le09'	16°Li01'
01/09/2012	08°Vi58'	05°Sc24'
01/10/2012	08°Li13'	25°Sc41'
01/11/2012	08°Sc58'	17°Sg58'
01/12/2012	09°Sg12'	10°Cp35'

Date	Sun	Mars
01/01/2013	10°Cp44'	04°Aq41'
01/02/2013	12°Aq17'	29°Aq09'
01/03/2013	10°Pi34'	21°Pi12'
01/04/2013	11°Ar25'	15°Ar14'
01/05/2013	10°Ta47'	07°Ta50'
01/06/2013	10°Ge40'	00°Ge24'
01/07/2013	09°Cn20'	21°Ge26'
01/08/2013	08°Le55'	12°Cn21'
01/09/2013	08°Vi44'	02°Le30'
01/10/2013	07°Li59'	21°Le15'
01/11/2013	08°Sc44'	09°Vi44'
01/12/2013	08°Sg57'	26°Vi25'
01/01/2014	10°Cp29'	11°Li39'
01/02/2014	12°Aq02'	23°Li09'
01/03/2014	10°Pi19'	27°Li32'
01/04/2014	11°Ar11'	21°Li52' R
01/05/2014	10°Ta33'	11°Li25'
01/06/2014	10°Ge27'	09°Li54' D
01/07/2014	09°Cn07'	18°Li21'
01/08/2014	08°Le42'	03°Sc09'
01/09/2014	08°Vi30'	21°Sc34'
01/10/2014	07°Li45'	11°Sg41'
01/11/2014	08°Sc29'	04°Cp07'
01/12/2014	08°Sg42'	26°Cp55'
01/01/2015	10°Cp14'	21°Aq03'
01/02/2015	11°Aq47'	15°Pi17'
01/03/2015	10°Pi04'	06°Ar54'
01/04/2015	10°Ar57'	00°Ta14'
01/05/2015	10°Ta19'	22°Ta06'
01/06/2015	10°Ge13'	13°Ge54'
01/07/2015	08°Cn53'	04°Cn20'
01/08/2015	08°Le28'	24°Cn49'
01/09/2015	08°Vi16'	14°Le47'
01/10/2015	07°Li30'	03°Vi41'
01/11/2015	08°Sc14'	22°Vi48'
01/12/2015	08°Sg27'	10°Li46'
01/01/2016	09°Cp59'	28°Li33'
01/02/2016	11°Aq33'	14°Sc58'
01/03/2016	10°Pi50'	28°Sc03'
01/04/2016	11°Ar42'	07°Sg21'
01/05/2016	11°Ta03'	07°Sg46' R
01/06/2016	10°Ge56'	28°Sc29'
01/07/2016	09°Cn36'	23°Sc04' D
01/08/2016	09°Le11'	29°Sc21'
01/09/2016	08°Vi59'	13°Sg56'
01/10/2016	08°Li15'	02°Cp25'
01/11/2016	09°Sc00'	24°Cp00'
01/12/2016	09°Sg13'	16°Aq09'

Date	Sun	Mars
01/01/2017	10°Cp45'	09°Pi31'
01/02/2017	12°Aq19'	02°Ar49'
01/03/2017	10°Pi35'	23°Ar27'
01/04/2017	11°Ar27'	15°Ta42'
01/05/2017	10°Ta49'	06°Ge35'
01/06/2017	10°Ge42'	27°Ge33'
01/07/2017	09°Cn22'	17°Cn20'
01/08/2017	08°Le57'	07°Le24'
01/09/2017	08°Vi45'	27°Le12'
01/10/2017	08°Li01'	16°Vi14'
01/11/2017	08°Sc45'	05°Li50'
01/12/2017	08°Sg59'	24°Li44'
01/01/2018	10°Cp30'	14°Sc10'
01/02/2018	12°Aq04'	03°Sg21'
01/03/2018	10°Pi21'	20°Sg15'
01/04/2018	11°Ar13'	08°Cp03'
01/05/2018	10°Ta35'	23°Cp26'
01/06/2018	10°Ge28'	05°Aq22'
01/07/2018	09°Cn08'	09°Aq07' R
01/08/2018	08°Le43'	02°Aq51'
01/09/2018	08°Vi31'	28°Cp44' D
01/10/2018	07°Li46'	05°Aq57'
01/11/2018	08°Sc30'	21°Aq10'
01/12/2018	08°Sg43'	09°Pi28'

Date	Sun	Mars
1/01/2019	10°Cp15'	29°Pi56'
1/02/2019	11°Aq49'	20°Ar54'
1/03/2019	10°Pi06'	09°Ta48'
1/04/2019	10°Ar59'	00°Ge29'
1/05/2019	10°Ta21'	20°Ge11'
1/06/2019	10°Ge15'	10°Cn13'
1/07/2019	08°Cn54'	29°Cn23'
1/08/2019	08°Le29'	19°Le04'
1/09/2019	08°Vi17'	08°Vi46'
1/10/2019	07°Li32'	27°Vi57'
1/11/2019	08°Sc16'	18°Li01'
1/12/2019	08°Sg29'	07°Sc42'
1/01/2020	10°Cp01'	28°Sc23'
1/02/2020	11°Aq34'	19°Sg24'
1/03/2020	10°Pi52'	09°Cp19'
1/04/2020	11°Ar44'	00°Aq49'
1/05/2020	11°Ta05'	21°Aq38'
1/06/2020	10°Ge58'	12°Pi42'
1/07/2020	09°Cn38'	01°Ar46'
1/08/2020	09°Le13'	18°Ar13'
1/09/2020	09°Vi01'	27°Ar34'
1/10/2020	08°Li16'	25°Ar03' R
1/11/2020	09°Sc01'	16°Ar22'
1/12/2020	09°Sg15'	17°Ar03' D

♡♡

Appendix 3
Linked Cycles
1000 - 2500

The first and last conjunction in each cycle 1000-2500

NEW CYCLE NUMBER	FIRST CONJUNCTION	DEGREE OF PASSION	END CYCLE NUMBER	LAST CONJUNCTION	DEGREE
14R	25 Feb 1723	28°Cp23'	44R	4 Oct 2010	12°Sc40'
14D	6 Apr 1723	29°Aq33'		AFTER 2500	
	BEFORE 1000		38D	2 Jul 1692	26°Le02'
10R	6 Dec 1436	20°Sc54'	38R	10 Aug 1692	20°Vi14'
10D	19 Jan 1437	22°Sg10'		AFTER 2500	
	BEFORE 1000		26D	14 Mar 1056	15°Ta44'
	BEFORE 1000		26R	20 Apr 1056	09°Ge46'
	BEFORE 1000		32D	8 May 1374	10°Cn00'
4R	12 Oct 1118	25°Vi28'	32R	8 Jun 1374	29°Cn15'
4D	27 Nov 1118	24°Li42'	46D	5 Apr 2271	00°Ge45'
18R	19 Sep 1983	23°Le42'	46R	4 May 2271	20°Ge15'
18D	26 Oct 1983	16°Vi19'		AFTER 2500	
23R	19 Nov 2301	18°Li04'		AFTER 2500	
23D	7 Dec 2301	29°Li01'		AFTER 2500	
	BEFORE 1000		39D	17 Nov 1698	12°Cp29'
6R	14 Jun 1347	19°Ta16'	39R	1 Jan 1699	17°Aq44'
6D	29 Jun 1347	29°Ta35'		AFTER 2500	
	BEFORE 1000		42D	1 Feb 1985	28°Pi21'
11R	29 Jul 1665	03°Cn23'	42R	28 Feb 1985	18°Ar39'
11D	8 Sep 1665	29°Cn49'		AFTER 2500	
24R	15 Apr 2308	17°Pi26'		AFTER 2500	
24D	28 May 2308	20°Ar28'		AFTER 2500	
	BEFORE 1000		35D	8 Sep 1412	11°Sc13'
3R	28 Mar 1093	06°Pi31'	35R	21 Oct 1412	12°Sg11'
3D	11 May 1093	10°Ar32'	49D	10 Aug 2309	02°Li32'
19R	17 Feb 2022	16°Cp55'	49R	19 Sep 2309	28°Li34'
19D	6 Mar 2022	00°Aq04'		AFTER 2500	

	BEFORE 1000		**29D**	18 Jul 1094	16°Vi17'
	BEFORE 1000		29R	4 Sep 1094	18°Li09'
	BEFORE 1000		**31D**	22 Feb 1355	28°Ar17'
2R	21 Aug 1067	29°Cn22'	31R	6 Apr 1355	27°Ta10'
2D	23 Sep 1067	19°Le50'	**47D**	4 Jan 2284	00°Pi39'
16R	17 Jul 1964	21°Ge01'	47R	21 Feb 2284	07°Ar14'
16D	27 Aug 1964	17°Cn44'		AFTER 2500	
	BEFORE 1000		**43D**	24 Jun 1991	16°Le43'
15R	29 Nov 1735	05°Sc26'	43R	26 Jul 1991	06°Vi34'
15D	13 Jan 1736	05°Sg45'		AFTER 2500	
	BEFORE 1000		**37D**	4 May 1673	29°Ge09'
8R	18 Oct 1385	24°Vi20'	37R	31 May 1673	15°Cn57'
8D	30 Oct 1385	01°Li19'		AFTER 2500	
22R	4 Sep 2282	10°Le13'		AFTER 2500	
22D	17 Oct 2282	07°Vi03'		AFTER 2500	
	BEFORE 1000		**27D**	18 Dec 1068	20°Aq48'
	BEFORE 1000		27R	4 Feb 1069	26°Pi52'
	BEFORE 1000		**45D**	14 Nov 2029	07°Cp50'
12R	19 May 1678	22°Ar57'	45R	24 Nov 2029	15°Cp08'
12D	3 Jul 1678	25°Ta19'		AFTER 2500	
	BEFORE 1000		**40D**	3 Sep 1711	26°Li13'
9R	26 Mar 1392	00°Pi59'	40R	18 Oct 1711	27°Sc30'
9D	3 Apr 1392	07°Pi03'		AFTER 2500	
25R	7 Jan 2353	15°Sg58'		AFTER 2500	
25D	2 Mar 2353	24°Cp27'		AFTER 2500	
	BEFORE 1000		**28D**	21 May 1075	19°Cn57'
	BEFORE 1000		28R	27 Jun 1075	12°Le33'
	BEFORE 1000		**33D**	4 Jul 1393	05°Vi47'
5R	23 Dec 1137	06°Sg21'	33R	18 Aug 1393	04°Li01'
5D	11 Feb 1138	12°Cp40'	**48D**	14 Jun 2290	07°Le37'
20R	12 Nov 2034	20°Li37'	48R	9 Jul 2290	22°Le53'
20D	31 Dec 2034	22°Sc19'		AFTER 2500	
	BEFORE 1000		**41D**	21 Apr 1972	16°Ge24'

13R	5 Oct 1684	07°Vi38'	41R	17 May 1972	02°Cn52'
13D	2 Nov 1684	24°Vi43'		AFTER 2500	
	BEFORE 1000		36D	9 Feb 1654	07°Ar36'
7R	4 Aug 1366	16°Cn08'	36R	2 Apr 1654	14°Ta28'
7D	11 Sep 1366	10°Le23'		AFTER 2500	
21R	8 Jul 2263	09°Ge17'		AFTER 2500	
21D	12 Aug 2263	03°Cn13'		AFTER 2500	
	BEFORE 1000		34D	7 Dec 1399	10°Aq49'
1R	21 Jun 1048	28°Ta16'	34R	30 Dec 1399	28°Aq52'
1D	21 Jul 1048	18°Ge04'	50D	20 Oct 2328	12°Sg58'
17R	16 May 1977	14°Ar09'	50R	20 Nov 2328	05°Cp38'
17D	7 Jun 1977	00°Ta37'		AFTER 2500	
	BEFORE 1000		30D	30 Sep 1113	29°Sc50'
	BEFORE 1000		30R	4 Nov 1113	26°Sg10'
	BEFORE 1000		44D	21 Aug 2010	13°Li35'

Appendix 4
Venus-Mars Saros
1000-2500

Dates and degrees for the first conjunction in each cycle. Degree of Passion.

Group One	First conjunction	Degree of Passion
1R	21 Jun 1048	28°Ta16'
1D	21 Jul 1048	18°Ge04'
2R	21 Aug 1067	29°Cn22'
2D	23 Sep 1067	19°Le50'
3R	28 Mar 1093	06°Pi31'
3D	11 May 1093	10°Ar32'
4R	12 Oct 1118	25°Vi28'
4D	27 Nov 1118	24°Li42'
5R	23 Dec 1137	06°Sg21'
5D	11 Feb 1138	12°Cp40'

Group Two	First conjunction	Degree of Passion
6R	14 Jun 1347	19°Ta16'
6D	29 Jun 1347	29°Ta35'
7R	4 Aug 1366	16°Cn08'
7D	11 Sep 1366	10°Le23'
8R	18 Oct 1385	24°Vi20'
8D	30 Oct 1385	01°Li19'
9R	26 Mar 1392	00°Pi59'
9D	3 Apr 1392	07°Pi03'
10R	6 Dec 1436	20°Sc54'
10D	19 Jan 1437	22°Sg10'

Group Three	First conjunction	Degree of Passion
11R	29 Jul 1665	03°Cn23'
11D	8 Sep 1665	29°Cn49'
12R	19 May 1678	22°Ar57'
12D	3 Jul 1678	25°Ta19'
13R	5 Oct 1684	07°Vi38'
13D	2 Nov 1684	24°Vi43'
14R	25 Feb 1723	28°Cp23'
14D	6 Apr 1723	29°Aq33'
15R	29 Nov 1735	05°Sc26'
15D	13 Jan 1736	05°Sg45'

Group Four	First conjunction	Degree of Passion
16R	17 Jul 1964	21°Ge01'
16D	27 Aug 1964	17°Cn44'
17R	16 May 1977	14°Ar09'
17D	7 Jun 1977	00°Ta37'
18R	19 Sept 1983	23°Le42'
18D	26 Oct 1983	16°Vi19'
19R	17 Feb 2022	16°Cp55'
19D	6 Mar 2022	00°Aq04'
20R	12 Nov 2034	20°Li37'
20D	31 Dec 2034	22°Sc19'

Group Five	First conjunction	Degree of Passion
21R	8 Jul 2263	09°Ge17'
21D	12 Aug 2263	03°Cn13'
22R	4 Sep 2282	10°Le13'
22D	17 Oct 2282	07°Vi03'
23R	19 Nov 2301	18°Li04'
23D	7 Dec 2301	29°Li01'
24R	15 Apr 2308	17°Pi26'
24D	28 May 2308	20°Ar28'
25R	7 Jan 2353	15°Sg58'
25D	2 Mar 2353	24°Cp27'

Venus-Mars Saros. 1000-2500.
Dates and degrees for last conjunction in each cycle. Degree of Separation.

Group One	Last conjunction	Degree of Separation
26D	14 Mar 1056	15°Ta44'
26R	20 Apr 1056	09°Ge46'
27D	18 Dec 1068	20°Aq48'
27R	4 Feb 1069	26°Pi52'
28D	21 May 1075	19°Cn57'
28R	27 Jun 1075	12°Le33'
29D	18 Jul 1094	16°Vi17'
29R	4 Sep 1094	18°Li09'
30D	30 Sep 1113	29°Sc50'
30R	4 Nov 1113	26°Sg10'

Group Two	Last conjunction	Degree of Separation
31D	22 Feb 1355	28°Ar17'
31R	6 Apr 1355	27°Ta10'
32D	8 May 1374	10°Cn00'
32R	8 Jun 1374	29°Cn15'
33D	4 Jul 1393	05°Vi47'
33R	18 Aug 1393	04°Li01'
34D	7 Dec 1399	10°Aq49'
34R	30 Dec 1399	28°Aq52'
35D	8 Sep 1412	11°Sc13'
35R	21 Oct 1412	12°Sg11'

Group Three	Last conjunction	Degree of Separation
36R	9 Feb 1654	07°Ar36'
36R	2 Apr 1654	14°Ta28'
37D	4 May 1673	29°Ge09'
37R	31 May 1673	15°Cn57'
38D	2 Jul 1692	26°Le02'
38R	10 Aug 1692	20°Vi14'
39D	17 Nov 1698	12°Cp29'
39R	1 Jan 1699	17°Aq44'
40D	3 Sep 1711	26°Li13'
40R	18 Oct 1711	27°Sc30'

Group Four	Last conjunction	Degree of Separation
41D	21 Apr 1972	16°Ge24'
41R	17 May 1972	02°Cn52'
42D	1 Feb 1985	28°Pi31'
42R	28 Feb 1985	18°Ar39'
43D	24 Jun 1991	16°Le43'
43R	26 Jul 1991	06°Vi34'
44D	21 Aug 2010	13°Li35'
44R	4 Oct 2010	12°Sc40'
45D	14 Nov 2029	07°Cp50'
45R	24 Nov 2029	15°Cp08'

Group Five	Last conjunction	Degree of Separation
46D	5 Apr 2271	00°Ge45'
46R	4 May 2271	20°Ge15'
47D	4 Jan 2284	00°Pi39'
47R	21 Feb 2284	07°Ar14'
48D	14 Jun 2290	07°Le37'
48R	9 Jul 2290	22°Le53'
49D	10 Aug 2309	02°Li32'
49R	19 Sep 2309	28°Li34'
50D	20 Oct 2328	12°Sg58'
50R	20 Nov 2328	05°Cp38'

Selected Bibliography

Barrow, John D., *Cosmic Imagery*, The Bodley Head, 2008.

Bobrick, Benson, *The Fated Sky*, Simon and Schuster, New York, 2005.

Bolen, Jean Shinoda, *Goddesses in Everywoman*, Harper Perennial, New York, 1984.

Campion, Nick, *The Book of World Horoscopes*, The Aquarian Press, 1988.

Davison, Ronald, *Synastry*, Aurora Press, New York, 1983.

Finey, Michele, *Secrets of the Zodiac*, Allen and Unwin, Sydney, 2009.

Friday, Nancy, *My Mother My Self*, Fontana/HarperCollins, London, 1979.

Greene, Liz, *Relating*, Samuel Weiser Inc., York Beach, Maine, 1984.

Hand, Robert, *Planets in Transit*, Para Research Inc., Rockport Massachusetts, 1976.

Hill, Lynda, *The Sabian Symbols as an Oracle*, Hill and Hill P/L, Avalon, NSW, 1995.

Kollerstrom, Nick, *The Metal-Planet Relationship*, Borderland Sciences Research Foundation, California, 1993.

Martineau, John, *A Little Book of Coincidence in the Solar System*, Walker Publishing Co., New York, 2001.

Nauman, Eileen, *The American Book of Nutrition and Medical Astrology*, Astro Computing Services, San Diego, 1982.

Rudhyar, Dane, *An Astrological Mandala: The Cycle of Transformations and its 360 Symbolic Phases*, Vintage Books, New York, 1974.

Ruperti, Alexander, *Cycles of Becoming*, Earthwalk School of Astrology, Santa Monica, USA, 2005.

Sullivan, Erin, *Retrograde Planets*, Samuel Weiser Inc., York Beach, Maine, USA, 2000.

Tierney, Bil, *Dynamics of Aspects Analysis*, CRCS Publications, California, USA, 1983.

Vogler, Christopher, *The Writer's Journey*, (Third Edition) Michael Wiese Productions, California, 2007.

Index

Also by The Wessex Astrologer - www.wessexastrologer.com

Patterns of the Past
Karmic Connections
Good Vibrations
The Soulmate Myth: A Dream Come True or Your Worst Nightmare?
The Book of Why
Judy Hall

The Essentials of Vedic Astrology
Lunar Nodes - Crisis and Redemption
Personal Panchanga and the Five Sources of Light
Komilla Sutton

Astrolocality Astrology
From Here to There
Martin Davis

The Consultation Chart
Introduction to Medical Astrology
Wanda Sellar

The Betz Placidus Table of Houses
Martha Betz

Astrology and Meditation
Greg Bogart

The Book of World Horoscopes
Nicholas Campion

Life After Grief : An Astrological Guide to Dealing with Loss
AstroGraphology: The Hidden Link between your Horoscope and your Handwriting
Darrelyn Gunzburg

The Houses: Temples of the Sky
Deborah Houlding

Through the Looking Glass
The Magic Thread
Richard Idemon

Temperament: Astrology's Forgotten Key
Dorian Geiseler Greenbaum

Nativity of the Late King Charles
John Gadbury

Declination - The Steps of the Sun
Luna - The Book of the Moon
Paul F. Newman

Tapestry of Planetary Phases:
Weaving the Threads of Purpose and Meaning in Your Life
Christina Rose

Lightning Source UK Ltd.
Milton Keynes UK
UKOW031559290612

195255UK00001B/1/P